CW00556187

ELITE PANZER STRIKE FORCE

Germany's Panzer Lehr Division in World War II

Franz Kurowski

Pen & Sword
MILITARY

English translation © 2011 by Battle Born Books and Consulting

First published in English in the United States of America in 2011
by Stackpole Books

Republished in Great Britain in 2011 by
Pen & Sword Military
An imprint of
Pen & Sword Books Ltd
47 Church Street
Barnsley
South Yorkshire
S70 2AS

Copyright © Franz Kurowski, 2011

ISBN 978 1 84884 803 0

Printed and bound in the United States of America.

Pen & Sword Books Ltd incorporates the Imprints of Pen & Sword Aviation, Pen &
Sword Family History, Pen & Sword Maritime, Pen & Sword Military, Pen & Sword
Discovery, Wharncliffe Local History, Wharncliffe True Crime, Wharncliffe Trans-
port, Pen & Sword Select, Pen & Sword Military Classics, Leo Cooper, The Praetorian
Press, Remember When, Seaforth Publishing and Frontline Publishing

For a complete list of Pen & Sword titles please contact
PEN & SWORD BOOKS LIMITED
47 Church Street, Barnsley, South Yorkshire, S70 2AS, England
E-mail: enquiries@pen-and-sword.co.uk
Website: www.pen-and-sword.co.uk

Contents

Acknowledgments iv

Chapter 1   Roots of the Division 1

Chapter 2   Activation of the Division 6

Chapter 3   In Vienna and Budapest 12

Chapter 4   The March to the Front 25

Chapter 5   The Fighting for Tilly 39

Chapter 6   Days of Horror 66

Chapter 7   A New Major Attack 80

Chapter 8   Westward 87

Chapter 9   Hell 106

Chapter 10   Retreat 118

Chapter 11   At the *Westwall* and Beyond 159

Chapter 12   Victory Lost: The Fighting in the Ardennes 169

Chapter 13   To the Bitter End 207

Appendices 217

Select Bibliography 235

Acknowledgments

Special thanks are in order for *Generalleutnant* Fritz Bayerlein, who provided his entire manuscript concerning the operations of the *PLD*.

The division's veterans association helped clear up matters wherever there were discrepancies and placed me in contact with various veterans.

CHAPTER 1

Roots of the Division

O ne of the core formations of the future *Panzer-Lehr-Division* was the
Panzer-Lehr-Regiment, which had been established at the Armor School
at Wünsdorf (Berlin) in 1938.[1] Elements of the regiment were attached to the
3. Panzer-Division for participation in the campaign in Poland.[2] Elements of
the regiment also participated in the campaign in the West in 1940. In the fall
of 1940, the regiment consisted of the following three battalions:
- 1st Battalion: Tank (1st through 4th Companies)
- 2nd Battalion: Motorized Rifle (later Mechanized Infantry) (5th
  through 8th Companies)
- 3rd Battalion: Antitank (9th through 12th Companies)

In the summer of 1941, the regiment was again alerted for operations in
the field, this time in the Soviet Union. The 1st Battalion was attached to an
armored division. It was never decisively engaged, however, and returned to
Wünsdorf a few months later, after transferring its weapons and equipment
to other forces in the field.

Soon thereafter, the *Lehr-Brigade 900 (mot.)* was formed in East Prussia.[3]
This formation was established using the 2nd Battalion of the *Panzer-Lehr-
Regiment*, augmented by the 1st Battalion of the *Infanterie-Lehr-Regiment
Döberitz* of *Oberst* Müller-Bülow, one artillery battalion from the *Artillerie-
Lehr-Regiment*, a signals instructional company from Halle, and the medical

---

1. Translator's Note: The term *Lehr* refers to a training and demonstration function on
   the part of a formation. There were numerous such formations within the German
   Army, each authorized to wear a Gothic "L" on the shoulder board and shoulder
   strap insignia as a form of honorific. In the case of some of the combat formations,
   such as the *Panzer-Lehr-Regiment*, there was still a home-front training element of the
   same name in Germany, causing some confusion about what formation is meant
   when treated out of context.

2. Translator's Note: Even though the original *Panzer-Lehr-Regiment* was considered a
   "schoolhouse" establishment, the German Army's policy was to rotate subordinate
   elements into the field so that the school cadre would remain current with trends
   on the battlefield.

3. Translator's Note: 900th Instruction Brigade (Motorized).

1

instruction company in Berlin-Reinickendorf. Also assigned was a troop from the *Aufklärungs-Lehr-Abteilung* in Krampnitz.[4]

The commander of this brigade was *Oberst* Walther Krause. The brigade's tactical insignia was a tower with a Gothic "L," with the tower representing the tower at the National Playing Fields in Berlin. The brigade was completely motorized with both wheeled and tracked vehicles. None of the elements of this *ad hoc* formation had ever trained together before.

On the day of its arrival in the Soviet Union, the brigade was partially committed. It advanced through Thorn and Suwalki in the direction of Vilna. It was employed in the pocket battles at Minsk, Lepel, Vitebsk and Smolensk. It was outside of Smolensk, along the Wopj, Wotrja and Zarewitsch Rivers that the brigade was employed in its entirety, and it suffered heavy casualties as it screened against Soviet forces attempting to break out of the Smolensk Pocket to the northeast. There was heavy fighting in the Duchowtschina area.

After three weeks of defensive fighting, it participated in the advance across the Beloj in the direction of Rshew. It was frequently thrown into the line when the Soviets attempted to break through the German main line of resistance with strong armored forces on 5 August.

It was during that round of fighting that *Unteroffizier* Kintzel of the 2nd Company of *Panzerjäger-Lehr-Abteilung 900* was employed with his *PaK 38*, a 5-centimeter antitank gun, in one of the most threatened areas. He had just gone into position when the first Soviet T-34's and KV-I's came rolling up in attack. The antitank gunners opened fire at 800 meters. After two rounds, Kintzel's gun had knocked out the first T-34. In quick succession, two more T-34's suffered the same fate. Then, a KV-I appeared barely 200 meters off to the right. The gun turned to face the opponent, but it fired five rounds without effect, with the remaining enemy closing to within 50 meters in the meantime. Kintzel was able to observe one of his rounds penetrate cleanly through the turret of another T-34, but the weight of the Soviet attack proved too much for the infantry in the sector. Kintzel soon found himself and his crew alone. When the Soviet infantry closed in to assault, the gun had to be abandoned. Since there were no demolition charges available, the Soviets captured it intact, along with ten rounds of ammunition. The German lines

---

4. Translator's Note: Döberitz is the name of the town where the regiment was garrisoned (in contrast to normal German Army policy of naming formations after their commanders). *Aufklärung* = Reconnaissance. *Oberst* = Colonel. For those unfamiliar with German ranks, there is a table in the appendices.

were pushed back several hundred meters. Despite the setback, Kintzel was eventually awarded the Iron Cross, First Class, for his bravery in slowing down the Soviet onslaught in his sector.

Following an intensive artillery preparation, the Soviets broke through in the sector of the 2nd Battalion of *Infanterie-Regiment 56* in the Gorbatowsky area two days later, early on the morning of 8 August. Soon, the lead Soviet elements were three kilometers east of Lossewo. The brigade, which was serving as the ready reserve of the *V. Armee-Korps*, was committed to an immediate counterattack and moved out with its 2nd Battalion at 0900 hours. Once again, the 2nd Company of the antitank battalion was attached to the infantry, since enemy armor was expected.

At 1400 hours, the 2nd Battalion's attack bogged down in the vicinity of Sujewa, where it established a defensive perimeter. The battalion was able to fend off several Soviet infantry attacks in seesaw fighting, but the heavy tanks that accompanied the infantry could not be dislodged. They positioned themselves around the German defensive positions and fired at anything that moved.

Kintzel's platoon was alerted, and the men briefed by an officer from the regiment. Kintzel's platoon leader was *Leutnant* Oventrop. The young officer raced ahead of his platoon to find the command post of the 2nd Battalion. After being briefed there, he established contact with the 7th Company, where the bulk of the enemy tanks were located. Oventrop ordered two guns manhandled forward.

The gun crews pushed their pieces forward between trees and vegetation and through practically impenetrable underbrush. The enemy tanks kept changing positions. Eventually, however, they managed to get one gun to within thirty meters of an enemy tank. Oventrop later provided the following firsthand account:

> Fire mission—Round out—Hit!—A shot of flame. One tank, then another and then a third were engulfed in flames. The crews were dead or wounded. A couple were able to escape by virtue of the terrain. The enemy artillery started to come alive. They started to cover our guns with fires of all calibers. Despite that, the crews only suffered minor casualties. Obstinacy, courage and decisiveness on the part of the antitank gun crews forces the enemy to pull back. Towards 1900 hours, the platoon was limbered up one kilometer east of Sujewa, ready for another mission.

✠

At the beginning of October, the brigade was attached to the *14. Infanterie-Division (Mot)* and advanced on Kalinin. After that town was taken, there was heavy fighting at Thoshok, to the northeast. The route of advance then took the brigade in the direction of Klin. For its part in the drive on Moscow, the brigade advanced to within thirty-five kilometers of the Soviet capital. Like the rest of the Germany Army, it was surprised by the bitter winter of 1941–42, which turned out to be the coldest in more than 150 years. The Soviet counteroffensive started in December. In the course of its withdrawal, the brigade reached Kalinin. In the fighting around that city, *Major* Georg Scholze, the acting commander of the 1st Battalion, set the example and helped stand firm against the Soviet onslaught.

At the beginning of March 1942, the remaining elements of the brigade were pulled out of the line and returned to Wünsdorf and Döberitz. The brigade was disbanded. Later that same year, however, the 1st Battalion of *Infanterie-Lehr-Regiment Döberitz* and the 2nd Battalion of the *Panzer-Lehr-Regiment* were consolidated to form *Lehr-Regiment 901*, which would later be absorbed into the *Panzer-Lehr-Division* as *Panzergrenadier-Regiment 901*.

The regiment was sent to the Soviet Union, where it was initially employed in operations around Starobjelsk during the winter fighting of 1942–43. The regiment distinguished itself under *Oberst* Scholze in the increasingly difficult fighting. On 31 December 1942, *Major* Kübler's 2nd Battalion was also cited for its valorous actions.

On 19 February 1943, Scholze received orders to pull his regiment back. In the days that followed, the regiment performed screening missions in front of the main line of resistance. The snowed-over roads turned into a morass with the early onset of a thaw, and the "mud period" of 1943 commenced. On 17 February, the actions of the regiment were recognized through the award of the Knight's Cross to *Oberst* Scholze, whose simple motto—"Be more than you appear to be"—had inspired his men. Scholze had led from the front during those difficult weeks in the Soviet Union. His soldiers not only knew him as a commander whose decisions revealed great tactical proficiency, but as a man who took his responsibilities for his soldiers to heart—a good man and a good comrade. Scholze considered his high award as more recognition than that which was necessary for simply performing his duty. But his soldiers knew that no one deserved the award more than he did. The regiment had formed bridgeheads at the focal points of the fighting. Under his leadership, it had defended stubbornly, held continuously and always performed its duty.

On 27 March, the grenadiers of the regiment were able to toss the attacking enemy back across the Donez in an immediate counterattack. Once again, it was *Major* Kübler's 2nd Battalion that was principally involved in that success. At the end of April, the regiment was pulled out of the line and returned by rail to Wünsdorf for reconstitution. The *Panzer-Lehr-Regiment* was there at the same time. This time, *Lehr-Regiment 901* remained intact. Together with the tank regiment, it was moved to Fallingbostel/Örbke starting in the middle of July 1943, since the German Army High Command needed the facilities at Wünsdorf. By October, all of the units had departed Wünsdorf.

While these moves were going on, *Panzergrenadier-Lehr-Regiment 901* also received orders to form two new companies: a heavy infantry gun/self-propelled gun battery (9th Company) and a machine-gun antiaircraft company (10th Company). *Oberleutnant* Hennecke became the commander of the gun battery, with his personnel cadre coming from the Infantry Gun Replacement Company at Burg (Magdeburg). The 10th Company was formed from personnel coming from *Panzergrenadier-Regiment 69*, which had been destroyed in Africa in May.

On 8 June, both of the companies were visited by the regimental adjutant, *Hauptmann* Weber, in Ludwigsburg. After moving to Wünsdorf, the heavy-gun battery received its complement of weaponry. They were ex-Czech light tanks that had been converted for the purpose to mount 15-centimeter heavy infantry guns: *15cm schweres Infanteriegeschütz 31/1 auf Sfl 38*. At the beginning of August, the battery reported itself ready for combat operations and conducted a gunnery exercise as proof. The regimental commander, still *Oberst* Scholze, viewed the exercise. The battery then moved to Fallingbostel along with the rest of the regiment.

On 16 September 1943, the regiment received deployment orders for Italy, with the rail load commencing the next day. The train was routed through Hanover–Magdeburg–Munich–Vienna–Postumia, finally reaching its destination of St. Pietro del Carso some days later. It was quartered in a former Italian military facility and was soon dispatched for operations against partisans in Dalmatia.

From 20 September 1943 through 14 January 1944, the regiment conducted anti-partisan operations, some of it resulting in bitter fighting, especially in the Fiume, Dugaresa and Tuzla areas. One of the company commanders, *Oberleutnant* Philipps, received the Knight's Cross to the Iron Cross on 7 April 1944 in recognition of his leadership and the heroic fighting of his company in the region. The regiment employed its mechanized flamethrower platoon for the first time, consisting of flamethrowers mounted on armored personnel carriers.[5]

On 16 January, the regiment was loaded on trains in Agram (Zagreb) and was moved to Nancy via Vienna–Munich–Straßburg (Strasbourg), where it joined the *Panzer-Lehr-Division*, which was in the process of being formed.

---

5. Translator's Note: Officially the *Sd.Kfz. 251/16*, of which six were authorized for each *Panzergrenadier* regiment.

CHAPTER 2

Activation of the Division

The official date for the activation of the *Panzer-Lehr-Division* can be traced to 30 December 1943.[1] The training regiments at *Panzertruppenschule I* in Bergen and *Panzertruppenschule II* in Krampnitz, as well as the command staff of the latter schoolhouse, were ordered to France to form the division.

The advance party of the *Panzer-Lehr-Regiment* was sent to Lunéville, while *Panzergrenadier-Lehr-Regiment 901* and the command staff of the armor school were dispatched to Nancy.[2] On 5 January, elements started to filter in from Bergen and Krampnitz. One day later, the Inspector General of the Armored Forces, *Generaloberst* Guderian, requested a change to the quartering plan for the division. According to the telegram, the elements were to be located as follows:

In Nancy: divisional headquarters; division escort company;[3] portions of *PGLR 901* (regimental staff; regimental troops and the regiment's 1st Battalion).

In Verdun: *PLR*; 2nd Battalion of *PGLR 901*; *Panzerjäger-Lehr-Abteilung 130*; *Panzer-Pionier-Lehr-Bataillon 130*; 2nd Battalion of the divisional artillery; *Heeres-Flak-Artillerie-Abteilung 311*.[4]

---

1. Translator's Note: Telegram from OKH/Chef H.Rüstung und BdE/AHA Gr. (I) Nr. 7190/43 g.Kdos. = Oberkommando des Heeres/Chef Heeres-Rüstung und Befehlshaber des Ersatzheeres/Allgemeine Heeres-Abteilung Gruppe (I) Nummer 7190/43 geheime Kommandosache = High Command of the Army/Chief Army Armament and Commander-in-Chief of the Replacement Army, Group (I), Number 7190/43, SECRET COMMAND MATTER.

2. Translator's Note: Hereafter referred to as *PLR* and *PGLR 901*, respectively.

3. Translator's Note: Not to be confused with the headquarters commandant and the Headquarters Company. The escort company was a combat company formed to protect the division command post and battle staff and, in a pinch, function as a ready reserve for the division.

4. Translator's Note: Some confusion exists as to the "official" designations of these formations and whether they actually had numerical designators or used the additional designation of *Lehr*. Some sources list the *PLR* as being *PLR 130*. For simplicity, it will be referred to as *PLR*. In the case of the two mechanized infantry regiments of the division, these will be referred to as *PGLR 901* and *PGLR 902*. *Panzerjäger-Lehr-Abteilung 130* (130th Antitank Instructional Battalion) will be shortened to *PJLA 130*. Likewise, *Panzer-Pionier-Lehr-Bataillon 130* (130th Armored Combat Engineer

In Lunéville: *PGLR 902.*

In order to transport the *PLR* to Verdun, it was first necessary to reinforce the railway bridge over the Meuse to support the weight of *Tiger* and *Panther* tanks.[5] The twenty-ton-capacity road bridges in the area had to be strengthened to accept seventy tons by a bridging battalion.

The first trains arrived in Verdun and Lunéville on 7 January. Additional elements followed the next day. On 9 January, *PGLR 902* marched by road from Verdun to Lunéville.

The commander of the advance party was *Major i.G.* Kurt Kauffmann, the former liaison officer for *Generalmajor* Fritz Bayerlein. Kauffmann was now the operations officer for the division. Bayerlein, who was earmarked by Guderian to command the newly forming division, had served under the pioneering armor officer during the first year of the campaign in the Soviet Union. As the Chief of Staff of *Panzer-Armee Afrika* under the Italian General Messe, he had been instrumental in saving the Axis forces around the Mareth Position and pulling them back in time to avoid capture. Bayerlein was flown out of Africa prior to the capitulation, where he returned to command the *3. Panzer-Division* later that year. At the beginning of January 1944, he turned over command of the division to *Oberst* Rudolf Lang, entered the officer reserve manpower pool and was quickly picked up to command the newly forming division, which was intended to be the strongest and best-equipped division of the German Army.

During Bayerlein's first briefing with Kauffmann and his staff, the new commander discovered there were serious deficiencies in the activation order for the division. Several troop elements were not part of the activation, and those were forthwith requested from the Inspector General of the

---

Instructional Battalion) will be *PPLB 130.* The divisional reconnaissance squadron, *Panzer-Aufklärungs-Lehr-Abteilung 130,* which is not listed with the order of battle above, will be shortened to *PALA 130.* For some reason, the divisional artillery does not generally insert *"Lehr"* into its designation and is simply referred to as *Panzer-Artillerie-Regiment 130* or, for the book's purposes, *PAR 130.* Other divisional troop elements analogously bore the numerical designator of 130. *Heeres-Flak-Abteilung 311 = HFA 311.*

5. Translator's Note: It was originally planned to issue the regiment a company of *Tiger* tanks, but these plans were never fully realized, with a "company" of *Tigers* planned for employment with the division being sent to Normandy during the invasion. The "company" consisted of five of the brand-new *Tiger II's* with the early Porsche turret. There were so many "teething" problems associated with the deployment that the tanks were soon lost in their initial combat commitment. This unit never officially linked up with the division.
Editor's Note: This is *Panzerkompanie (Funklenk) 316,* equipped with five *Tiger II's* (p), three *Tiger I's,* ten *Sturmgeschütz III's* and fifty-one *Sd.Kfz. 301* demolition charge carriers. Prior to the move to Hungary the ten *StuG's* were turned over to *3./Panzerjäger-Lehr-Abteilung 130,* which had not yet received its *Panzerjäger IV's.*

Armored Forces. This led to a telephone conversation on 15 January between Kauffmann and Guderian's Chief of Staff, *Generalmajor* Thomale. Generous support was promised. Instead of the designated *Pionier-Lehr-Bataillon (mot)*, which had no armored assets, a full-fledged armored engineer battalion was substituted, along with a bridging column. A self-propelled artillery battalion was requested from the Armed Forces High Command, and the request was approved. A company of *Tiger II's* was also promised.

Although Guderian had intended for the division to be a counterattack force that would drive any intended Allied invasion along the Atlantic coast back into the sea, all of the groundwork for forming the division encountered difficulties.

After discussing issues with the commander of the *PJLA 130*, *Major* Barth, Kauffmann requested that the battalion be equipped with the new *Panzerjäger IV* if the intended issuance of the *Jagdpanther* could not take place in the foreseeable future.[6] The requests were always sent either by telegram or radio in order to shorten the process. One of the requests read:

1. Request a maintenance and repair platoon be established for the *Panzerjäger-Lehr-Abteilung*. Since repairs of the two fully tracked companies (table of organization and equipment) cannot be guaranteed alone by the [authorized] maintenance section, it is

2. requested that a complete fully tracked company be authorized instead of the armored maintenance company (minus the 2nd Platoon) of the *Panzer-Lehr-Regiment*, so that the regiment, which is being reinforced by *Tiger* and radio-controlled companies, may be assured of maintenance and repair and, moreover, the promised self-propelled artillery battalion can rely on the *Panzer-Lehr-Regiment* for maintenance and repair.[7]

---

6. Translator's Note: The *Panzerjäger IV* was a tank destroyer armed with an L/48 7.5-centimeter main gun, using the chassis of the *Panzer IV* as its undercarriage. Editor's Note: In May 1944, *Panzerjäger-Lehr-Abteilung 130* was equipped with three mixed *Panzerjägerkompanien* consisting of ten *Jagdpanzer IV (Sd.Kfz. 162)* armed with the 7.5-cm *PaK 39*, L/48 guns and four 7.5-cm *PaK 40* towed guns per *Kompanie*. *Panzerjäger-Lehr-Abteilung 130* did not begin to be equipped with the 7.5-cm L/70 *Panzer IV/70 (V)* until November, 1944.

7. Translator's Note: The radio-control company—*Panzerkompanie (Fkl) 316*—referred to was for a tank company equipped with radio-controlled Borgward demolition carriers, officially known as *B-IV's*. The tanks guided the demolition carriers to targets, directed the offloading of a demolition charge, retrieved the carriers and then ignited the charges. That was the theory, although the practice was often less than successful, since enemy gunners would target the carriers as soon as they saw them, since they knew what they contained. Further, the science of radio control

According to telephonically received instructions on 17 January, the mechanized infantry regiments, the reconnaissance battalion and the *Panther* battalion were to be organized under the *freie Gliederung* organizational concept, which consolidated all of the logistics elements of the battalions into separate companies and supposedly "freed" the combat commander—hence the word *frei*—from being concerned about anything but the conduct of combat operations.[8]

One day later, the Inspector General of Engineers informed the division that the division's engineer battalion would be formed in Holzminden, with personnel being provided from the engineer school at Dessau-Roßlau.

Gradually, the designated formations began to arrive in the staging area for the activating division. When the 2nd Company of *PGLR 901* reached Nancy on 23 January 1944, the staging of that regiment was marked as complete. The regimental commander, *Oberst* Scholze, had arrived on 19 January.

On 24 January, the Commander in Chief of *Panzertruppe West, General der Panzertruppen* Geyr von Schweppenburg, arrived at the division command post.[9] The commanding general emphasized the following with Kauffmann:

1. Educating the battle group commanders in battlefield command language.

2. Dispersed combat formations; not only troop movements but their fires must be carefully planned. The planning must not only cover the start of the fighting but also continue on through the course of the fighting.

3. Offensive operations to be conducted in width and depth.

The Commander in Chief also stressed that entraining and detraining practice be conducted both during the day and the night, as well as on open stretches of rail and in close coordination with the air force liaison officer at *Heeresgruppe D.*[10]

left much to be desired at the time, and the demolition carriers were not always responsive to the remote commands. After a while, the tank companies so equipped went into action solely as normal tank companies, although German interest in the prospects for remote control continued until the end of the war.

8. Translator's Note: The *PLR* consisted of two tank battalions, one of which was equipped with the *Panzer IV* and the other with the *Panther*.

9. Translator's Note: *Panzertruppen West* was a corps-level command and consisted of various armored divisions that were assigned with defense in the West.

10. Translator's Note: Army Group D.

The difficulties encountered in the formation of the division were outlined in correspondence to Guderian on 27 January. In the meantime, the division ordered route reconnaissance of the surrounding area in the event of an early deployment. Two main and two auxiliary routes were designated within the movement zone of the division. The routes were capable of supporting both *Tigers* and *Panthers*. Following the recommendation of Kauffmann, Bayerlein requested the movement of the divisional artillery into the division's staging area so that it could begin its necessary coordination with the combat formations of the division.

When *HFA 311* arrived in Verdun on 29 January, Kauffmann breathed a sigh of relief, since Bayerlein had only the day before emphasized the necessity of providing air defense for the division.

On 1 February, Guderian informed the command that he would visit the division for the first time on 18 February. In a division order-of-the-day published on 3 February, Guderian's directives to the new formation were repeated:

> Training: The most pressing mission is to have the division coalesce into a cohesive fighting formation; the interaction of all of the troop elements is emphasized. The central focus of the training is offensive in nature: that is the same for all weapons systems; for example, it is also applicable for the *Panzerjäger-Lehr-Abteilung*. The uncompromising concentration of all forces to form a main effort for combat operations is the basic focus of leadership. The entire division is to conduct night marches after receiving short-notice alerts. The division has until 1 March to be deployable.

On 4 February, Bayerlein officially took command of the division. He directed an exercise take place the following day. The exercise conducted by *Oberst* Gerhardt's initiated a period of extremely intensive training. Everything that the division would have to do in the event of combat operations was practiced. Everything was done to instruct the soldiers and prepare them for combat. Bayerlein did everything in his power to take the diverse elements of the division, which had come together from all points of the compass, to form them into a cohesive and powerful whole.

When it looked like *HFA 311* was going to be pulled from the division, Bayerlein fought to keep it. Aside from the complete mechanization of the division, the best possible air defense was a guarantor for its successful employment.

On 17 February, the division's logistics officer, *Hauptmann* Berend Werncke, arrived from the War Academy. The same day, Bayerlein discovered that the Armed Forces Command intended to move the division into the area of operations of the *19. Armee* after its activation period was over. Writing to Guderian, Bayerlein took exception to this plan. The main point of his argument:

> A movement of the division without it being fully deployable for combat operations could lead to catastrophes similar to those that befell two other armored divisions on the Eastern Front. That would be lamentable based on the unique equipping of the division and the great expectations that have been placed in it by the highest levels of command.

After Guderian visited on 18 February, he forbade any offices of his inspectorate from establishing timelines for ending the training and the activation period. He reserved that right to himself.

In three days of exercises, Guderian was able to convince himself that the division commander had done everything possible to train his division in the best manner possible. At the *Grand* Hotel in Nancy, Guderian expressed his belief that the division would be able to accomplish its intended mission— the turning back of any Allied invasion. In order to ensure that the division would have all means at its disposal to do so, he had it placed under his direct command on 26 February.

On 6 March, the operations officer of *Panzergruppe West* called the division. He informed his counterpart: "The division's being moved into the area around Vienna. Start on 8 March at 2400 hours. End [of movement] on 13 March." The written movement orders soon followed. The advance party was formed. It was ordered to move out by road march at 0600 hours on 7 March. That brought ten weeks of training to a close.

CHAPTER 3

In Vienna and Budapest

TRAINING AND MORE TRAINING

By the end of February 1944, there were reports filtering in to Berlin from the Hungarian capital that talked about an impending crisis. The danger was present that the Hungarian allies would be "toppled" in much the same way that the Italians had fallen at the beginning of September 1943.

Since there were hardly any German forces in Budapest at the time that were capable of representing German interests and securing the logistical lines of communication to the southern portion of the Eastern Front, it was decided to move the *PLD* to Hungary. On the one hand, that meant that no combat divisions had to be pulled out of the line on the Eastern Front. On the other, the High Command was convinced that the division, which was still not considered combat deployable, was capable of accomplishing the aforementioned missions.

The *PLD* was directed to the assembly area of the *LVIII. Reserve-Panzer-Korps* of *General der Panzertuppe* Krüger. Since the position of the Hungarian Army was still not clear, it was feared that there might be some conflict there. The division was directed to put down any resistance by means of force. If possible, however, it was intended to employ the Hungarian forces in support of German interests.

It was not certain what would follow the occupation of Budapest and the disarming of the Hungarian forces, if the latter case were necessary. Would a new national government be installed or would there be a military administration? The only thing that was certain was that the division would practically be on its own and that it would have a difficult situation to master as a "guest of the Hungarian armed forces."

On 8 March 1944, the advance party of the division arrived in Vienna. It met with and was briefed by the staff of Krüger's reserve corps and the logistics officer of the hosting *XVII. Armee-Korps* rear-area command. The division was assigned a quartering area north and east of Lake Neusiedel. Since there were few opportunities for establishing quarters there, many elements, especially *PGLR 901*, were put up at the Bruck an der Leitha Training Area. By means of telegram, Kauffmann asked all military agencies involved with the division's activation to reroute logistics to Bruck an der Leitha. That same day, *PALA*

130, under its commander, *Hauptmann* Gerd von Born-Fallois, arrived at the training area.

During the briefing on 10 March with Krüger, the division was given directives concerning its possible employment. The corps had been directed to occupy Hungary as a precautionary measure to prevent that nation from falling away from the Axis. Forces were being assembled in Belgrade, Vienna and Breslau to that end.

The *PLD* received orders to establish two battle groups—*Kampfgruppen*—under the command of a regimental staff. They were to be loaded on six trains during the morning of 17 March and sent by express to Budapest by evening of that same day. The most important buildings were to be occupied there and the Hungarian forces disarmed. Bayerlein was to receive more detailed information on 13 March from *General* von Pfuhlstein, the commander of "Operation Margarete," as the occupation operation was to be called. The *16. SS-Freiwilligen-Panzer-Grenadier-Division "Reichsführer SS"* was to advance to the right of the *PLD* into the industrial area on Budapest's west side.[1]

During a briefing with Guderian on 11 March, the Inspector General decided to request that the field-army group release the *PLD* from its mission within "Margarete," since it would lead to the splitting up of the division. The field-army group turned down the request, with the result that both *Kampfgruppen* were formed on 12 March and placed under the command of Knight's Cross recipient *Oberst* Joachim Gutmann, the commander of *PGLR 902*.

While the planning was proceeding, units and formations of the division continued to pour into its designated assembly areas. In order to provide cover for the movement of the division into the area southeast of Vienna, the corps published an order announcing that its new mission was preparation for a spring offensive in the east.

On 15 March, the *Kampfgruppen* for "Margarete" were loaded on trains. Guderian, who visited the division that same day, spoke to the assembled men of the 3rd Battalion of the divisional artillery, *PALA 130* and the 1st Battalion of *Panzer-Regiment 6*.[2] Guderian outlined Germany's situation, with special emphasis on the situation in the East. He emphasized the strength of

---

1. Translator's Note: 16th *SS* Volunteer Mechanized Infantry Division *"Reichsführer SS."*

2. Translator's Note: At the end of 1943, the 1st Battalion of *Panzer-Regiment 6* (*3. Panzer-Division*) was detached from the division and sent to Erlangen for new-equipment training on the *Panther*. In January 1944, the battalion was attached to the *PLR* to act as its *Panther* battalion until the actual 1st Battalion of the *PLR* could finish its training. Eventually, the battalion was redesignated as the *I./PLR* and served with the regiment and division until the fall of 1944, when it was returned to its parent division and redesignated as the *I./Panzer-Regiment 6*. In August 1944, the *PLR* formed its own *Panther* battalion, which then joined the division as the "new" *I./PLR*.

the division and the necessity of concentrating all forces. In conclusion, he stated:

> I am firmly convinced that this division will accomplish great things with its terrific commanders and exceptional equipment. I call for you to take special care of the equipment and demand loyalty to your combat arm and a will for victory. There is only one thing for us: Victory or defeat—but no compromise.

✠

As the result of a bombing raid on 17 March on the southeastern portion of Vienna and the surroundings, the quartering area of *PPLB 130*—the village of Deutsch-Haslau—was also hit. The engineers suffered one dead and three wounded. There was no doubt that the raid was directed against the German forces concentrating in Vienna for the upcoming operation against Hungary.

On 18 March, as part of a commanders briefing, the division order entitled "Advance on Budapest" was issued. At 2330 hours, there was a briefing by Guderian's adjutant indicating that a march into Hungary had been arranged with the regent of Hungary. The order was that the Hungarian forces were not to be disarmed. It was only in instances where resistance was being offered that harsh measures were to be taken. The lead elements of the *PLD* reached Raab (Györ) at 0605 hours the next day. Under the leadership of Bayerlein, the Hungarian garrison was interned in its facilities without a hitch. At 0715 hours, Komaron (Komárom) was reached.

The division's immediate objective of Pilisvörösvár was reached by the main body of the *Kampfgruppe* around 1405 hours. At 1500 hours, the lead elements were in an area west of Budapest. The Hungarian garrison at Gran (Esztergom) was interned in its facilities by a battalion of *PGLR 901*. Around 2230 hours, orders arrived from corps directing the division to occupy the area Komaron–Stuhlweißenburg (Székesfehérvár)–Ascod by 20 March. The division headquarters was established in Pilisvörösvár.

The march on Budapest was a good exercise for the division. Deficiencies in march discipline came to light, which the division commander used as the basis of further training.

On the following day, *Generalfeldmarschall* von Weichs, the Commander in Chief of *Heeresgruppe F*, visited the division command post and had Bayerlein brief him on how the operation went. At the conclusion of the briefing, the field-army group's chief of staff noted that the *PLD* would only spend a short while in Hungary prior to being shipped back to France.

That afternoon, the division command post moved to Gran. *General der Panzertuppe* Krüger held a conference with all of the division commanders there on 21 March. The commanders were informed that the developing political situation in Hungary made it inopportune to disarm the Hungarian forces. Since things were still percolating under the surface, however, the German forces were to remain on alert. At the same time, the forces were to consider themselves guests of the Hungarian forces and not their conquerors. That said, any affronts were not to be tolerated. Good appearances and behavior were considered to be the best propaganda.

The division was issued the following order:

1. Immediate measures: Seal off Budapest to all German formations and elements. Start at 1800 hours on 23 March 1944. Later on, it is intended to conduct regular inspection tours. General officers and general-staff officers may pass through the cordon; everyone else only with written permission of the commanding general.

2. The corps is preparing for the occupation of other portions of Hungary.

3. The division is to prepare to occupy Budapest. The task organization of the forces is to be determined and the approach march controlled.

To that end:

a) Immediately attached to the division: *Regiment Brandenburg* (in the area southeast of Budapest); *SS-Fallschirmjäger-Bataillon* and *Fallschirmjäger-Bataillon Brandenburg* (in the vicinity of 412).[3]

b) Attached to the division upon arrival: *Grenadier-Regiment (mot) 92* in the Czeged [Szeged] area.[4]

---

3. Translator's Note: The *Brandenburg* elements were special operations forces; *Fallschirmjäger* were airborne forces. The *SS* battalion referred to was officially designated *SS-Fallschirmjäger-Bataillon 500*.

4. Translator's Note: This formation may have been mistakenly referred to as a regiment in the order when, in fact, it had apparently been redesignated as a brigade on 5 June 1943 according to the website *Lexikon der Wehrmacht* (www.lexikon-der-wehrmacht.de/Gliederungen/Grenadieregimenter/GR92.htm). As a brigade, it received a light artillery battery and a light engineer company. It still had only two battalions of infantry, the *I.* and *II./Sonderverband 287 (Deutsch-Arabische Legion)*. Apparently, there were some Arabs assigned to the battalions. The regiment/brigade was intended as a general headquarters force and was allocated to *Heeresgruppe F.* An

Additional details concerning the occupation to be provided by the military attaché, *General* von Greifenberg.

Task organization of the forces:

West bank: 1 mechanized infantry regiment; 1 artillery battalion; 1 tank battalion; and 1 airborne battalion.

East bank (southern sector): *Grenadier-Regiment (mot) 92; 4./Regiment Brandenburg;* 1 artillery battalion; 1 tank company.

East bank (center sector): 1 mechanized infantry regiment; 1 artillery battalion; 1 tank company

East bank (northern sector): 1 engineer battalion; 1 tank company.

Details for conduct in Hungary:

a) Care is to be taken when invited to functions by civilian and military authorities.

b) Requisitions only in emergencies and approved by regimental commanders.

c) Military courtesies to be exchanged with Hungarian armed forces.

d) The division is directed to send liaison officers to the Hungarian I Corps in Budapest and the II Corps in Stuhlweißenburg. Missions for the liaison officers: Taking care of all difficulties that surface.

PGLR 901 was given the mission of executing the cordon around Budapest. The corps also ordered the division to occupy Stuhlweißenburg. By 1700 hours on 21 March, the *PLR* had completed that mission, focusing on industrial areas and railway facilities.

Major Joachim Barth, the commander of *PJLA 130*, reported on the condition of the combat vehicles of his battalion on 22 March.[5] The thirty-

---

extensive discussion of this interesting formation can be found at *Axis History Forum* (forum.axishistory.com/viewtopic.php?t=64436).

5. Author's Note: Barth received the Knight's Cross on 17 December 1942 while serv-ing as the commander of *Panzerjäger-Abteilung 13* of the *13. Panzer-Division.* At the time, he was a *Hauptmann.*

one *Panzerjäger IV's* his battalion had been issued were only incompletely outfitted. His request for replacement parts and equipment for the vehicles, some of which had been damaged while being transported to the battalion, was approved by the division commander and forwarded to the appropriate division of the Army High Command. That same day, *Major* Kauffmann was summoned to *LVIII. Panzer-Korps* to see the chief-of-staff. He was informed that the division had to be prepared to march into Budapest with six hours' notice.

In "Division Order No. 3," Bayerlein directed his forces to move up to the restricted zone of Budapest by 1800 hours on 23 March so as to be able to immediately occupy the city, if ordered to do so. Four approach routes were designated. The occupation was to take place upon receipt of a code word—*Donaustadt* ("Danube City")—and be conducted in three phases. By then, the division had received the forces designated to be attached to it. At 1300 hours on 23 March, the division command post was moved to Budakezy (Budakeszi).

By the evening of 23 March, the division had closed on the outer ring of Budapest. Nothing happened on 24 March or the next day. Around 2245 hours on 25 March, Kauffmann was informed by the corps chief of staff that the *16. SS-Freiwilligen-Panzer-Grenadier-Division "Reichsführer SS"* was being moved immediately through Budapest to eastern Hungary and that the *PLD* was being given the additional mission of securing the area the *SS* division had previously occupied. To that end, the *PLD* was directed to form an *ad hoc* element out of reserves. The *Sonderverband* was ordered to report directly to the corps. Augmenting the *ad hoc* formation were *Pionier-Bau-Bataillon 798* and a militia battalion from Ödenburg.

In the end, Bayerlein intervened and contacted the corps chief of staff, arranging for *Grenadier-Regiment (mot) 92* to assume this mission, thus preventing the division from being split up.

In the end, however, there was no massive march into Budapest. A half hour past midnight, the corps announced that the requirement to "bind" the Hungarian forces had been lifted and that the only mission left was the securing of bridges, railway facilities and industrial areas. That same day, Bayerlein started up the training program for his division again. For instance, the *PLR* received a training mission: "Breaching a minefield with tanks, engineers and mechanized infantry." The breaching of minefields was a special concern for Bayerlein and he, in turn, was only reacting to Guderian's directive that all soldiers, especially mechanized infantry, be schooled in detecting, clearing and emplacing mines. Bayerlein told his commanders:

Attacking across a defended minefield requires intensive practice within the units and close coordination across the formations. I am therefore ordering in the next few days that all mechanized infantry battalions repeat this exercise, together with tanks, armored engineers and artillery support.

The divisional engineers were instructed to offer short courses on detecting and clearing mines with at least one officer, two noncommissioned officers and eight enlisted personnel participating from each company. In addition, the engineers were told to practice building bridges and ferries, in conjunction with corps bridging assets. The divisional artillery conducted gunnery training with its heavy battalion.

During the evening of 27 March, the division received a route reconnaissance mission from the corps. It was to reconnoiter two passes through the Carpathians: the Tatar (Jablonitza) Pass and the Stiel Pass. It was directed to determine the following: condition of the roads (width, traffic patterns, grades and curves and bridge capacities); obstacle employment options; snow conditions; trail network aside from main roads and suitability for infantry, motorized forces and tanks; and how long would it take to make the passes trafficable and what means would be needed.

The reconnaissance was to be completed within three days, with ongoing results being reported to corps by landline or radio starting at Debrecin. This mission seemed to indicate the potential employment of the division in especially poor terrain for armored forces. *Major* Kauffmann correspondingly called the Guderian's offices on 28 March and echoed these concerns. Guderian was able to allay those fears, however, by assuring Kauffmann that the division would be sent back to France in about four weeks to continue its training.

On 29 March, Bayerlein and his operations officer accompanied the commanding general to view Hungarian tank gunnery training at the ranges at Gran. On 1 April, the reconnaissance elements that had been sent to the Carpathian passes—*PPLB 130*—returned and forwarded their findings by radio to the corps.

That same day, Bayerlein requested that *HFA 311* be permanently attached to the division. He needed the valuable antiaircraft assets to protect his equally valuable ground formations. *Hauptmann* Gustav Weinkopf's battalion had four heavy batteries, each with six 8.8-centimeter dual-purpose antiaircraft/antitank guns. In addition, there was a light battery with four 2-centimeter automatic cannon. The entire battalion was motorized. Bayerlein's request did not fall on deaf ears, and the battalion was eventually assigned to the division.

On 6 April 1944, Kauffmann was notified that the corps headquarters would be moved to the west and that the division would assume the command and control functions of the corps. To that end, the division was to move its command staff to Budakezsi, the site of the corps command post. That move took place the following day. Effective as of 2400 hours on 8 April, the division assumed its new responsibility. The only area that it did not receive was that of the *298. Infanterie-Division*. Since the mission could be accomplished from Gran, Bayerlein requested and received approval to move his "corps" headquarters there.

During this time period, another report was sent to the Inspector General of the Armored Forces and the Army Procurement Agency concerning the thirty-nine *Panzerjäger IV's* of *PJLA 130*. Basically, the report stated that the vehicles were not ready for employment at the front. Bayerlein wanted to prevent any of his men from going into combat with ineffective weapons. He wanted only the best for his men and his division. At the same time, Guderian was requested to change the table of organization and equipment of the battalion's 3rd Company to reflect the *Jagpanzer IV* instead of the *Jagdpanther*, since replacement parts for the former would be considerably easier to receive than the latter.[6]

The amount of detail work never seemed to end while getting the division ready for combat. The Commander in Chief of *Heeresgruppe F* visited the division on 11 April. Von Weichs was briefed by Bayerlein on the division's quartering area, its organization and its relationship with the Hungarians, which Bayerlein characterized as good. The field-army group commander finished up his visit by informing Bayerlein that the division had been directed to release the division by the Armed Forces High Command/West; the only detail left was when the division would depart.

Bayerlein had the intensive training continue while waiting for the movement orders. He placed special emphasis on gunnery exercises and marksmanship training. He also emphasized field training (to include dismounted drills) and night training. It was important to him that fires be coordinated and concentrated. Above all, he stressed that every soldier in the division must be well versed in both active and passive air-defense measures.

On 13 April, bomber formations of the U.S. Eighth Air Force bombed the areas around Budapest and Raab. Because not only the Hungarian military but also the local civilian populace were unable to combat the conflagrations, the *PLD* had to take the lead. That same date, the field-army group informed the division that the command staff created for *Operation "Margarete"* would

---

6. Translator's Note: The *Jagdpanther* was based on the chassis of the *Panzer V Panther*. Editor's Note: Late in the war, the 5th and 8th Companies of the *II./Panzer-Lehr-Rgt. 130* were equipped with *Jagdpanther* while the 6th and 7th Companies were equipped with *Panthers*.

soon be disbanded. That effectively placed command of all German forces in Hungary under the military attaché in Budapest, *General der Infanterie* von Greiffenberg. On 14 April, *Major* Kauffmann was informed by Guderian's staff that the division's move to the Bergen Training Area could be expected soon. Guderian's staff was then requested to reconsider the location of the transfer and shift it back to France. Conditions were more favorable for the division there in terms of quartering arrangements, training opportunities and rations. Furthermore, the division would not be exposed to air attacks as much as it would be in Germany. Finally, it was requested that the move be held back to 22 April at the earliest, in order to allow exercises that had already started and were being planned by the division to be completed. Guderian's staff provided assurance to that effect.

The training continued. Every man in the division realized that he had a commander in charge of the division who had learned his craft on the battlefields of the East and North Africa and who placed the values of good training above everything else. The tank regiment conducted gunnery training on the ranges at Gran and Vezsprem. The mechanized infantry regiments and the reconnaissance battalion practiced at the other training areas within the division's assigned area. Coordination and concentration of fires were stressed. The divisional artillery moved its 2nd and 3rd Battalions to the Vezsprem Training Area.

On 17 April, two soldiers of *PGLR 902* were killed during a bombing raid on Budapest.

During an exercise designed to practice coordination between armor forces and artillery that was held on 18 April, Bayerlein stressed the importance of both active and passive antitank measures. When selecting positions, he stressed, it was especially important to safeguard the tanks. All weapons systems needed to be versed in the art of destroying tanks. Drawing on his experience in Africa, he emphasized the use of mines as an anti-armor deterrent.

Guderian's staff was requested to provide estimates on how long the division would remain in Hungary so that the training plan could be adjusted to fit the available time. On 22 April, the *Panther* battalion conducted gunnery exercises involving moving targets. During the period from 24 to 30 April, night operations were on the schedule, as well as exercises conducted during twilight. In addition, there were formation-level training, river-crossing exercises (in conjunction with the divisional engineers) and a live-fire exercise involving all of the combat arms of the division. For the mechanized infantry, there was an exercise involving "smoking out enemy pockets of resistance with support of flamethrower vehicles while following a friendly armor attack."

Just after planning for the exercises from 1 to 6 May had been finished, orders arrived from Guderian's staff on the evening of 29 April for the division to be moved by expedited rail to France and the area of operations of the Commander in Chief West starting on 1 May.

Starting on 30 April, *PGLR 901* began loading on trains at the Buda-West station. The train movement was given highest priority, and it passed through Vienna, Munich, Straßburg and Nancy without stopping on its way to Orleans. Due to the danger from fighter-bombers there, the units detrained rapidly and reached their staging areas around Illiers by road march.

A few hours earlier the same day, the division advance party moved out to Meaux, the headquarters of *Panzergruppe West*. The formation structured their individual trains so that each formed a combat-ready element. The troops were warned about the increased danger from the air in the western part of the *Reich* and in the occupied territories and the concomitant requirement for increased readiness. By 15 May, the entire division with all of its equipment and vehicles reached France, using seventy trains in the process. The division's troops and subordinate formations were quartered at Illiers and around Nogent-le-Rotrou and the area between Le Man and Chartres. In all, only two low-level aerial attacks were made against the movements, and the division was able to reach its new assembly area without appreciable casualties.

Despite the initial difficulties, the six weeks spent in Hungary had given the division the opportunity to bring its activation and training efforts to a qualified conclusion. Even if unit-level training still needed some additional practice, the units themselves had made good progress in individual skills training and weapons familiarization, gunnery and marksmanship. The exercises had increased understanding among the soldiers of the peculiarities of employment for individual formations.

On 1 May, Bayerlein was promoted to *Generalleutnant*. Once the division's troop elements had settled in, training was resumed. The staff officers war-gamed defensive options and reconnoitered along the Atlantic Wall between the Cotentin Peninsula and Le Havre.

Bayerlein insisted that his elements conceal themselves from the air. He had experienced firsthand the devastating effect of Allied airpower in North Africa, and the constant aerial reconnaissance being flown by the Allies over western France indicated that the upcoming campaign would be no different. He was convinced that his division could not be allowed to be discovered by the enemy after its return from Hungary. No vehicles were allowed to move along the roads during the day, unless it was absolutely necessary. The main body of the division was bivouacked in woods, with some smaller elements scattered among the surrounding villages. During the entire month of May, there were no attacks in the divisional assembly area.

U.S. Flying Fortresses flew over the division's area on a daily basis on their way to Germany. Bayerlein was unable to resist that temptation, and he allowed his *Flak* battalion to engage the B-17's. *HFA 311* was able to shoot down four of the aircraft. On 2 and 3 June, however, it became obvious that the division's location had been discovered when aircraft began to appear— medium bombers and, above all, fighter-bombers—which shot up roads and targets in the division's area of operations, which contained 260 armored fighting vehicles and 800 *SPW's*. Despite the attacks, losses were minimal.

Thanks to the fact that all four of the division's mechanized infantry battalions were completely outfitted with *SPW's*, the *PLD* could boast that it was the only German armored division that had 100 percent mechanized or armored combat elements. That had been Guderian's intent, since he wanted to create an elite strike force to thwart the invasion. He once told Bayerlein: "Your objective is not the coast! It is the sea!"

Thanks to its outfitting, the *PLD* had the strength of about three normal Army armored divisions at that point in the war, especially since all of the others had been in the field and were never able to receive a full complement of replacement personnel, materiel and equipment. Had it been employed in the vast expanses of the Soviet Union, it would have been able to deploy in a tactically and doctrinally sound manner. In the broken hedgerow country of Normandy, however, its deployment options were much more limited.

There proved to be an additional disadvantage for the division in that the *PLR*, which was the slowest element to move, was arrayed the farthest away from the potential invasion front. Despite requests, Bayerlein was not allowed to regroup his forces. Although the division was also in the potential invasion area, the Armed Forces High Command continued to hold the powerful formation under its direct control as an operational-level ready reserve. Numerous requests were made to the High Command's chief of staff, *General* Warlimont, in this regard, but they were all turned down. In addition to the *PLD*, the *21. Panzer-Division*—reconstituted after the division had surrendered in North Africa in 1943—and the *12. SS-Panzer-Division "Hitlerjugend"* were also held back as a reserve force. Together, those three divisions represented enough combat power that they probably would have been capable of throwing a newly landing enemy into the sea in an immediate counterattack if they had been released by the Armed Forces High Command in a timely manner.

Did the Armed Force High Command really have that chance?

A member of *Admiral* Canaris's espionage agency (the *Abwehr*) who was also a member of the French underground—which was to open a sabotage campaign just before the start of the invasion after receiving a code word—brought Canaris a poem. It was the "Autumn Song" of Paul Verlaine. The poem held the key to the actions of the underground. Whenever the first line of the poem was read on the BBC, the invasion was just around the corner. When the second line was read, the invasion would start within forty-eight hours. From that point forward, the radio intercept battalion of the *15. Armee* in Tourcoing stayed glued to the BBC broadcasts. From 1 to 3 June, the first line of the poem was read. The second line was heard by a radio-intercept operator at 2115 hours on 5 June. All military channels were immediately notified. Less than an hour later, the Armed Forces High Command and Hitler were informed that the invasion was imminent. Of course, they did not know exactly where the landings would come.

Nonetheless, German countermeasures should have been initiated. The *PLD*, which had been formed and trained for this express purpose, could have moved out. It would have been possible for the division to be on the invasion beaches on the morning of 6 June. It would have been able to strike at the enemy when he was the weakest: immediately after the initial landings. Of course, that presupposes that the right beaches would also have been picked.

In the end, both the *Führer* Headquarters and the headquarters of *Heeresgruppe B* failed to give credence to the invasion being "announced" by means of a poem. Forces were not alerted and, on the morning of the invasion, the *PLD* was 150 kilometers from the beaches.

At 0111 hours on 6 June, the telephone rang in the main command bunker of the *LXXXIV. Armee-Korps* of *General der Artillerie* Erich Marcks, the commanding general. Marcks, who had just enjoyed a drink with his staff on the occasion of his birthday, lifted the receiver. The operations officer of the *716. Infanterie-Division* was at the other end. What the commanding general heard was alarming: "Enemy paratroopers have jumped east of the mouth of the Orne. Primarily in the Breville–Ranville area and the northern edge of the woods at Bavant. Countermeasures underway."

A short while later, at 0145 hours, the *709. Infanterie-Division* reported from Valognes: "Enemy paratroopers south of St. Germain de Varreville and at Ste. Marie-du-Mont. Second group west of the main road from Carentan to Valognes on both sides of Merderet Creek and along the road from Ste.-Mère-Église and Pont-l'Abbé. Fighting for the crossing points."

That same day, at 0230 hours, the telephone rang at Bayerlein's command post in Dogent-le-Rotrou. *General* Warlimont from the Armed Forces command staff directed Bayerlein to alert his division and have it move in the direction of Caen. Further orders would be received through *Heeresgruppe B.*

Bayerlein swung into action immediately. The invasion had started.

CHAPTER 4

The March to the Front

THE STREET SWEEPERS OF FRANCE

The exact message that Bayerlein's staff later received stated:

> Enemy airborne landings on the Calvado Coast and the east coast of
> the Cotentin Peninsula. Perhaps the expected invasion. Probably only
> part of a deception, however, since the aircraft reporting centers at
> Cape Gris and Cape d'Albrecht, as well as the radio intercept station
> at Le Touquest–Paris–Plage, are also reporting the approach of large
> fleets across the water. The *PLD* is to go on alert and be prepared to
> march in the direction of Caen.

In the surrounding villages, the feverish work began. It now turned out
to have been ill-advised that the division had not been allowed to move since
it had returned from Hungary without direct orders from the Armed Forces
command staff. The coastal area was nearly 150 kilometers away. While the
division prepared to move, it did not receive any further orders that night or
the next morning. The German Armed Forces High Command wavered. It
still was not convinced that the invasion was actually taking place. Perhaps it
was a deception operation. It continued to cling to its previous assessments
that the actual invasion would take place at the Pas de Calais. It was aided in
that delusion by the Allied deception campaign, "Operation Fortitude," the
aim of which was to attack all tactical targets between Calais and Le Havre,
especially the likes of the fortifications and coastal batteries at Cape Gris Nez,
Fort Mahon and Pointe du H-Blanc.

Bayerlein spent the night trying to recall the *I./Panzer-Regiment 6*, which
had been released back to its parent division. The tanks were in various
locations, all *en route* to the east. Without the *Panther* battalion, he lost more
than half of his tank combat power, since the *Panthers* were qualitatively
superior to his remaining *Panzer IV* battalion. With luck, he was able to get
the transports stopped and turned around, but it would be three days before
the entire battalion was back with its adopted division.

Bayerlein was tireless in trying to get information on what was happening
and how his division might be employed. The men, who had been sitting in

their vehicles since the middle of the night, started to get tired in the hot June sun. The uncertainty of the situation was getting on their nerves. They searched the skies constantly. Fighter-bombers were swooping above without pause, but none of them were German.

Bayerlein took off to Le Mans with his liaison officer. He wanted to visit the headquarters of the *7. Armee* personally to see what was going on. *Unteroffizier* Kartheuß was the driver. Once they got there, Bayerlein was hit with yet another surprise. *Generaloberst* Dollmann, the Commander in Chief of the field army, informed Bayerlein that the *PLD* was attached to him, effective immediately. The same news awaited the *12. SS-Panzer-Division "Hitlerjugend."* Dollmann ordered Bayerlein to start his division moving at 1700 hours. Bayerlein protested; he wanted to wait until it had at least turned dusk. Dollmann did not relent, however. After the division had remained stationary for such a long time, it was now being ordered to move out almost immediately. *Generalmajor* Pemsel, the chief of staff of the *7. Armee*, read aloud from a telegram the headquarters had received:

> The Commander in Chief West refers to the desire of the Armed Forces High Command that the enemy be destroyed in his bridgehead by the evening of 6 June, since there are fears that the air and sea landings will be reinforced. In accordance with orders from *Generaloberst* Jodl, all forces are to be sent to the [beachhead] on the Calvados coast. The penetration there must be cleared up today.

Bayerlein pointed out that the division had been stationary for more than nine hours. He did not hide the fact that he considered the absurd order the same thing as a death sentence for his division and that nothing at all could be achieved by executing it.

Dollmann insisted the order be carried out: "The *PLD* must be in an area south of Caen by the early morning of 7 June. The British 185th Brigade under Lieutenant Colonel Maurice has already broken through the high ground at Périers and is marching on Caen. Caen is of the greatest importance to us."

Bayerlein pointed out that the rate-of-march for his elements could not exceed eight kilometers an hour under the existing air threat and that his forces would not be able to reach the area south of Caen the next tomorrow morning. In all seriousness, it was then recommended to Bayerlein that his forces take the most direct route to Caen. To do that, however, would require rerouting the entire division.

Bayerlein went back to his command post in Nogent-le-Rotrou and summoned his commanders. He briefed them on what was required, trying hard not to show his displeasure at the orders he had received. In conclusion, he said: "Move on or near the roads and try to get there as fast and as unruffled as possible!"

At 1700 hours, orders were issued within all of the subordinate elements: *"Panzer marsch!"*

The best-equipped armored division in the German Army started to move out. It was imperative for the division to establish contact with the *21. Panzer-Division*, which was already in contact with the enemy.

The fully tracked, half-tracked and wheeled vehicles resembled a moving forest. They snuck from position to position in order to avoid being observed from the air. But even the best of camouflage was not of great value. Gigantic clouds of dust rose skyward behind the vehicles and marked the five advance routes of the division.

Bayerlein later recalled his feeling on that first day in action in Normandy:

> I moved ahead of the middle column—*PGLR 901*—in two staff cars and two radio trucks of my battle staff along the Alencon–Argentan–Falaise road. A fighter-bomber attack forced us to take cover as early as Beaumont-sur-Sarthe. Things went well that time. But the columns were being torn farther and farther apart. Since the field army had ordered no radio traffic, there was only contact by means of messengers—as if no radio traffic were going to stop the fighter-bombers and reconnaissance aircraft that were loitering in the air from identifying us. The only thing it did was ensure the division command was prevented from gaining an impression on the status of the advance, whether it was fluid, whether there were delays or casualties, where the lead elements were. I had to constantly send officers out and personally go to the formations.
>
> All of the five march routes were occupied by my elements. There was no question that the advance had been identified by the enemy's aerial reconnaissance. Soon, the bombers were loitering over the roads, destroying crossings, villages and cities that were along the advance route and diving on snaking vehicle columns. At 2300 hours, we passed through the village of Sèes. It was lit up like a "Christmas tree" and heavy bombs were already bursting in the small town. Get through!
>
> Around 0200 hours, we approached Argentan. It was as light as day from fires and explosions. The city was quivering under the hail of bombs from the rolling attacks. We got as far as the southern suburb, where it was then impossible to proceed. All of Argentan was burning. We were in a witch's cauldron. The road behind us

was blocked as well. We were enclosed in the burning city. Dust and smoke robbed us of vision.

Sparks flew over the vehicles. Glowing beams and collapsed houses blocked the ways. The aircraft were still loitering in the skies. Their illumination bombs covered the burning houses in blazing light. Biting fumes took our breath away. We had to find a way out on foot. Engineer sections were working on the badly damaged bridge over the Orne. At 0300 hours, we succeeded in breaking out of the burning prison across the fields in the direction of Flers. Towards morning, the bombing slowed up. The road going through Ecouché–Briouze–Flers was in good shape. We were in Flers at 0400 hours; it had also suffered terribly. At 0500 hours, we reached Condé-sur-Noireau. Far and wide, nothing could be seen of the march columns of the division. They were working their way with difficulty across the bombed-out roads. Just as in Argentan, all of the transportation hubs behind the invasion front had been blown to bits, apparently with the intention of preventing the advance of reserves to be employed around Caen.[1]

What was the status of the tanks of the *PLR* on that first day of terror on their way to the invasion front? Bayerlein continues:

The tanks thundered north. The crews searched the skies continuously. Suddenly, they were there. No one knew where they had come from. The fighter-bombers roared in. They flitted over vegetation and hedgerows at low altitude. A nearby quad *Flak* opened fire. As a result of the concentrated fires, the oncoming machines were thrown off course. Up front, at the head of the column, there was the first detonation. Those who heard it looked at each other.

"Is that one of ours?"

You could read those thoughts off of the faces of the men.

Moving forward, the crewmembers appearing in their hatches again saw a shot-down fighter-bomber next to the road. The fuel pouring out was blazing brightly. On-board ammunition was bursting with a loud racket. But there was death among the friendly ranks as well. A *Kübelwagen* was the victim of the low-level attack.[2] Two men were killed there. The gunner on the *Flak* was killed. The first combat dead of the division. The [tank regiment] had to endure three more air attacks before it turned dark. But there was no thinking about

---

1. Author's Note: The Allies' intent was to capture Caen on D-Day+1.

2. Translator's Note: The *Kübelwagen* was the German equivalent of the U.S. "jeep."

rest. The march continued. It was not until midnight that the low fuel situation forced a short halt. The tank crews refueled. The other combat vehicles were topped off as well. Track pins had to be swapped out. Engine covers slammed open. The drivers bent over them. An hour later, everyone mounted up.

"*Panzer marsch!*" was heard instead of the [words giving the] desired break.

PGLR 901 rolled along its designated route of march: Illiers–Domfront–Rennes–Falaise–Condé St. Marie (Caen). When the elements of the regiment moved through built-up areas, they had already been bombed by Allied bomber squadrons. In Falaise, entire blocks had been leveled. It was not until 1800 hours on 8 June that the regiment closed on St. Marie, just south of Caen.

Caen was ablaze. Naval gunfire from Allied vessels placed fires throughout the approach march of the division. The 9th Company of *PGLR 901*—the self-propelled heavy infantry gun company—went directly into position in St. Marie under its commander, *Hauptmann* Hennecke. That company had also suffered its first losses. Two ammunition trailers being towed by *Maultier* prime movers were hit by rockets from fighter-bombers and destroyed, sending 100 shells up into the air.[3] Trucks in the trains were also being targeted by fighter-bombers. One of the drivers, *Obergefreiter* Griethe, could not be extracted from his shot-up driver's cab; he was burned alive. After darkness fell, the self-propelled guns moved on to Vendés, where they again went into position.

Oberst Gutmann's *PGLR 902* had moved out of Vibraye at 1700 hours on 6 June. Its tortured journey started early on the morning of 7 June. The fighter-bombers arrived at first light. In the bright sunlight of 7 June, the Thunderbolts could identify every target, no matter how well it had attempted to camouflage itself.

In their open *SPW's*, the mechanized infantry were constantly being targeted and shot out of their vehicles. The 1st Battalion was especially hard hit. In the end, it was forced to seek temporary concealment in a nearby woods a few kilometers outside of Brouay and wait for darkness.

Gutmann established his command post in a 1.5-meter-deep dugout. Shortly after digging the hole, an Allied aerial artillery observer started circling overhead. A short while after that, naval artillery began to fall on the positions from out of the sector of the two British corps that had landed.

---

3. Translator's Note: "Mule." The *Maultier* was developed for use on the Eastern Front, where road conditions left much to be desired. It was a fully tracked prime mover, also capable of hauling logistics in addition to towing trailers.

The naval barrage of heavy-caliber guns lasted an hour, with the regiment taking heavy losses. And it still had not directly engaged the enemy.

While the *PLD* was attempting to inch its way forward into the beachhead area, the Allies had already established a firm beachhead on nearly thirty miles of the Calvados Coast. In some instances, the German coastal installations were already in the hands of the Allies. Only "Utah," one of the two U.S. beaches, was still isolated.

Along the beaches, in the area of operations of Marcks's *LXXXIV. Armee-Korps*, the *709. Infanterie-Division* was defending the eastern flank of the Cotentin Peninsula. To the east was the *353. Infanterie-Division*, headquartered in Littry. Inserted between the two divisions was *Fallschirmjäger-Regiment 6* of *Major Freiherr* von der Heydte.[4] Farther to the east were the *711. Infanterie-Division* (Caen) and the *716. Infanterie-Division* (Lisieux). The only armored division directly in the corps sector was *General* Feuchtinger's *21. Panzer-Division* in Falaise.

By first light on 6 June, the Germans had already determined that three enemy airborne divisions had dropped into the Normandy area: the British 6th Airborne and the U.S. 82nd and 101st Airborne. At "Utah" beach, the U.S. had started to put the VII Corps ashore, initially consisting of the U.S. 4th Infantry Division. The U.S. V Corps landed at "Omaha," the other U.S. beach, which was located between Vierville and Port-en-Bessin, starting with the 29th Infantry Division and nine companies of Rangers. The British/Canadian beaches were "Gold," "Juno" and "Sword." The beachheads were some thirty kilometers across, in all. "Gold" was the landing area of the British 50th (Northumbrian) Infantry Division and the 8th Armoured Brigade. "Juno" saw the Canadian 3rd Infantry Division land. Finally, the British 3rd Infantry Division landed at "Sword."

The immediate objective of the British 2nd Army was to take the Caen–Bayeux road, which served as important lines of communication for the Germans. Ever since first light on 6 June, Marcks had been attempting to get the nearby armored formations released to him. That was especially true of the *21. Panzer-Division*, which was the closest formation of that type. The *716. Infanterie-Division* was fighting for its life and urgently needed some heavy firepower support.

It was not until 1700 hours on that day that Marcks saw some success. He personally led the *21. Panzer-Division* from its assembly area forward. Towards 2200 hours, *Panzer-Regiment 100* of *Oberst* von Oppeln-Bronikowski, a

---

4. Translator's Note: The regiment was assigned to the *2. Fallschirmjäger-Division* but was in the Bretagne undergoing reconstitution at the time of the invasion. It was tactically attached to the *91. Luftlande-Division* for defensive operations within the Cotentin Peninsula. The *Luftwaffe* ground division's main body was positioned behind the airborne regiment's lines.

highly decorated armor officer and prewar Olympic equestrian, had its lead elements at Luc on the coast.[5] The regiment was able to establish contact with the hard-fighting infantry.

If the *PLD* had also been on hand, then the *21. Panzer-Division* attack might have succeeded by dint of considerable combat-power reinforcement. As it was, *Panzer-Regiment 100* lost 25 percent of its operational strength and had to pull back to the area north of Caen.

By that evening, the Allies had broken out of the beachhead at Vierville. Then a second road leading off the coast was forced open. Despite that, the Allies' position was still precarious. If the three armored divisions had been given a green light early enough, the whole invasion could have been called into question. As we have already discovered, however, neither the *PLD* nor the *12. SS-Panzer-Division "Hitlerjugend"* were released early enough to do anything substantive in nature, especially since they were situated so far from the actual invasion front.[6]

Another factor hindered the deployment of the *PLD*. At the start of the landings, its organic *Flak* battalion, *HFA 311*, was in and around Paris, assisting in the air defense of that city. As it turned out, it was the only formation of the division that received permission to move early on 6 June. Of course, it was too far away to rejoin the division for its initial march towards the coast.

Even the *Flak* battalion paid a price in casualties to Allied airpower that day. The approaching fighter-bombers, which were coming out of the sun, were misidentified as *Bf 109's*. The column was strafed, and the battalion suffered its first dead. Several vehicles were set alight or badly damaged and had to be towed. Battered and bruised, the battalion was still able to reach its new area of operations along the coast relatively quickly.

By the end of the first day of movement, the division had lost some thirty vehicles. But the worst was yet to come. Those attacks from the air were but the prelude.

The *PLD* was then transferred to the operational control of the *I. SS-Panzer-Korps* of *SS-Obergruppenführer* Josef "Sepp" Dietrich. Bayerlein attempted to establish contact with the *SS* general and his headquarters, but initial attempts

5. Translator's Note: By the end of the Normandy campaign, the regiment was effectively wiped out and never reconstituted. For its part, the *21. Panzer-Division* later received *Panzer-Regiment 22* to replace the destroyed regiment.

6. Translator's Note: Since the *12. SS-Panzer-Division "Hitlerjugend"* and the *21. Panzer-Division* occur so often in the text concerning Normandy, they will be referred to hereafter as the *HJ* and *21PD*.

were in vain. It was not until late in the afternoon of 7 June that he succeeded in discovering that the corps headquarters was in Thury-Harcourt.

Dietrich then gave the division orders to establish two battle groups and reach the Caen–Bayeux rail line by the morning of 8 June and be prepared to operate around Norrey and Brouay. Dietrich concluded his orders: "You have to have reached this line by early tomorrow. From there, you will conduct an attack across a broad front, together with the 12th and 21st to throw the enemy into the sea."

The corps operations officer provided additional instructions regarding the planned attack. According to him, *SS-Brigadeführer* Fritz Witt's *HJ* already had enemy contact, as did Feuchtinger's *21PD*. The start time for the attack was set at 1205 hours. Von Oppeln-Bronikowski's forces would lead the attack for the *21PD*, while *SS-Standartenführer* Kurt *"Panzer"* Meyer's *SS-Panzer-Grenadier-Regiment 25* would lead the *HJ* elements.

Bayerlein ordered Kartheuß, his driver, to take him back to the division command post. While returning there, the men once again saw the devastation that had ben wrought by the Allied air forces. The road was lined with burned-out and shot-up vehicles. Mess vehicles had been tipped over next to prime movers. Fuel trucks were glowing, block clouds of oily smoke riding from them. The Chaumont–Villers-Bocage resembled a scene from hell.

It was 2200 hours when the headquarters vehicle reached the crest of Hill 238. Suddenly, three fighter-bombers appeared in the nighttime sky. They dove steeply and approached just above the surface of the road, approaching the vehicle head on along the road that ran as straight as an arrow.

"Three *Jabo's, Herr General!*" *Hauptmann* Hartdegen yelled out.

"Stop, Kartheuß. Get out!"

The brakes screeched, and the vehicle slid along the righthand side of the road. Far ahead, Bayerlein could see the impacts from the aircraft machine guns, whose bullets penetrated into the asphalt. He jumped out of the still-rolling vehicle with a single bound and landed parallel to the road in the ditch. In front of him he recognized the silhouette of Hartdegen, who had disappeared into the thick walls of a concrete drainage ditch. The driver also swung out of the vehicle. At that moment, the aircraft cannon started to fire. The rounds sprayed around the ears of the men and forced Bayerlein to take full cover, as he had been forced to do so many times before.

The vehicle was engulfed in flames after a mighty detonation. Kartheuß called out: "Crawl farther from the ditch, *Herr General!*" Anything else he attempted to yell was drowned out in the fury of cannon and machine-gun fire. The second fighter-bomber flew right along the ditch. Rounds slammed into the earth to both sides, in front of and behind Bayerlein. He was hit by shrapnel. He pressed himself even more desperately into the soft earth.

The fighter-bombers repeated their attack and then came in a third time. They only stopped when they thought they had extinguished all forms of life in the attack zone. Bayerlein heard the aircraft turn off and then disappear to the north. He collected himself and then moved up to the road. At the same time, Hartdegen was dragging himself out of the drainage pipe. The vehicle was a smoking wreck on the road.

The general officer called out: "Kartheuß!" But the driver was incapable of answering. He had fallen victim to the inferno of fire form the Thunderbolts. Bayerlein wiped away the blood on his forehead, which was coming from his own shrapnel wounds. It was a miracle that he had escaped with his life.

"How are you, Hartdegen?" he asked his liaison officer, who was kneeling next to Kartheuß.

"Kartheuß is beyond help, *Herr General!*"

"We need to cover him up."

Hartdegen removed his pullover and covered the face of the driver. Both of the officers presented arms. Hartdegen then turned to his commander: "*Herr General*, we need to get away from this smoke. They might send more bombers after us."

Bayerlein nodded in agreement. They went another 100 meters and then collapsed into the ditch. They were still trembling after the attack. It got darker and soon turned to night.

"How do we get from here to the division command post, Hartdegen? Kauffmann is certainly waiting impatiently for us there."

"I think it would be best if I went to Coulvain and the command post of the *902* and get a vehicle from *Oberst* Gutmann, *Herr General.*"

But Hartdegen didn't get a chance to set out for the hike to Coulvain. A *Kübelwagen* came racing up the road from the direction of Coulvain. Gutmann had observed the fighter-bomber attack from his command post and sent out the staff car as a precautionary measure.

The *Kübelwagen* moved out at speed in the direction of Proussy, where Kauffmann had been waiting for more than twenty-four hours for his division commander. The operations had assembled the loss reports of the divisional troops and formations as they started to filter in. As of 1930 hours on 7 June, the division had lost the following vehicles: five tanks, forty fuel trucks (each with 2.5-ton capacity), eighty-four *SPW's* and self-propelled guns and ninety other vehicles of all types.

That was the equivalent of 10 percent of the division's authorized vehicular strength. Up to that point, not a single vehicle had had a direct encounter with the enemy. The Vire–Beny-Bocage road had become a shooting gallery for fighter-bombers.

Together with his battle staff, Bayerlein went over the orders he had received for the attack planned for the next day. It was directed that *PGLR 901*, reinforced by the 5th and 6th Companies of *Major* Wilhelm's battalion of *PLR*, attack in the area of Norrey. *PGLR 902*, also reinforced by the 2nd Battalion of *PLR*, was directed to attack in the area of Brouay. The latter regiment was to link up with the *HJ* after achieving its attack objective, with the *HJ* having been directed to head for the coast. It finally appeared that a major attack was about to be launched. But Bayerlein knew—and knew all too well—that it was coming two days too late.

To a certain degree, Bayerlein had feared that would happen. The Allied air superiority would hamper operations—that he knew. What he didn't know beforehand was the extent of Allied air superiority, which could more accurately be referred to as air supremacy. While the addition of *HFA 311* to the division had been indispensible, it was no more than a pinprick against the vast aerial armada it faced. Other than the failure to align and employ the German armored reserves properly, it was the Allied air superiority that contributed the most to the initial German setbacks. On 6 June, 10,585 combat sorties were flown, which does not include the 1,730 sorties of transport commands. On the evening of 6 June, the Commander in Chief of the *7. Armee* made a bitter call to *Generalfeldmarschall* Rommel: "The *Luftwaffe* has not shown up."

Author Chester Wilmot, the author of *The Struggle for Europe*, wrote in his book:

> The value of the combined Allied air superiority cannot be overestimated. Of the individual factors concerning the success of the invasion, it was without doubt the most important; its effect was felt in almost every enemy plan and almost all enemy operations. Strategy and tactics of the Germans, fortifications and equipment, troop movements and logistics, psychological state and combat morale—all of that was influenced by the air superiority of the Allies.[7]

---

7. Author's Note: Chester Wilmot, *Der Kampf um Europa*, 281. Translator's Note: Kurowski uses the German translation of the original title, which has been reverse-translated into English, with the result that it might not literally match the original text.

It was not until 7 June that Bayeux fell into Allied hands. The British 50th Infantry Division dug in on the high ground south of the town. Total Allied casualties on the first day of operations came to 11,000.

Naval gunfire opened the morning of 8 June with a thunderous roar. *Oberst* Scholze had just reached his assembly area at Norrey with *PGLR 901*, while the battle groups of *PGLR 902* had to fight to obtain their jumping-off positions at Brouay. Tanks of the Canadian 3rd Infantry Division, which had the mission of taking the airfield at Capriquet, were already in Brouay with their lead elements. In difficult night fighting, *PGLR 902* took its staging area, but it suffered heavy casualties in the process, since determining friend and foe proved nearly impossible. Finally, in close combat, the grenadiers knocked out the enemy tanks and took the village. *Oberst* Gutmann was wounded. *Major* Willi Welsch, a Knight's Cross recipient, assumed acting command of the regiment.

The divisional artillery of *Oberst* Luxenburger had not yet reached its staging area. Together with two of his battalion commanders, *Oberstleutnant* Zeißler and *Hauptmann Graf* Clary-Adringen, and several noncommissioned officers and enlisted personnel, he moved forward on the morning of 8 June to reconnoiter the best advance route for his regiment. They ran into a group of tanks from the Canadian "Inns of Court" Regiment and were all taken prisoner. At that point, things turned ugly.

Luxenburger, who had lost an arm in the First World War, was tied up by two Canadian officers, knocked unconscious and bound to the front of one of the tanks as a shield. Zeißler, who succeeded in escaping during the barrage fire that the British were laying down, reported the unbelievable incident when he reached German lines. Clary-Adringen was later found badly wounded by members of *Panzer-Grenadier-Regiment 2* of the *2. Panzer-Division.* The next day, Luxenburger was found. He was still bound to the Canadian tank, which had been knocked out by a German antitank gun in the meantime. He died three days later in a German field hospital.

✠

Reports began filtering in to the division command post at Le-Mesnil-Patry by noon on 8 June. All of the combat elements had reached their designated staging areas by then. Despite that, the division still did not receive any attack orders. An inquiry at the corps command post yielded the information that *SS-Panzer-Regiment 12* and *SS-Panzer-Grenadier-Regiment 25* had taken Bretteville but that they had to pull back due to the heavy enemy pressure. The corps staff wanted to await the arrival of the commanding general, *General* von Geyr, before making decisions. He was expected at any moment.

Afternoon turned to evening. At 1905 hours, *Generalfeldmarschall* Rommel appeared at the division headquarters. After the exchange of greetings between the two old friends from Africa, Bayerlein discovered that the anticipated attack would not take place.

"Bayerlein," the Field Marshal told the division commander, "all of our positions have been turned aside. The British 50th Infantry, our familiar friends from Africa, has taken Bayeux." In his excitement, Rommel occasionally slipped into his Swabian dialect.

"What are we going to do, *Herr Feldmarschall?*"

"You have to regroup your two battle groups and your artillery tonight farther to the west into the area around Tilly. It's eleven kilometers from Tilly to Bayeux. Bayeux's your new attack objective. You are to take it on 9 June."

The regrouping of the division was accomplished as instructed. Unnoticed by the enemy, the division's armored vehicles rolled into their new assembly areas. By pure chance, however, German aircraft identified troop movements in Fontenay-Le-Pesnel (due east of Tilly) and bombed the moving forces, thinking they were Canadian. Fortunately, there was only negligible damage. By morning on 9 June, the regrouping had been accomplished.

Because the first British tank forces were already rolling on the road from Bayeux to Tilly, the division had to conduct its attack west of the road. Bayerlein, together with his battle staff, moved with the lead elements, which were formed by *Hauptmann* Gerd von Born-Fallois's *PALA 130*, in the attack on Bayeux. Going around Ellon at noon, the battalion reached Arganchy an hour later. The division battle staff set up in a patch of woods there to direct the final attack on Bayeux, five kilometers away.

The British began firing naval artillery into the approach routes and staging areas of the division. The dismounted mechanized infantry sought cover behind the advancing armored vehicles. A thick cloud of gunpowder smoke spread across the terrain, from which the impacts of heavy artillery sent mushroom clouds skywards. But the armored vehicles continued to advance.

The 2nd Battalion of the *PLR* rolled forward with its four companies. Towards noon, the church tower of Ellon appeared to the north. The flat-topped high ground at Ellon was taken. The grenadiers of *PGLR 901* followed closely behind the tanks. The Germans started to receive ground fire from the elements of the British 49th Infantry Division positioned in the town.

The tanks advanced on a broad front and collapsed the resistance. The first enemy tank appeared in front of *Panzer IV 602*.[8] It rolled forward from behind the church. The first antitank round that was fired against another enemy tank in this engagement shattered one of the enemy's tracks. The

---

8. Translator's Note: *602* = Sixth Company (6)—Headquarters Section (0)—Second Tank (2). The tanks of the companies were numbered analogously.

second round sent it ablaze. An English squad attacked *604*, but it was cut down by the tank's machine guns. Two hand grenades exploded harmlessly on the tank's frontal armor.

The enemy's artillery fires started to then concentrate on Ellon proper. They increased in intensity. Shells of all calibers crashed down on the houses and tanks without pause. Heavy mortar rounds smashed into the cobblestones with violent blows. Shrapnel raced through the air, seeking the sideskirts and turrets of the tanks. The tanks of the 7th and 8th Companies continued rolling to the northern edge of the village. The grenadiers, who were following, assembled the prisoners and sent them to the rear. Ellon was finally cleared of the enemy. The 5th and 6th Companies remained in the village and surveyed the damage to their vehicles—ripped off sideskirts and bent sheet metal—after they dismounted.

Major Prinz Schönburg-Waldenburg, the 2nd Battalion commander, removed his sun-faded cap as the dead of his formation were gathered together. A few of the dead had been with him in the famous *Panzer-Regiment 31* of the *5. Panzer-Division*. They had been part of his 1st Company when he had received the Knight's Cross.

By taking Ellon, the division had obtained a good position for continuing its attack towards Bayeux. But at that point, orders arrived from the corps, which negated all of the previous success: "Call off the attack on Bayeux. Pull the division back to Tilly."

The men of the division cursed. The objective had been palpably near. *Hauptmann* Hauck, the commander of the division signals battalion, had all of the stations on the division net notified.

The corps order was not without its reasons, however. Strong Canadian forces had infiltrated along the boundary between the *12. SS-Panzer-Division "Hitlerjugend"* and the *PLD*. They had penetrated into the area bounded by Tilly–Audrieu–Christot. *Major* Uthe's 1st Battalion of *PGLR 901* remained in Ellon, and the 5th and 6th Companies of the *PLR* screened for them. The 7th and 8th Companies headed out immediately to launch an immediate counterattack against the enemy forces that had broken through.

Around 1400 hours, *Hauptmann* Reche, the commander of the 8th Company, received orders from his battalion commander to stand by for operations in the Fontenay area. Both of the companies—the 7th and the 8th—were to eject the enemy forces and then, once again, continue the advance to the coast.

Bayerlein immediately went to the corps command post. He received orders there to transition to the defense in the Tilly area with his division. It was imperative that he hold a line running Christot–Verrières, which had

Tilly as its middle point. The orders still stood, even if two British divisions—the 50th and 51st Infantry—attacked Tilly frontally, as was expected.

The tanks moved out. Evening fell. The sounds of the moving tanks were amplified in the night air. Widely dispersed, they headed towards the new front. The battalion reached the villages of Audrieu and Chouain. *Hauptmann* Reche was not to participate in the next round of fighting, however. Sick for days by that point, he was driven to the rear by the battalion's physician's assistant and taken to the field hospital. *Oberleutnant* Walter assumed acting command of the company.

The 2nd Battalion stopped momentarily between the two villages. About 1.5 kilometers in front of the tanks, which were well positioned, the dense vegetation transitioned into two thick patches of woods, which were separated by a small band about 300 meters wide.

The two companies then moved out again. At that point, no one knew that the British had taken the northern portion of Tilly that day. *Panzer IV 801* of *Leutnant* Stöhr advanced along the left flank of the battalion. The tanks reached freshly dug enemy positions, but nothing was to be seen of the enemy himself. Apparently, he had evacuated the positions when he heard the approaching tanks. The first tanks reached the open space between the woods and slowed down. The tanks that followed closed up.

Massed artillery fire rained down on the tanks as they entered the bottleneck. Since the trail tanks had closed up too much, it was impossible for the lead vehicles to turn around. They had to continue moving through the narrow passageway.

Major Schönburg-Waldenburg moved at the head of his two companies. He approached Hill 103 at full speed, where he thought he could gain a good vantage point. Two hundred meters in the distance, an enemy antitank gun opened up, and the gun's report could be heard clearly. Its round penetrated the front armor of the turret. The battalion commander fell to the side; he was immediately killed. All of his crew was badly wounded. Tank main guns fired in response. A duel ensued between the tanks and the enemy's artillery and antitank guns. *Hauptmann* Ritgen assumed acting command of the battalion.

The enemy's artillery placed a deadly curtain of fire and steel over the German tanks. Any effort to continue the advance would have been suicide. Ritgen decided to pull the tanks back.

By the evening of 9 June, it was obvious that the English main effort had shifted to the area around Tilly. After Field Marshal Montgomery had failed to take Caen in a frontal assault, he decided to advance from the Bayeux area in the direction of Tilly, take the high ground around Villers Bocage and then turn on Caen.

A new chapter in the history of the invasion was starting.

CHAPTER 5

The Fighting for Tilly

During the night of 9–10 June, the division, which finally had all of its elements, was directed into a line running Christot–Tilly (north)–Verrières and Bernières–La-Belle-Èpine–Torteval–St.-Germain-d'Ectot. The division was directed to hold a seventeen-kilometer-wide sector. The division command post was established in a farmer's house in Sermentot.

Bayerlein directed all measures necessary be taken to hide the location of the command post from the enemy so that it would not be discovered and destroyed. That fate had befallen the command post of *Panzergruppe West*, whose radio transmissions had been intercepted. A fighter-bomber squadron promptly attacked it, with twelve officers of the staff being killed and *General* von Geyr being badly wounded.

Correspondingly, Bayerlein directed that his communications center be established some 2,000 meters from the command post proper. Vehicles were only allowed to approach no closer than 500 meters to the command post during the day. The camouflage was checked several times each day.

✠

The British preparations for the attack on Tilly started on 10 June with an unbelievable concentration of naval gunfire. Surprisingly, however, there were no air attacks. Bayerlein later commented:

> It was a typical British attack. It started, as always, with a concentrated and heavy artillery preparation and relatively little air support. This was in contrast to the typical American attack, which was preceded by scattered artillery with relatively little effect but with unbelievably heavy air attacks.

On 10 June, the U.S. Army Air Force attacked the fuel trains of the division, still located west of the St. Lô sector, with entire squadrons.

✠

To cover the approach route of the entire division to the west and northwest, the 1st Company of *PGLR 901* of *Oberleutnant* Monz was employed in the Balleroy area to screen the division's left flank. The men of this company would soon make a name for themselves.

The company worked its way forward in an inverted wedge. The 3rd Platoon, which was in the lead, advanced along the road, reaching the edge of some vegetated pastureland, behind which there was the typical hedgerow. While the 2nd Platoon moved up on the right, the 3rd Platoon stayed concealed on the lefthand side of the road in some vegetation. A hundred meters farther back was the 1st Platoon and the 4th Platoon, which had the company's heavy weapons, consisting of heavy machine guns and 8-centimeter mortars. Monz was upfront with his 3rd Platoon.

Unteroffizier Rudi Brasche, a highly decorated veteran of the Eastern Front, had an *Ofenrohr* with his squad.[1] Off to his left, he saw a defile that joined the road. He could see about 100 meters into it, since it curved off to the north at that point. He had moved another three steps when he heard the voice of Jasper Langemann, causing him to pause: "Tanks to the left, Rudi!"

Brasche raced back a few meters. At the same moment, all of them heard the roar of numerous tank engines. Brasche saw the lead tank rolling forward. He recognized the flat and seemingly too-wide turret of a Sherman with its short main gun and coaxial machine gun. On the left front slope was another machine gun manned by the radio operator. Brasche then saw more tanks behind the first one—first one, then another and finally four in all. They were rolling around the bend in the defile and heading for the road.

"Becker! Take a report to the CO. Tanks to the left. Rolling right into the flank of the company."

Obergefreiter Becker raced up front to the 3rd Platoon. Brasche raced over to the righthand side of the defile and jumped into the ditch. He aimed the *Ofenrohr* at the lead tank, whose tracks rattled so loudly that they were pounding against their eardrums. The colossus approached ever closer. The wind blew in their direction and, with it, the smell of engine fumes.

Brasche took aim and fired the *Ofenrohr*. A stream of flame shot to the rear, and the projectile arched its way to the tank. It hit the lower part of the turret. As if lifted by unseen hands, the turret was dislodged from its race. It flew a few meters through the air and smashed into the turret of the second tank with a loud crack. The battle for Tilly had been joined.

---

1. Translator's Note: Brasche received the Knight's Cross as an *Obergefreiter* assigned to the 4th Company of *Panzergrenadier-Regiment 93* of the *13. Panzer-Division* on 9 November 1942. The *Ofenrohr*—"Stovepipe"—was the German version of the bazooka.

Brasche yelled out for his men to follow him. He grabbed the *Ofenrohr* and headed west, parallel to the defile. Hannes Keck appeared, as if out of nowhere. He was followed by Hill, and Lagemann rallied the rest of the squad. They saw the reports of the main guns on the Shermans and then felt the impact of the rounds landing dangerously close.

They had just reached the bend in the path along the defile when a few automatic cannon and some more main guns opened fire. The tracers were headed northwest, towards the positions of the 3rd Platoon.

"Keep going!" Brasche wanted to knock out the last tank in the defile in order to trap all the tanks in the middle.

They worked their way forward, bent over. They were being greeted by sprays of machine-gun fire. They then passed the beaten area. The muzzle flash of a main gun helped him orient back to the tanks. Brasche worked his way through the brush. All of a sudden, he saw the turret of a tank through the vegetation. He figured he was at the position of the last tank. The *Ofenrohr* was brought into position.

The deadly cargo of the *Ofenrohr* flew through the air towards its intended target. It hit and penetrated into the turret, where the ready racks were immediately ignited with a tumultuous explosion. Everyone and everything in the immediate vicinity of the fire-spewing volcano involuntarily pulled back.

From the positions of the 4th Platoon, the mortars suddenly came to life. It wasn't a second too soon, since the British infantry that had been following the tanks soon started advancing. The 8-centimeter shells started landing among the tightly bunched groups of infantry, forcing them to take cover.

"Hill and Lagemann, follow me. Everyone else cover us."

Brasche then ran through the vegetation. Tree branches struck him in the face. His hands emerged bloody from an encounter with a boysenberry bush. He then reached the steep wall of the defile. Right next to him, the main guns of the tanks were going off. They were sending their deadly salvoes of steel towards the lead elements of the company.

Brasche saw a squad of dismounted British. He swung his submachine gun around and let loose with three short bursts. While the British took cover, Hans Hill raced towards the closest Sherman. He was carrying a bundled charge consisting of three hand grenades. With a quick leap, he was on the tank. The crew had foolishly not locked down its hatches, and Hill was able to drop the charge into the turret. He then closed the hatch the best he could and jumped from the tank. Seconds later—the surprised crew did not react fast enough—the sound of a tremendous explosion in a confined space could be heard above the din of the rest of the battlefield.

Rounds echoed through the defile. Lagemann and Brasche fired with everything they had to keep the enemy down, thus enabling Hill to make it to the safety of the embankment. Brasche then ordered the men to cover him, as he disappeared into the underbrush and raced farther down the length of the defile.

Brasche crawled through thick hazelnut brush. He moved through weeds to the top of the brush and then saw that he had estimated correctly. Barely five meters in front of him was another Sherman. The Sherman was preoccupied with firing towards the more distant enemy, this time to the south where the heavy weapons were. The German heavy weapons platoon was wreaking havoc among the groups of British infantry and scattering it.

Brasche hesitated for a second. He knew he was risking it as soon as he left the concealment of the vegetation. The enemy was crawling all around the defile as well and waiting for the chance to repay the blows the Germans had delivered.

He pulled some hand grenades from his belt. He unscrewed the safety cap from one of them and crawled forward. Fortunately for him, the interior wall of the defile was covered with boysenberry bushes. Off to his side, a few men with the typical flat British trench helmet appeared. Lagemann and the remaining men of the squad started firing from their overwatch positions. The enemy infantry disappeared behind the second tank, which was still smoking. With a leap, Brasche reached the rear of the tank. For a fraction of a second, he heard voices. Then a clink, as the breech slammed shut.

He jammed the hand grenades underneath the turret overhang above the thinly armored rear deck. He hit the igniter and raced away in long strides away from the doomed machine. He tripped over a tree root and landed flat on his face.

The hand grenades went off with an ear-shattering roar. A shot of flame emerged from the engine compartment. Hatches were popped open. Submachine guns began to bellow again.

Crawling, Brasche disappeared into the dense vegetation. It was not a moment too soon, since enemy infantry squads started appearing behind the last tank. They fired blindly into the underbrush.

Brasche thought to himself: "They've seen me. . . . They're going to try to smoke me out!"

He crawled off to the side as quickly as he was able to. A machine gun began to fire in long bursts. All of a sudden, hand grenades exploded at the location of the enemy machine gun. They firing abruptly stopped.

Brasche continued crawling up the embankment. By the time he reached the top, his back was drenched in sweat. He was greeted by Lagemann: "Rudi, the rest of the platoon has caught up. We're all in position."

Oberleutnant Monz was also there. He had returned from the 3rd Platoon to be with the main body of the company. Monz ordered Brasche's squad

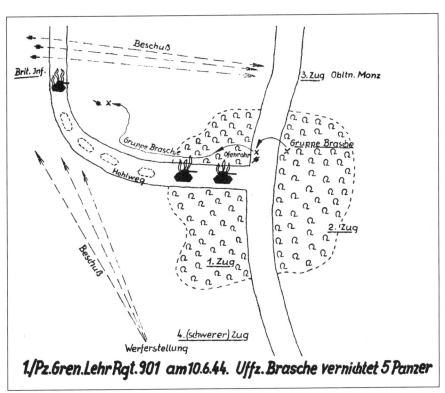

1./Pz.Gren.Lehr Rgt.901 am 10.6.44. Uffz.Brasche vernichtet 5 Panzer

The *1./Panzergrenadier-Lehr-Regiment 901* on 10 June 1944. *Unteroffizier* Brasche destroys five enemy tanks. Legend: *1. Zug* = 1st Platoon (analogous for remainder); *4. (schwerer) Zug* = 4th (Heavy) Platoon; *Obltn* = *Oberleutnant*; *Beschuß* = Firing; *Hohlweg* = Defile; *Gruppe Brasche* = Brasche's Squad; *Ofenrohr* = "Stovepipe" (bazooka); *Werferstellung* = Rocket-launcher position.

to the far end of the defile. The other squads closed in on the right. Staying under the concealment offered by the bushes and underbrush, they eventually reached the end of the defile.

"Damn, that's a whole infantry battalion!" Lagemann exclaimed when he saw the assembled British along the edge of a patch of chestnut trees.

"We'll keep 'em busy with the *Ofenrohr!*"

The round from the German bazooka took the enemy completely by surprise. It exploded in the middle of a dense pack of men and extracted a corresponding toll. The British forces immediately pulled back into the woods.

"Cover here!"

The men remained in position. The 4th Platoon continued firing. Whenever the Tommies tried to approach the five knocked-out and burning or smoldering tanks, they were taken under fire by the heavy machine guns, which grazed their flanks. The British were forced to pull back over and over again. The 1st Company had not only survived its first baptism of fire, it had done quite well. Despite that, the 3rd Platoon, which had borne the brunt of most of the British fire, had taken heavy losses.

The enemy's breakthrough attempt at that location—a weak point in the already overextended lines of the *PLD*—had been thwarted. Brasche's squad had knocked out five enemy tanks with the *Ofenrohr* and hand grenades. The feat of arms was singled out for praise by the division in its order of the day on 11 June.

12 June 1944. The German defensive effort around Tilly had solidified. The British had moved out on their expected offensive on 11 June. In Tilly proper, the 5th Company of *PGLR 901*, under its commander and Knight's Cross recipient, *Hauptmann* Philipps, turned back the English.[2] The 1st Battalion of the regiment was in position at Verrières, west of Tilly. The 1st Company was repositioned to a patch of woods near Lingèvres. Monz then decided to move a little farther east, where he deemed the defensive options were better, once his battalion commander had given him the option of determining his final defensive positions.

The company moved out at noon on 12 June. The 1st Platoon moved forward on the right, orienting along a road. The 2nd Platoon followed, a bit

---

2. Translator's Note: Philipps had received the decoration in the same capacity—albeit as an *Oberleutnant*—on 7 April 1944. He had received the German Cross in Gold on 2 July 1942 and would later receive the Honor Roll Clasp on 7 August 1944.

offset to the left. The 3rd Platoon formed the left flank, with the 4th Platoon bringing up the rear.

As it turned dusk, the men of the company heard the sound of shells impacting around Tilly. The British were hammering away at the ruins of the city with artillery and naval gunfire. The darker it became, the more the sky was lit up by the "lightning" caused by the artillery to the north of the advancing company.

"They're getting ready to land a punch!" Hill practically shouted.

"The poor bastards in the 5th!" Lagemann added.

Becker wanted to get the last word in: "The same thing can happen to us any moment!"

Brasche chimed in: "I don't think we're there yet. It doesn't look like Tommy has formed up in our sector yet."

Monz issued orders to the company: "Move up to the pasture land and dig in. Southern edge of the pasture, the 2nd and 3rd Platoons. The 1st Platoon on the eastern edge. The 4th Platoon behind the 3rd."

The men worked their way through the vegetated terrain. The squad *Ofenrohr* seemed to weigh a hundred pounds. Brasche could see the silhouette of the pasture land ahead, along with some low-lying bushes. The 2nd Platoon then reached a hedge that adjoined the pastureland.

"Hey, great ditch, Rudi! You're making it easy for us. We'll have enough cover here!"

Brasche jumped into the ditch. He tried to look out into the pastureland through the hedgerow, but he could not force his way through.

"Dig in a bit deeper, anyway, guys. The deeper the better!"

Muttering, the squad went to work, while Brasche made a hole through the hedgerow, through which he inserted the snout of the *Ofenrohr*. He was unable to identify anything in the darkness, although he could make out the dark shadows of bushes, which seemed to be distributed in an unusually symmetrical pattern across the pasture land.

"Get going, Hannes. Cut yourself a second hole for the other *Ofenrohr*."

"Man alive. Why this drill?"

"Get going before the old man comes along and rips you a new one because we haven't set up properly."

"He's over there with the 1st"

"I'm going around."

Brasche disappeared around the hedgerow. He saw that the ditch on the eastern end wasn't half as deep as around his positions. The men of the 1st Platoon were also busy digging in.

"What's going on, Karl-Heinz?" Brasche asked his friend *Unteroffizier* Görenz.

"Nothing much . . . I think we can probably play some cards with Wetterau in the 4th Platoon. We can meet him in the radio vehicle."

When Brasche saw the old man, he made himself scarce and returned to his squad. But the maneuver did not help. He had barely returned when Monz also showed up.

"Everyone up, Brasche!"

"*Jawohl, Herr Oberleutnant!*"

The acting company commander continued his rounds. Brasche could hear his voice over in the location of the 3rd Platoon. Five minutes later, he returned with the company headquarters section leader, Peter Kollmannsberger. The two disappeared around the corner of the hedgerow.

"Damn, Rudi! What's that?"

Barely forty meters in front of the positions, a tank engine fired up. Flames shot out of the exhaust, and the broad shadow that had looked like a giant bush, started to move, rolling past the 2nd Platoon and heading in the direction of the hedgerow to the east. Looking through his hole in the hedgerow, Brasche was momentarily paralyzed. But then he noticed that all of the shadows on the pasture land had started to move, heading in the same direction. If they ejected the men of the 1st Platoon from their positions there, they would then be able to wipe them out at their leisure on the open flat ground.

Brasche grabbed the *Ofenrohr*. Lagemann moved over and helped him. They ran in the ditch to the point where the hedgerow turned. They were able to move past the slow-moving tank. At the corner, Brasche noticed a gap in the hedgerow. He set up with his *Ofenrohr* and waited for the tank. He did not have to wait too long. He soon saw its silhouette off to the side. When the tank came up around the corner, Brasche fired.

The howl of the rocket-propelled grenade launching and the shrill crack of the metal being hit were as one. A brilliant flame shot out of the tank. Then the night was peppered with the glowing red muzzle flashes of main guns reporting. The tanks that had been rolling directly towards the eastern hedgerow thought they had been attacked from the front, and they stopped in place. Brasche was thus able to get off another shot at the tanks. The tank was hit and began to burn brightly. The remaining tanks backed up, leaving two burning torches on the open field.

"Rudi, get back here!"

The two men ran back to their platoon and jumped into the ditch.

It wasn't a second too soon, since the night was turned into day by the combined fires of thirty, perhaps forty, tank main guns. Machine guns joined the fray and sent lightning-like tracers through the night skies.

"Good thing we dug in. That must be a tank regiment!"

"Looks like we almost walked into their assembly area."

"If you hadn't gotten the two tanks, Rudi, they would have marched right through to the 1st and chewed it up."

"Nonsense!"

The mortars of the heavy platoon started firing. The impacting rounds landed in the middle of the pasture land. In the flames of the detonations, the men around Brasche could see that there was also infantry there in the background. They linked up with the tanks that had beaten a hasty retreat.

The *MG 42's* began to rattle. They fired half a meter above the ground, mowing down anything in their path.

Occasionally, an *Ofenrohr* would fire, joined by the sporadic firing of *Panzerfäuste*.[3] The rounds from the main guns tore the hedgerow apart. Steel clanged. The night had turned raving mad. The tanks started firing broadsides into the hedgerows. One of the *MG 42* nests was hit and blown apart.

The men disappeared into the ditches. Only Brasche stuck his head up occasionally to see if the enemy were attempting to sneak up. He observed one of the tanks advancing at the southeast corner of the pasture land. For a fraction of a second, he thought he saw a couple of figures in the garish light of the main gunfire. He thought he saw *Oberleutnant* Monz. Then one of the figures jumped up onto the tank. Rounds were fired. The man who had jumped on the tank was caught by a burst of machine-gun fire and swept to the ground.

Brasche raised his submachine gun and fired at the point where he thought the enemy had to be. He instantly received return fire. He was forced to ground by several bursts of fire. He disappeared into the ditch and crawled a few meters off to one side. Then he tried again.

He wormed his way through the shredded hedgerow. He pushed his way another quarter of a meter forward. He saw the muzzle flash of a machine gun. That was followed by the brilliant flash of a main gun firing. He raised his submachine gun and fired. While firing, he saw the muzzle flash of a rifle. Then tracers from a machine gun passed overhead. Something hit him in the upper arm, and he was thrown backward. He remained in place—pressed to the ground—for a few moments before he crawled back to the ditch, collapsing.

---

3. Translator's Note: The *Panzerfaust* was a one-shot rocket-propelled unguided anti-tank weapon with a hollow-charged projectile. It was the precursor of the world-famous RPG-7 and had a maximum effective range of about 100 meters.

"Man, you're wounded!" Lagemann called out. Hannes Hill crawled over as quickly as he could. They removed Brasche's field blouse and dressed his upper arm.

"Not too bad . . . you were lucky!"

"The war's over for you!" Lagemann added laconically.

"Shit!" Brasche mumbled. He bit his lips as the pain started to settle in.

The small-arms fire, which had only started hesitantly before, began to reach epic proportions.

A report came in: "*Oberleutnant* Monz was wounded engaging a tank." It had been Monz, after all, that Brasche had seen.

The men held on.

Major Uthe, the commander of the 1st Battalion of *PGLR 901*, had established his command post in the Chateau Fontenay, just west of the village of the same name. The palace grounds, with their gnarly old trees, looked like an area devastated by a hurricane. The palace proper was nothing but ruins after having been bombed and hit by naval gunfire. Uthe had set up shop in the palace basement. A couple of candles were burning on an old keg.

Not too far away, *Oberst* Scholze had also erected his command post, although he was rarely there, since he was constantly going to the front to check on his men and the situation. They were men he had served with in the Soviet Union, and there was a special place in his heart for them.

As previously noted, the British started the artillery preparation for their offensive at 0500 hours on 10 June. The bottomland along the Vire was soon saturated with shell craters. *Major* Uthe worked his way forward through the wasteland along with two messengers. The ground seemed to grow wings constantly. In the middle of the craters, he climbed to the high ground. The foxholes of his grenadiers were on the reverse slope. *Oberleutnant* Mersiowski and his 2nd Company were there, along with *Hauptmann* Salzmann and the 3rd Company. Uthe's 1st Company had received other orders from the regiment and was not in the lines there.

Salzmann reported to his battalion commander that the enemy had established positions in the Ferme Cheval Rouge and was firing on the German positions with antitank guns from there whenever there was any movement along the German lines. Uthe immediately contacted the divisional artillery and had counterbattery fires placed on the enemy positions.

Especially heavy artillery fire was placed on the sector of *Hauptmann* Philipps's 5th Company in the regiment's 2nd Battalion. The enemy was pounding Tilly mercilessly with his artillery. Despite the intense pressure, the grenadiers continued to hold in the town. They weren't about to let themselves be shot out of their positions.

The situation was even more threatening in the sector of the 1st Battalion of *PGLR 902*, which was committed north of Tilly. The 1st and 3rd Companies had just gone into position in the hilly countryside, when the British started forty-five minutes of barrage fire. Since they had not yet dug in, they were practically without cover and were exposed to the full fury of the artillery. The barrage was a real test of nerve, especially for the younger soldiers.

When a few of the men jumped up and started racing towards the rear, they were soon joined by others. It looked like the lines might fold, but *Oberleutnant* Ritter, the acting commander of the 4th Company, raced towards the panicky men. He collected them up and sent them back to the front. Fortunately for *PGLR 902*, the enemy did not launch any attacks at that critical moment, otherwise a breakthrough might have been possible at that location, which would have had incalculable consequences.

Another critical situation arose towards noon on 10 June when a group of five enemy tanks that had broken through made a surprise appearance at the command post of the 1st Battalion of *PGLR 902* west of Tilly. At first, the Germans thought they were friendlies. When the tank commander of the lead tank quickly disappeared from his open hatch and the turret began traversing towards the command post, followed by the garish muzzle blast of the main gun that rent the midday air, the men knew that enemy tanks had broken through.

Fortunately for the otherwise helpless command post, the 1st Company of *PJLA 130* was positioned nearby. The company had just received its self-propelled antitank guns.[4] *Leutnant* Werner, the acting company commander, gave battle. The enemy tank that was the farthest away was sent up in flames. Two rounds destroyed the tracks of another tank, immobilizing it. When it continued firing like mad into the surrounding area, a third round sealed its fate, hitting the vehicle between the turret and hull and killing the crew. A third tank was hit and set alight, after it had bottomed out in a ditch. The remaining two tanks also got stuck. They were fired upon and, suffering significant battle damage, were not longer combat effective. The crews bailed out and attempted to make their way back to their unit. They were engaged

---

4. Editor's Note: *Panzerjäger IV L/48.*

by the men of the command post escort section. Several were killed; the rest surrendered.

When the news of the surprise appearance of the enemy tanks reached the division command post in Sermentot, Bayerlein immediately had his staff car ready to move out. He knew it was important to get a firsthand glimpse at what was happening up front in that broken terrain. He personally headed out to reconnoiter, accompanied solely by his liaison officer and driver. The vehicle soon left the relative security of the forward defensive positions and reached the open plains north of Tilly.

For the general, it was clear that if there were enemy tanks in the vicinity, it meant that a large offensive was about to start. The vehicle shot through a depression and then started to climb out of it. The driver suddenly stopped at the crest and then pulled the vehicle into a concealed position.

"Tanks, *Herr General!*"

"Damn it! Hartdegen, that looks like an entire regiment. They're set up as though they were on peacetime maneuvers." After a pause, the general continued: "Get whatever you can together. I'll stay here."

The liaison officer disappeared at high speed. He succeeded in finding four *Panthers* and a couple of 88's and brought them forward quickly. The tanks and antitank guns were able to occupy good firing positions without being noticed. They then commenced firing, the tanks first, followed by the powerful antitank guns.

Without a few seconds, the enemy concentration looked like an anthill. The first rounds impacted in the middle of the laager, causing the crews to mount hurriedly and attempt to leave the death trap. A few of the tanks succeeded in escaping through the wild confusion and vehicles that were already burning. Red tongues of flame rose skyward. Three enemy tanks attempted to attack the high ground. Before they even got close, however, they were knocked out by the powerful 8.8-centimeter rounds. Smoke rose from the wreckage.

Smoldering tanks, burning trucks and brightly flaming fuel trucks littered the plain. Then hell broke out for the German tankers and gunners. The first salvoes of heavy naval gunfire began howling in and transformed the position on the hill into a fire-spitting volcano. The impacts from the shells tossed trees and vegetation into the sky. The steel shells burst apart with an unbelievable crash, and the shrapnel slammed into the armor of the tanks and the shields of the guns.

"Naval gunfire, *Herr General!*"

"Pull back!" the general ordered.

The tanks and the two antitank guns rolled back, followed by the hammering, droning and crashing of ton upon ton of steel that was raining down on that small piece of terrain north of Tilly. They had just left the hilltop when the tempest from the sea increased in intensity. The hilltop was plowed up, meter by meter. The small battle group was able to reach the German lines unscathed, however. As a result of the timely intervention, the British plans north of Tilly had been disrupted. There would be no attacking by that tank regiment in the immediate future.

✠

The 9th Company of *PGLR 901*, the heavy infantry gun company (self-propelled), which was in position west of Tilly, was able to identify the assembly area of a Scottish battalion in front of the German lines on 10 June. *Hauptmann* Hennecke had his guns place concentrated fires on the patch of woods populated by birch trees, where the Scots had set up their assembly area. In the course of the day, the guns were able to advance as far as Tilly-sur-Seulles, but they had to stop there, since the friendly forces to the right were unable to close up. They established a defensive perimeter.

✠

During the early-morning hours of 11 June, Bayerlein summoned his commanders to his command post in Sermentot. He had received a report from a German radar station at Douvres, which was still holding out behind enemy lines:

Concentration of—so far—200 enemy tanks at Anguerny, with transportation elements arrayed to the south. Continuous movement of heavy and medium tanks to the southeast. More than 80 tanks counted in an hour.

At about the same time, the assembly areas of the *PLD* were reported to the Commander in Chief of the British 2nd Army, General Dempsey. From Dempsey's perspective, it signaled preparations for the German counteroffensive, which had long been expected. Dempsey immediately ordered heavy aerial bombardment of Caen and ordered General Crocker, the commanding general of the British I Corps, to hold off on the planned southern envelopment of Caen and be prepared to defend against the anticipated German assault. The final words of Dempsey's orders: "The patch of ground is the heart of the British Empire. Never pull your tanks back from there."[5]

Bayerlein issued his orders to his commanders at Sermentot. *Major* Uthe was with his 1st Battalion of *PGLR 901* at Fontenay and *Hauptmann* Philipps was with his 5th Company of the regiment in the front lines just north of Tilly. Other elements of the 2nd Battalion were also with his forces.

The armor reserves were positioned to the south, to include the antitank forces of *Hauptmann* Oventrop and the 9th Company of *PGLR 901*, with its self-propelled infantry guns. The artillery had occupied its positions the previous night. The reconnaissance battalion of *Hauptmann* von Born-Fallois was located in La-Bellè-Èpine.

Shortly after the German forces had repositioned or improved their already existing positions, the British launched their attack. The British main effort was intercepted by the mechanized infantry of *Hauptmann* Philipps. *Stabsgefreiter* Gerhard Kunze, who experienced the fighting with the British 49th and 50th Infantry Divisions and the 7th Armoured Division, has provided the author with a direct account of his experiences defending the palace grounds from his positions.

✠

"That's right! Just keep on sending them over!" *Stabsgefreiter* Kunze called out in an attempt at gallows humor when the naval gunfire and artillery hammered down on Tilly. The firestorm rained down ceaselessly on the improved positions. Already plowed up once, the positions increasingly took on the features of a moonscape.

Kunze's assistant gunner on the *MG 42* chimed in: "They're firing at every foxhole individually!"

"Oh, it's not so bad!" *Oberfeldwebel* Brombach said with a forced grin.

When another salvo landed right in front of their dugouts and showered them with steel, stones and soil, the men involuntarily pressed themselves deeper into their holes.

"Well, I hope the shells also know it's not so bad, either!" Martin Schwab said hurriedly when the men had a short break in the fire and could peer out again.

"The Tommies are going to attack . . . that's for sure."

"Where's our AT? Where are *Hauptmann* Oventrop's guns?"

---

5. Translator's Note: This is reverse-translated into English, so the original wording may have been different.

"We have our pocket AT, pal!" Pfeiffer pointed to the *Panzerfäuste* stacked nearby.

"Oventrop will be here when we need him. He's always been there when we needed him, even back when he was a *Leutnant* in Russia with the *LB*!"[6]

Oberfeldwebel Bromberg, the prewar career soldier, peered out into the terrain ahead, trying to make out anything among the fountains of explosions, the gunpowder smoke and the clouds of dirt that were being sent skyward.

"Another pull, guys?" Max Niehüser asked his friends of the machine-gun section. He was the "procurer" of the bunch and had found some wine in the chateau. "It's the stuff from the chateau. Pretty good!"

"Hmmm . . . not bad! An old *Fine de Charente*. Great brand! Are there some more bottles from there, Niehüser?"

"Another five bottles. Besides, once they're gone, we just have to go back into the chateau's basement."

"Until the ceiling collapses on us!"

They passed the bottle around, interrupted only by the shells ranging in.

When the preparatory fires suddenly shifted farther to the rear, all of them extended their heads out of the positions at practically the same time. No words were necessary. Everyone was on high alert in all of the dugouts at that point. The attack had to kick off at any moment.

The platoon was ordered to get prepared for combat, as if the orders were necessary. There was some murmuring, but no one spoke loudly. The air was so thick with tension, you could cut it with a knife. Despite all that, the enemy did not attack. He was still not certain whether the artillery had adequately weakened the resistance of the Germans in the ruins of Tilly.

"*Jabos!*" Kunze yelled out.[7] He was the first to see silvery birds swooping down from the north. A few seconds later, the aircraft engines combined to form a background cacophony to the impending destruction.

The divisional *Flak* started firing. The detonations looked like gray, serrated clouds in the sky. One of the approaching fighter-bombers was hit by an 88, and it blew apart in a garish red ball of flame. The others continued their approach, however. The flitted over the moonscape at barely fifty meters of altitude. Their wing mounts spit out red tongues of flame. Then the rockets were launched. One of the first rockets slammed into the dugout of a forward observer. It collapsed in a brilliant detonation. One of the antitank guns was also hit and rendered combat ineffective.

When Kunze raised his head, he saw that the rockets and machine-gun salvoes were tracing a way directly to their positions. The sound of the rockets

6. Translator's Note: *Lehr-Brigade 900*.

7. Translator's Note: *Jagdbombers* = fighter-bombers.

grew ever more shrill. The impacts of rockets hammered at his ears. The ground seemed to sway drunkenly in a circle.

About ten meters from their position, the impacts suddenly ceased. The Thunderbolts raced above their heads, described a wide circle and then headed back north to their bases. They were replaced by another wave of fighter-bombers, however. The 88's were joined by all available antiaircraft guns this time. The fingers of blazing light caused by the tracers seemed to wait to impale the afternoon sky. A pattern of red light was woven in the air above the men, through which the Thuderbolts moved like bobbins.

Brilliant tongues of flame emanated from the wings. Bombs were released, competing with the Thunderbolts in velocity as a result of the laws of inertia. But they always eventually fell and exploded with an earth-shuddering roar. A forest of *Flak* puffs colored the sky gray. One of the approaching machines was hit in the wing near the fuselage by a 2-centimeter gun. The rounds sawed the wing off, and the heavy fighter-bomber plummeted to the earth like a projectile and exploded in a fiery ball upon impact.

"Take cover!" *Oberfeldwebel* Brombach yelled. The men pressed themselves farther into the floor of their dugout. They clawed their way into the dirt in an effort to escape the approaching death and destruction. The rockets exploded all around them with ear-deafening bursts. One of them exploded in a crater where Bergmann's squad had set up. None of the men survived. Then that wave of fighter-bombers disappeared like a ghost in the night.

Then, all at once, they heard the certain din of death: enemy tanks were approaching from their attack positions.

"They're coming!"

The call moved from one dugout to the next. And in places where all signs of life appeared to have been wiped out, the mechanized infantry of *Oberst* Scholze started manning their positions.

Kunze placed his machine gun in the embrasure of the dugout that had been prepared for it. Säuberlich, his assistant gunner, loaded a belt. Schwab was preparing belts.[8]

The attackers worked their way forward through the terrain that was saturated with craters and shredded vegetation. A sound near the dugout, barely audible above the din, startled the men. It was *Oberleutnant* Mahr, the commander of the 7th Company, coming in from the neighboring sector.

"Everything ready, Brombach?"

"Everything ready, *Herr Oberleutnant!*"

Just as quickly as he had come, he also disappeared. He headed in the direction of the 3rd Platoon.

---

8. Translator's Note: Unlike the U.S. Army, ammunition in the German Army did not come pre-belted for machine guns and had to be loaded manually.

"Fire when ready!"

The first of the enemy figures with their flat helmets could be recognized as silhouettes through the battlefield haze. Almost simultaneously, the *MG 42's* positioned throughout the sector began to open fire on the charging enemy. The machine guns were set for grazing fire and barely cleared the ground.

Kunze was manning his machine gun. He saw a squad of British jump up barely 200 meters away. They approached as a group. He let loose with a burst, traversing from left to right. The enemy disappeared. The gun jammed and the weapon fell silent. Kunze attempted to clear the stuck round. He burned his fingers in the process, but he got the job done.

Obergefreiter Säuberlich made sure the gun had a clean feed and the belt did not drag through the dirt. He watched as the bolt ate the steel rounds and spat out the empty cartridges. He saw the enemy soldiers fall and the attack lose steam. The lead elements bogged down in the defenders' fires.

A few minutes later, a second wave moved out. They had not yet closed to firing range when there was a mighty shock wave that spread over the men from the rear, heading in the direction of the British. There were brilliant fiery tails behind the 30-centimeter rockets as they plummeted towards the enemy. They had been fired about 2,000 meters behind the lines by the men of the heavy rocket battalion of the *7. Werfer-Brigade* of *Oberst* Tzschökell. The twenty-four rockets of the four launchers slammed into the middle of the British attack sector and shattered everything that was in their effective radius. The heavy infantry guns of the 9th Company of the regiment then started firing. They had taken up positions along the Vire bottomland between the 1st and 2nd Battalions. Once again, the British attack stalled.

"Tanks!"

The tanks approached from the north, coming from the ruins of a farm. They were Cromwells, a recently introduced fast British tank. Brombach had a messenger go to the palace and make a report to *Hauptmann* Philipps. A few seconds later, Philipps was on his way to *Hauptmann* Oventrop, who was standing by with his antitank battalion. Oventrop dispatched six *Jagdpanzer* through the bottomland and had them go into position along a reverse slope.[9]

From his position, Kunze pointed over to the left: "Over there . . . that's where they're coming from . . . from the patch of woods!" The shattered tree trucks could be seen. It was the same place the enemy had penetrated the previous day, in the vicinity of the Ferme Cheval Rouge.

The tanks advanced in a tight formation. Individual ones stopped to fire, with the muzzle flashes clearly visible despite the battlefield haze. Main-gun

---

9. Editor's Note: *Panzerjäger-Lehr-Abteilung 130* in Normandy had three "mixed" companies consisting of ten *Jagdpanzer IV 39* and four towed *7.5 cm PaK 40* per company.

rounds slammed into the German defensive belt. The heavy infantry guns began to direct their fires towards the advancing tanks. The lead Cromwell, which was appearing from out of the bottom of a gigantic crater caused by naval gunfire, was shoved back in as if by an unseen hand when it was hit. Soon a lance of flame rose skyward, followed by a mighty detonation as the ready racks of ammunition also went up. Two more of the new British tanks were knocked out. The remaining ones continued rolling forward, however. They advanced on a broad front, firing at the identified German positions.

"HE!" Brombach shouted when rounds started impacting in front of them, sending showers of hot shrapnel their way. That was followed by: "Infantry!"

The infantry was following behind the enemy tanks. The machine guns started a steady staccato beat as they fired into the exposed ranks. The breeze coming in from the sea brought with it clouds of stink: Hot oil and gunpowder smoke mixed with the smell of burnt earth.

"Pfeiffer, get some *Panzerfäuste . . .* show us what you've learned!" Kunze pointed to the two tanks that were barely eighty meters in front of them and emerging form a depression. They stopped to fire and then, with a jerk, they moved out again in the direction of the men. The tank farthest to the left suddenly turned in. Moving rapidly, it closed to within forty meters of the crater the men were in. Its main gun spit out an orange-red lance of flame. It was followed by a string of machine-gun tracers.

It seemed as though Pfeiffer had drawn the concentrated fires of the steel colossus directly towards him. It seemed to him that there was no way he could show himself if he didn't want to be swept away by the angry monster.

Despite those elemental fears, he righted himself. He brought up the *Panzerfaust,* placed it on his shoulder and took aim at the stationary tank that was still belching its fire.

"Firing with *Panzerfaust!*" he warned as he had been trained to do. The cracking voice had not been part of the training, however. The backblast from the ignited rocket sent a stream of flame a meter to the rear when he fired at the Cromwell.

"Take cover!" Niehüser yelled when he saw how Pfeiffer followed the rocket's trail, as if in a spell. Once again: "Cover!"

At that point, Pfeiffer fell backwards, hard. He barely heard the detonation, as the hollow-charge round tore the turret off its race when it struck at the sweet spot between the turret and hull. A burst from the turret's machine gun had shattered the young soldier's chest.

A moment later, the second tank was also burning. Niehüser had hit it with a *Panzerfaust.* Niehüser then turned to his comrade: "How are you, Heinz?"

"They got me, Max," the badly wounded man gasped. Blood was streaming out from both hands, which he had pressed tightly to his chest. He saw the light-colored bubbles of blood that formed on Pfeiffer's lips every time the dying soldier breathed. Niehüser crawled over to his comrade while the firing of the *Panzerfäuste* and the hammering of main guns reached a crescendo.

When he lifted his wounded comrade by the back, he could feel the large exit wounds. He could feel the warm blood flowing over his fingers, taking the life of his comrade with it. Niehüser no longer heard the firing of the machine guns. He no longer heard the orders being shouted by Brombach through the din of battle. He only reached for the dressing that Kunze handed his way during a short break in the firing.

"Is it bad?" Pfeiffer asked with difficulty. He looked at Niehüser with watery eyes.

"You're kidding," his friend lied. "It's just the ticket home for you! Just rest!"

Kunze crawled up to them along the dugout floor when the British attack bogged down and the tanks started to pull back. He looked down at his comrade. He saw that the red had left his cheeks. His whiskers looked so black that they looked as though they had been applied with charcoal for some sort of drawing. The dying man sucked in the air with difficulty in fits and spurts. The air had been contaminated with the stench of death.

"Water!" he begged.

Distraught, he looked at Brombach. The *Oberfeldwebel* nodded.

As Pfeiffer drank, Niehüser turned his head to the side. The efforts of his friends to grab some air overpowered even the noise of the rocket launchers, which had started firing again. This time, it was the enemy's. Pfeiffer lifted his face in the direction of the noise.

"What kind of noise is that?" he asked, each word separated by a slight pause.

"Just lay there, Pfeiffer!" Brombach answered, trying to sound like a stern disciplinarian, even though he was on the verge of tears.

"Cig . . . cigarette!"

The *Oberfeldwebel* nodded to his charges once more.

Kunze lit up a cigarette with trembling hands and placed it between Pfeiffer's lips. Pfeiffer took a deep draw. All of a sudden, he stretched out. The luster disappeared abruptly and irrevocably from the young man's eyes. It was replaced by the numbness of death.

As if it were the utmost of consideration, the barrage fires started up again. The men threw themselves under cover. All thoughts disappeared, except one: survival. They clawed their way back into the yielding earth. They wished they were as small as insects and could disappear into the cracks of the earth. They cursed and they prayed. They waited for death and hoped for salvation at the same time.

The steel fell from the heavens for thirty minutes and scorched the earth. Then the assault elements of the British 49th and 50th Infantry Divisions, supported by tanks, charged the German positions at Tilly once again. When the enemy armor had closed to within effective range, *Hauptmann* Oventrop thrust his arm into the air and pumped it three times.

The *Jagdpanzers* started firing almost immediately. The muzzle flashes extended almost a meter from the long-barreled main guns. The sounds of shrieking and bursting filled the air.

Legs spread, Oventrop had positioned himself forward in a crater in order to best direct the fires of his tank destroyers. After the initial volleys, he ordered his men to attack. The tank destroyers of the 3rd Company rolled forward under the command of *Leutnant* Schönrath. Following Schönrath in the second *Jagdpanzers* was the gun commanded by *Oberfeldwebel* Erich Stolz. His gunner was Eduard Job. It was an experienced crew. Job, for instance, had been awarded both classes of the Iron Cross while serving in *Panzerjäger-Abteilung 13* of the *13. Panzer-Division* under *Hauptmann* Barth. He had also been wounded three times. In a few minutes, Job would become the most successful gunner of the entire division.

"Get going, Ede!" Stolz ordered his gunner when he identified the enemy tank. The gunner observed the Cromwell in his optics. He fired, and the round slammed into the frontal armor of the Cromwell, cleanly penetrating it and killing the crew inside.

Krenstedt, the driver, shifted the vehicle to the right to aid the gunner in sighting additional targets.

Stolz announced another target: "400 . . . twelve o'clock . . . fire, when ready!"

A round soon left the barrel of the main gun, and another tank went up in flames. Heller, who served as both the radio operator and the loader, worked like an automaton. Covered in sweat, he rammed the rounds home into the gun's breech. Job took up another sight picture and fired.

The six tank destroyers rolled forward, stopping to cover one another and fire. They drove back the enemy tanks that had penetrated and cleared the terrain in front of them. Once again, the enemy had been turned back.

The mechanized infantry breathed easier and started to evacuate their wounded. They walked hesitantly back in the direction of the aid stations. A number of them had to be carried. The 7th Company, which had borne the brunt of the enemy's attack in the 2nd Battalion sector, had only forty-three combat effectives left.

Stabsarzt Dr. Selzer, the battalion physician, worked without pause.[10] All of the wounded at Tilly were initially seen by him. Farther to the rear, the division surgeon, *Oberstabsarzt Dr.* Wolfgang Schmidt, carried on a bitter fight against death. He was able to save men again and again who were previously thought to be "gone." He was aided by fellow physicians *Stabsarzt Dr.* Wilhelm Heinemann and *Stabsarzt Dr.* Hans-Joachim Schulz-Merkel. The latter physician was also a recipient of the Knight's Cross, the only medical doctor of the entire German Armed Forces so honored during the war, although his award was for acting command of the 1st Battalion of *Panzer-Regiment 35* of the *4. Panzer-Division* during a time when he was the senior officer present.

The elements of *PGLR 901* under *Hauptmann* Philipps also turned back the enemy. *Leutnant* Stöhr, a platoon leader in the 8th Company of the *PLR*, showed up at Philipps command post at precisely the right moment: the enemy was attacking for the third time with tanks. Advancing with his four tanks, Stöhr moved to the outer edges of the palace grounds, where the mechanized infantry were in their positions. His tanks took up position and began to return the enemy's fire. Eventually, they advanced and took on the enemy in one-on-one tank engagements against elements of the British 7th Armoured Division.

The enemy was turned back, and all of Tilly was clear of the enemy once more. With no rest for the weary, the mechanized infantry immediately set about improving their positions within the ruins of the town.

To the west of Tilly, however, a brigade of the British 50th Infantry Division, supported by tanks of the 7th Armoured Division, succeeded in taking the town of Verrières. Reconnaissance vehicles of the enemy immediately started rolling out of the large patch of woods north of the town along the road. Moving rapidly, they crossed pasture land and apple orchards. Lingèvres was in grave danger. There was the chance that the 1st Battalion of *PGLR 902* could be encircled. The 6th and 7th Companies of the *PLR*, which had been held back as the division reserve, were sent forward. *Leutnant* R. Ernst, a platoon leader in the 6th Company, participated in that action and the operations of the days that followed in his tank, the *Zitrone* ("Lemon").[11] His account follows:

It was a quiet and mature seriousness, you could almost say an almost happy quietude, with which I saw in the tank commanders and their

10. Translator's Note: *Stabsarzt* is a medical rank equivalent to *Hauptmann.* An *Oberstabs-arzt* was equivalent to *Major.*

11. Translator's Note: "Lemon" does not have a negative connotation in German. Moreover, in this instance, it is his codename on the radio, not the name of his tank. As will be seen later on, one of the other tanks of the company was code-named *Kirsche* ("Cherry").

men move out against the terrible experiences and the most horrific concentration of weapons in this war. It was something like that that I saw in one of my tank commanders, *Unteroffizier* M., as he lightly touched the white blossoms on the hedgerow as he strode to his tank in the middle of an ear-deafening artillery barrage after I had told the men to mount up. Perhaps he could perceive the decisive events ahead of him. A few minutes later, he found his own end in that coffin of steel. Or the blond *Leutnant*, punching a hole in the air, when he said: "That's the way . . . with a jolt . . . that's how it has to be done!"

A few weeks later, deadly shrapnel hit him in the forehead, right after the huge thunderclap blew apart his engine and set men and vehicle ablaze.

It was with those types of men that I went into combat with on 9 June, moving through Tilly—mentioned in the Armed Forces Daily Report—and against the enemy bridgehead at Bayeux. The assault on that old Norman city—famous as a result of its tapestry depicting William the Conqueror's invasion of England—misfired. The fighting west of Tilly started after that, fighting that filled the columns of the world's press at the time. For us, the fighting meant the village of Lingèvres. Lingèvres turned out to be hell for us and it started this way:

The alert sent us rolling forward. The massive church tower of Lingèvres, made out of unfinished fieldstone, jutted above the muddle of hedgerows with their ancient thorn bushes and the small, narrow pasture lands flanked by apple tress with their broad crowns.

An enemy remote-controlled vehicle was positioned under a linden tree in the middle of the village.[12] British armored forces had advanced as far as the large patch of woods north of the locality, and one of their reconnaissance vehicles had almost felt its way as far as the large road that went through the town without our being able to get it in the jungle of narrow gardens, pastureland and apple trees. We had just reached Lingèvres at that point, and we were immediately committed to a counterattack.

Our steel monsters waltzed through the narrow streets of the village with an ear-deafening noise caused by their engines and tracks. They squealed around in front of the church and on to the major road and left it again where the knocked-out remote-controlled

---

12. Translator's Note: Ernst must be mistaken in this instance, since the Allies had no such vehicle. It could have been a German *Goliath*, since those were employed in Normandy, and many of the German forces were not even aware of them.

vehicle was. We moved towards the patch of woods—about 300 meters away—along a field path.

"Be prepared to engage!" *Hauptmann* Ritgen ordered. That was followed by: "Button up!"

At that point, only a small section of hedgerows and trenches, the pasture land and the edge of the woods could be seen at any given time through the bulletproof glass of the vision blocks—about as wide as a hand—in the commander's cupola. All of the noises from the engine and the tracks were pleasantly muffled, and a tension-filled, expectant silence filled the fighting compartment.

"Both weapons loaded and ready to fire!" the loader reported over the intercom. He was referring to the coaxial machine gun and the 7.5-centimeter long-barreled main gun, which extended threateningly over the front slope of the tank and was about as long as a naval gun.

There were three vehicles moving ahead of us. All of them were in column. They were forced onto this narrow field path, from which they turned off to the left (west) on a side trail at the southern edge of the woods.

With the exception of a few gigantic deciduous trees, it turned out that the patch of woods consisted primarily of a mish-mash of hedges and bushes about as tall as a man and ancient, untended apple trees and small bits of pastureland that became visible under them.

All of a sudden, the lead tank turned sharply to the right into a larger bit of pasture land that was opening up within the patch of woods. The second vehicle followed immediately. Then the third. But it had not competed its turn when I started hearing excited reports and orders from several tank commanders at the same time in my headphones:

"Look out, enemy tanks!"

"Enemy tanks at eleven o'clock! Fire!"

The sounds of several rounds fired from our tanks penetrated through the double filter of tank steel and headphones.

"Turn right!" I ordered.

As I also entered the patch of woods after a hard turn, I saw our three tanks rolling or stationary right in front of me. Fifty meters farther up was a smoldering knocked-out Churchill tank.

Behind it were the outlines of some more enemy tanks, which were pulling back behind an abruptly climbing wall of smoke from a smoke pot. They immediately disappeared behind a hedgerow. At the same moment, I saw that the shapes of tanks that were also moving behind the hedgerow to the right behind us. After a few meters, they were undeniably British tanks. And almost at the same moment, I recognized sharp, angular lines in the vegetation to the left of me. At the same time, the Cromwell to the right of me fired.

"Fire!" I ordered the gunner.

Our round raced just a hair above the turret of the Cromwell. The enemy rolled back behind the hedgerow. Immediately following that, I received fire from the left.

"Swing left!"

The tank turned left with a jerk and rumble. The outlines of the enemy tank grew in the sights. With a powerful recoil that rocked the tank, the round raced into the vegetation. There was the sound of a hit and detonation. Smoke rose into the air. Nothing stirred. Apparently, the enemy had abandoned his tank after the first round—he was just as surprised as we had been—thus escaping his own death.

The Cromwells pulled back. The fire from the German main guns followed them. For the time being, the British breakthrough had been thwarted in this sector.

During the next two days, the fighting for this patch of woods continued. Short, sharp engagements took their toll of both sides.

The invasion forces continued to hammer Tilly and Lingèvres with naval gunfire, artillery and close air. Tanks hunted their prey in the impenetrable thickets and fired at pointblank range. With the absolute certainty of a hit, both friends and foes were knocked out. It just depended on who fired first.

Then the hotly contested woods were lost. The numerical superiority of the enemy proved to be decisive. The forwardmost lines—there, where the mechanized infantry of [*PGLR*] *902* had dug in—clung to the field path that led to the church. We felt it in our bones that the enemy was about to swing his decisive blow soon.

That day soon came. We were located with another tank in a rest position along the main road that led through Lingèvres. We had just started sizzling a giant country breakfast on the fire when there was a barrage laid down on Lingèvres from concentrated naval gunfire. Immediately following that, there were cries for help in the headphones of the tuned-in radio sets in both tanks: "*Kirsche* to *Zitrone* . . . encircled by enemy infantry . . . cannot move. *Zitrone* needed immediately! . . . *Zitrone* needed immediately!"

That was us. We tossed our breakfast into our mess tins. Blankets, bread bags and laundry went on the tank, followed by us. We cranked the engine; combat preparations needed to be made while moving out. How often had we already done this the last two days at Lingèvres?

We turned onto the field path past the remote-controlled tank. We didn't need to advance too far along its hedgerow. Right in front of us was our screening tank—stationary. The flat helmets and dark figures of the Tommies were visible along the edge of the hedgerow. We sent a few bursts of machine-gun fire into them, but we also started to receive fire from the wood line from armor-defeating weapons. The critical moment then arrived, when we had to open our hatches and dismount under direct fire while we hooked up the stranded tank in front of us and the second tank, which had followed us, gave covering fire. I saw that it had received a direct hit, but it was still firing.

Together with the men from the stranded tank, we hooked up the tank. At the same moment, a *Schütze* appeared in front of me, whose arms had been ripped off by a round. He was moaning something incomprehensible in the ear-deafening noise of battle. We lifted him up onto our tank to get him out of harm's way.

We then tried our first recovery effort. Slowly, carefully, we applied tension. We moved back a few steps when the tow cable snapped. The tank rounds from the edge of the woods increased in intensity. It was high time to get moving! Those were the types of moments during the war when things needed to be done despite little chance of success. A young radio operator helped me while round after round impacted into the hedgerow and burst with an ear-shattering din. It puzzled me why the guys "over there" didn't aim higher, but everything was probably happening in a matter of seconds. A voice in me said: "Nothing's working!"

I was as cold as ice as I directed this tank caravan on foot outside the entrance to the village. In moments like those, things took on a curious stillness. At the moment, I was only interested in getting the tanks through the obstacles there. There was more luck than skill involved. We got though by a matter of millimeters and then, a few meters later, we were safe.

The main line of resistance was held with difficulty over the next few days. Lingèvres remained in our hands. The month of June turned nicer and nicer; the green fullness of the hedges and pasture lands glowed in lush, vibrant colors. The moist fragrance of the soil and the dew on the opulent grass of a small garden invigorated us. Then, one evening, our riflemen discovered enemy antitank guns through the thick hedges. We exchanged a few rounds with them and then moved out through gardens and pasture land with trees in an immediate counterattack west of Lingèvres.

The company commander moved ahead of me—followed by some antitank gun rounds—across some pasture land, and I followed him as fast as I could. The gunner did not properly understand my command to traverse the turret, and I saw, to my horror, that the tank was rapidly approaching an apple tree with the gun off to the side. The driver—on edge because of the impacting antitank-gun rounds—was also not to be diverted from his course. The inevitable happened, and the five-ton turret was turned to the rear as a result of the collision with the apple tree by the main gun. At the same moment, as I was forced to look over at the enemy, a phosphorous round slammed into the side of our tank with a thunderous roar, and a narrow flame, about a meter in length, climbed high right next to me. I do not know what happened next, since I was beside myself as a result of the impact and practically paralyzed. I felt completely powerless and surrounded by the white heat of the gigantic flame. Comrades later told me that I had immediately jumped out at the moment of impact.

Two other tanks suffered the same fate. We tried to save our burning comrades. We succeeded in freeing a few from their pitiful situation. But it was an almost impossible undertaking to get the burning uniforms off the bodies fast enough or to smother the flames with blankets.

In the middle of all those efforts, someone approached this scene of horror. He was completely calm, but he was also completely naked and with a fire-blistered body. In response to our horrified questions, he would only answer: "But I really am Schmielewski! I really am Schmielewski!"

We had no time. We grabbed him as the artillery fire started to commence and placed him and the other wounded on the last remaining tank, which was packed to the gills in the fighting compartment and on the rear deck with tankers.

I will never forget that last movement from Lingèvres. The wounded squatted and lay on the rear deck, most of them with bad burns. They screamed when the exhaust stacks started to glow as the tank moved out of the artillery beaten zone at maximum speed. Schmielewski was right next to them with big, open eyes. He did not utter a sound; he was burned in the worst way imaginable.

My left hand had received burn wounds as a result of the lance of flame in my tank. It was only then that I started to feel the real pain. I counted the minutes until we reached the aid station and received first aid. We were then sent back to the main aid station, a nice country estate from France's better days. We were taken into a large Gothic hallway, fitfully lit by a few candles. In the flickering light and fleeting shadows, I recognized an almost life-sized portrait of a lady from Renaissance times that reminded me more of similar portraits from Elizabethan times in English palaces.

While the rumbling of the nighttime fighting rolled on threateningly outside, there was an almost ceremonious quiet inside. Most of the wounded had already been treated with shots to kill the pain; the shot they gave me had the same effect. The doctors and medics only spoke in whispers. As a result, I could only make out the doctor next to me with difficulty: "I cannot inject. His skin is completely gone."

Our Schmielewski was lying there, motionless and quiet. He died a soldier's death that same night.

That's how the first few days of the Battle of Normandy ended for us. The landing of the enemy had not been prevented, but the German defense had forced him to fight one of the biggest battles of the last war. Superhuman efforts were made in both the offense and the defense, and the memory of those who fought, of those who were sacrificed and those who were wounded will remain alive in those who participated in it.

CHAPTER 6

Days of Horror

While the British 49th and 50th Infantry Divisions attacked Tilly and Lingèvres without pause, Flying Fortresses plowed up the terrain into a crater moonscape over and over again and naval artillery of up to 38 centimeters in caliber put down fires worthy of purgatory, Bayerlein was presented with several prisoners captured by *Oberleutnant* Ernst Thies's divisional escort company at St. Germain d'Ectot. They were assigned to the British 7th Armoured Division, the famous "Desert Rats."

Bayerlein knew that formation all too well from his days in North Africa. The general took the three prisoners with him in his staff car to Sermentot. *Hauptmann* Hartdegen discovered from one of the men, who were to be interrogated by the division's intelligence officer, that he was the head gravedigger at a London cemetery.

The gravedigger turned out to be talkative. He stated that his division was already deep along the left flank of the *PLD* and was currently in the process and attempting to insert itself into the gap between the British and American beachheads.

"If that's true," *Major* Werncke, the division's logistics officer, stated, "then our situation is pretty serious. If the Desert Rats get behind the division, then our front could collapse."

On 13 June, the statements made by the gravedigger were confirmed.

While the British 50th Infantry Division continued to run up against Tilly and Lingèvres from the front, thus fixing the division, a strong battle group of the British 7th Armoured Division was moving past the left flank of the *PLD* in the direction of Villers-Bocage. It was only by luck that the front around Tilly did not collapse. Luck, in this case, came in the form of *SS-Obersturmführer* Michael Wittmann, the commander of the 2nd Company of *schwere SS-Panzer-Abteilung 501*.[1]

---

1. Translator's Note: The 501st SS Heavy Tank Battalion was a corps asset of the *I. SS-Panzer-Korps* and represented the corps' sole *Tiger* formation. The author's narrative of Wittmann's actions is based on the knowledge available at the time this book was written. Considerable research has since been conducted into what was to become one of the most famous individual small-unit actions of the war since then. The reader is referred to Wolfgang Schneider's excellent account in *Tigers in Normandy*, also published by Stackpole.

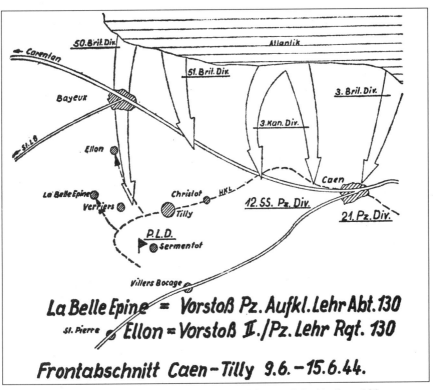

La Belle Epine = Advance of *Panzer-Aufklärungs-Lehr-Abteilung 130*
Ellon = Advance of the *II./Panzer-Lehr-Regiment 130*
Caen–Tilly Sector from 9 to 15 June 1944

Wittmann had been awarded the Knight's Cross on 14 January 1944 while assigned to the *Tiger* Company of the *1. SS-Panzer-Grenadier-Division "Leibstandarte SS Adolf Hitler,"* after having previously made a name for himself within the assault gun battalion of the same division during the early part of the campaign in the Soviet Union. That same month, he was awarded the Oak Leaves to the Knight's Cross. By then, he was credited with having knocked out 119 Soviet tanks and countless pieces of equipment.

On the morning of 13 June, Wittmann rolled forward to reconnoiter Villers-Bocage. His own tank was not operational, so he "borrowed" another and took along his trusted gunner from the Eastern Front, Balthasar Woll. The remaining four operational *Tigers* of his company were in a defile out of town, conducting maintenance and repairing damage they had suffered near Versailles on 8 June during a bombing raid.

Wittmann saw the tanks that were rolling down from Hill 212 in the direction of Villers-Bocage. They were vehicles from the 22nd Armoured Brigade and the 8th Hussars. Observing through his binoculars, Wittmann saw the enemy roll through the town unopposed. The lead elements started to turn on to the road leading to Caen.

Those enemy forces would roll into the rear of the German front like a tornado if no one held them up. Wittmann's tank approached the concentration of enemy vehicles all alone. When the lead enemy vehicle was about eighty meters from his position, he gave Woll orders to fire. After the first round, the Cromwell was engulfed in flames.

Moving rapidly, Wittmann's *Tiger* crashed out of the wooded terrain he had been hiding in. He stopped, fired and then moved out again, repeating the process over and over again. A round from a Cromwell ricocheted off the front armor of the *Tiger*. In the space of a few minutes, Wittmann's crew had knocked out the lead elements of the British armored force, forcing it to pull back. Wittmann pursued, firing with his main gun and machine guns. He overran antitank guns, motorcycles and Bren carriers as he moved along the abandoned vehicles of the British march column. He was then joined by the remaining four operational *Tigers*. Wittmann had been too busy engaging to render a report, but the remaining tankers knew something was up when they heard the report of the mighty 88. They started engaging reconnaissance vehicles that were attempting to bypass Wittmann.

All of the half-tracked and fully tracked carriers, the armored vehicles of the headquarters section and a troop of reconnaissance vehicles were engulfed in flames, immobilized or rendered combat ineffective. The confusion was indescribable. Wittmann's company then rolled into Villers-Bocage. The 1st Company of the *Tiger* battalion was notified of what was happening by radio.

SS-Hauptsturmführer Möbius rolled out to the sound of the guns with his eight *Tigers*.

Once Möbius's tanks arrived, the fighting around Villers-Bocage flamed up again. The track on Wittmann's tank was shot off, and he and his crew had to bail out. That signaled the end of Wittmann's direct involvement in the fighting there. But it was enough for the history books, with the British describing it as the "Battle for Villers-Bocage." The "battle" was decided by a handful of *Tiger* tanks. Montgomery's planned thrust into the flank of the *PLD* was thwarted.

Later that month, Wittmann was flown out of the battlefield area to the *Führer* Headquarters in East Prussia to be personally awarded the Swords to the Oak Leaves of the Knight's Cross to the Iron Cross by Hitler. He was only the seventy-first member of the German Armed Forces to be so honored at that point in the war.

Although the immediate danger at Villers-Bocage had been averted, it was not yet over.

Oberstleutnant Kauffmann, the operations officer of the *PLD*, rallied men from his headquarters and rear-area personnel. With his *ad hoc* force, supported by two 88's and three artillery pieces, he advanced from the north into Villers-Bocage, engaging the British infantry. A short while later, the advance guard of the *2. Panzer-Division* of *General* von Lüttwitz entered the town from the south.

The house-to-house fighting lasted until late in the evening on 13 June. At that point, the elements of the British 7th Armoured Division there pulled back to Livry. In the course of the fighting that day, the commander of the 22nd Armoured Brigade, Brigadier W. R. N. Hinde, lost 15 officers and 176 enlisted personnel, in addition to the many vehicles destroyed. The 1st Rifle Brigade had also taken heavy losses: 4 officers and 60 enlisted personnel.

Lieutenant General Bucknall, the commander of the British armored division, ordered Hinde to hold the high ground at Livry (Hill 174) for as long as was needed to provide relief to the forces of the 60th Infantry Division, which was attacking frontally against the Germans to the south.

The British plans were both ambitious and overly optimistic. The *PLD* was able to hold off the attacks of the three divisions that day, defending along a front that stretched from Tilly to La Belle Èpine. The latter town was defended by von Born-Fallois's *PALA 130*, with the commander setting the personal example for his men and rallying them constantly against the numerically superior enemy forces.

The British 50th Infantry Division stepped up its attacks on either side of Tilly, but the *PLD* held firm there as well.

"Operation Perch," as the unsuccessful venture had been named, demonstrated to both Montgomery and Dempsey that Caen could only be taken from the front. Dempsey came to the conclusion that

> No opportunity existed now for an envelopment operation with airborne forces to take Caen or to expand the beachhead in front of the XXX Corps. . . . It is now clear that Caen can only be assaulted from the front. At present, we have neither the men nor the ammunition for that.

Despite that conclusion, Dempsey needed to continue the offensive tactics that had been initiated, since they were fixing all four German armored divisions that had been committed so far. It was imperative to continue to fix them so that they could not be released for other operations, perhaps seizing the initiative and attacking themselves. With both sides in a stalemate of sorts, Rommel was incapable of fulfilling his mission: pushing the invasion forces into the sea.

Rommel knew what all of this meant. In fact, he knew as early as 12 June, when he sent the following report to the Armed Forces High Command:

> For the time being, the field army group must be content with the forces that are only gradually coming in being used to form a cohesive front between the Orne and Vire [Rivers] and allow the enemy to run against it. In the process, the remaining armored formations can be brought forward.
>
> The field army group is attempting to have the committed armored formations being relieved as soon as possible by infantry formations and forming a mobile reserve once again with them. In the coming days, the field army group intends to shift its main effort into the Carenten–Montebourg area, so as to destroy the enemy forces there and turn back the danger to Cherbourg. It is not until this happens that the enemy forces between the Orne and the Vire can be attacked.

Field Marshal Montgomery, for his part, reported the following to his superiors:

> My general tactic is to fix the enemy with the British 2nd Army so that it is easier for the American 1st Army to expand [its beachhead].

Both of these statements show an amazing correlation with regard to operational intent.

In the discussions being held at the *Führer* Headquarters at the time, both *Generalfeldmarschall* Keitel and the Commander in Chief of the Navy, *Großadmiral* Dönitz, came to the conclusion that all of France would be lost if the enemy succeeded in getting out of his beachheads and obtaining the freedom to conduct a war of maneuver.

After the setback for the British at Villers-Bocage, the overall situation took on the following dimensions:

The U.S. V Corps succeeded in reaching the southern tip of the woods at Cérisy (near Litteau). The American forces were clearly attempting to envelop the German defensive bulwark at St. Lô, manned along the frontage of the *3. Fallschirmjäger-Division*, and straighten out their own front lines. By doing so, they could establish contact with the British 2nd Army.

In the vicinity of Carenten, the *17. SS-Panzer-Grenadier-Division "Götz von Berlichingen"* was preparing its counterattack on the town, since it had to be abandoned by the decimated *Fallschirmjäger-Regiment 6*. The German counterattack failed, however.

Four German divisions remained committed in the area around Cherbourg as a result of a *Führer* order: the *77. Infanterie-Division*, the *243. Infanterie-Division*, the *709. Infanterie-Division* and the *91. Luftlande-Division*. After the Americans turned back the armored attack at Carentan, the U.S. 9th Infantry Division and the U.S. 82nd Airborne Division advanced west in the direction of Haye du Puits, threatening to split the forces of the *LXXXIV. Armee-Korps*.

In the British sector, Montgomery set about planning an operation to break through the German lines. Once again, the British 49th and 50th Infantry Divisions prepared for offensive operations. Early on 15 June, a hurricane of fire descended on the dugouts and foxholes of the men in the defensive positions in and around Tilly. It started at exactly 0430 hours, and every man in *Oberst* Scholze's regiment knew what was to follow.

When the artillery fire shifted towards the rear, it was followed by three fighter-bomber groups flying in a broad formation and showering the earth with their rockets. They blew everything apart that had withstood the last barrage fire.

✠

By the time the British tanks started rolling forward, *Major* Uthe had lost all contact from his command post in the palace at Fontenay with his forces in the front lines. Messengers that were dispatched came back without having made any contact. They were unable to get through. The engineer platoon

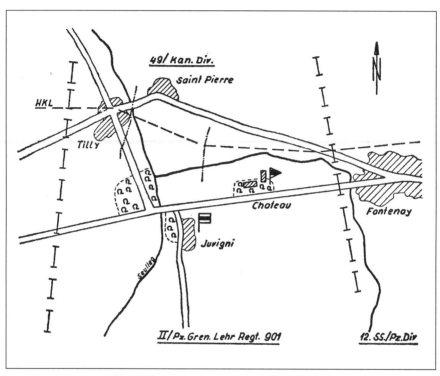

The Fighting around Tilly on 15 June 1944
Legend: *HKL* = *Hauptkampflinie* = Main Line of Resistance

that had been attached to Uthe's battalion was buried under mountains of debris. There were only a handful of men at the command post: *Oberleutnant* Gehrke (Uthe's adjutant), radio operators and signals personnel and three messengers.

They could hear the sounds of fighting echoing towards them from the front. They could hear the rapid fire of *MG 42's* and the dry bark of main guns.

Uthe did not hesitate: "Get ready to go . . . we're going up front!"

Uthe grabbed a submachine gun and slung it over his shoulder. The battalion operations NCO grabbed the documents in the command post and stowed them in the headquarters *SPW*. The junior NCO who drove the vehicle already had the engine running. The last men of the battalion jumped aboard, and the half-tracked vehicle took off with a lurch out of the hull-down position it had been in.

The *SPW* raced at high speed down the road leading from the palace. Not unlike a downhill skier, the driver skillfully made his way around the turned-up trees. They reached the main road running east to west.

"Brits up ahead, *Herr Major*!"

"Fire, Gehrke!"

The *Oberleutnant* took aim from behind the gun shield of the *MG 42* mounted on top of the vehicle. The remaining men opened fire with their rifles and submachine guns. The enemy quickly dove for cover, not expecting Germans to be racing up the road.

Making an abrupt change of direction, the young NCO behind the wheel spun the *SPW* around. The tracks squealed, the engine roared and the vehicle sped off in another direction. When they got close to Fontenay, the *SPW* stopped along the edge of a patch of woods. All of a sudden, they began to see the scattered troopers of the battalion, who had been thrown back. Uthe rallied the men and began to organize a new defense.

A company from the *12. SS-Panzer-Division "Hitlerjugend"* appeared out of the battlefield haze to the right. It was the divisional escort company. Its armored vehicles approached the woodline.

Speaking in military shorthand, the *Major* explained to the *SS-Untersturmführer* in command his intent to retake the original positions several hundred meters to the front. The *SS* officer nodded in agreement and then disappeared in his tank.

The tanks started to move with a thunderous roar, followed by the dismounted infantry. Aided by the tanks, the infantry were able to gain ground and wipe out pockets of resistance. Uthe moved at the head of his men, rallying them whenever they appeared to falter. The men reached the earthen wall several hundred meters short of the original main line of resistance. Uthe halted his men there in order to get a feel for the overall situation. Men that had been left behind originally began to surface out of the rubble. Most were wounded and almost all on the verge of exhaustion.

At that moment, enemy tanks that had broken through started to engage the small battle group. They had been hard to make out in the haze of the battlefield. Fountains of dirt sprayed high from the earthen wall. A hard blow sent *Oberleutnant* Gehrke reeling to the ground. It was concussion, and he was not wounded, but as he gathered himself up, he saw Uthe two meters away, bleeding slightly. A piece of shrapnel had ripped open his sleeve and grazed his arm. Otherwise, he was also relatively unscathed.

The German tanks responded to the enemy's fire. Two of them were soon set alight. The remaining ones decided to quit the battlefield and rolled towards their own lines.

"Men!" the *Major* called out. The soldiers tensed up; something was about to happen. "Let's go! Follow me!"

The battalion commander was the first one over the earthen wall, racing forward. The men jumped up and followed. With weapons at the ready, they charged the enemy forces that had broken through. Meter by meter, they took back their old positions. From some of the foxholes, "dead" Germans sprang back to life when they saw their comrades racing forward in the immediate counterattack.

Off to the right, the *SS* tanks rolled forward and supported the attack. The tanks fired their main guns and machine guns and tore big holes in the enemy's ranks. Soon the British were racing back, tank and small-arms fire nipping at their heels. The *SS* tanks were then called away to put out another fire.

The front lines started to become fluid. The British infantry did not stop, even when their own tanks launched an immediate counterattack from the north. That did not make too much of a difference, since there were already fresh forces mounted on the rear decks of the tanks with dismounted elements following closely behind.

By then, however, the German grenadiers had reached their former positions. Uthe had Gehrke help organize the defense. There were a few *Panzerfäuste* available. The enemy tanks started to take the Germans under fire. They approached ever closer, sure of their success. Once within range, however, one of the *Panzerfäuste* fired, sending a Sherman ablaze.

Despite losing one of their own, the other British tanks kept advancing. The muzzle flashes of the main guns could be seen, heard and felt. All of a sudden, the sound of engines could be heard to the rear. Gehrke spun around.

"*Herr Major!*" he called excitedly and with relief in his voice. "It's our AT guns!"

The 3rd Company of *PJLA 130* moved up the road towards the German positions. *Hauptmann* Oventrop was leading them in in his *Kübelwagen*, both standing and using hand and arm signals and radioing at the same time.

The ensuing engagement between the tanks and the tank destroyers was short. The enemy tanks turned around and rolled back to their lines. Once again, the enemy breakthrough attempt had been thwarted.

The enemy had been stopped at two locations where he had attempted to break through. The main line of resistance remained firmly in German hands. A few of the men who had been trapped as a result of the initial British success were freed.

Once again, the main brunt of the fighting was borne by the 2nd Battalion of *Major* Schöne and, within the battalion, by *Kampfgruppe Hauptmann Philipps*. All of the enemy's attacks against Tilly were stopped by the courageous men of the battalion. The enemy had to be ejected in bitter hand-to-hand and house-to-house fighting. The enemy's tanks, which had broken through, were taken out by means of close-in armor-defeating weapons and *Panzerfäuste*.

Neighboring the *PLD*, the young men of the *12. SS-Panzer-Division "Hitlerjugend"* also performed magnificently in defending against the British 49th Infantry Division. The fight was equally bitter and determined there as well. The defenders held out, but the question remained: How long?

On 15 June, La-Belle-Èpine was lost after final desperate fighting by *PALA 130. Major* von Born-Fallois's men were unable to hold the town in the face of overwhelming enemy superiority. At the same time, the British succeeded in advancing in a broad front across the Tilly–Balleroy road, where *Major* Willi Welsch's *PGLR 902* was in position. For a while, it appeared that the regiment's 1st Battalion was in danger of being encircled. Bayerlein, who happened to be at Welsch's command post at that critical time, looked at the situation map with the regimental commander.

"If the enemy breaks through here, *Herr General*," Welsch said, pointing to the map, "then things will get hot. We have to retake Hottot; otherwise, the enemy will break through and encircle us."

Bayerlein agreed: "Markowski has to retake the town." He was referring to *Major* Markowski's 1st Battalion of the *Panzer-Regiment 6 (PLR)*, which had just arrived back at the front. By the time Markowski had been notified of his new mission, he had already alerted his *Panther* battalion. Twenty-two of the tanks were ready to move. Grenadiers from the 2nd Company and part of the 3rd Company of *PGLR 902* had mounted the rear decks of the vehicles.

Markowski himself was at the head of his men in his command tank. The tanks moved through a shallow defile before they were outside of Hottot. The divisional artillery began to fire in support. Shells hissed overhead and slammed into the houses of Hottot. Heavy British defensive fires lashed out at the advancing Germans from basements, hedgerows and ruins.

Markowski gave his men permission to fire at will. The *Panther* main guns began to bark and fire at the glowing muzzle flashes of the enemy. The high-velocity rounds slammed into the house walls, smashing antitank guns and machine-gun nests, which were attempting to hold back the grenadiers, who were following the tanks at a safe distance by then, so the tank hunter/killer teams could go to work. The tanks rolled forward, meter-by-meter. "Tanks up front!" The report was submitted by the 1st Company commander to Markowski. Markowski was soon able to make out the first enemy tank. It was rolling forward from behind a thick hedgerow. Once out in the open, it quickly stopped to start firing. The round from the Cromwell grazed the side of Markowski's command *Panther*.

"One o'clock . . . 1,200 . . . Fire!"

"Target!" Markowski exclaimed when the round from his *Panther* immobilized the enemy tank. The Cromwell did not give up so easily. It soon fired another round, which burrowed into the soil ten meters in front of Markowski's vehicle, throwing up rocks and dirt. Shrapnel rained against the walls of the tank as well.

"Continue to engage!"

The gunner adjusted his sight picture, and the second round soon left the barrel. The tank rocked from the recoil, and the round slammed into the enemy tank between the turret and the hull, causing the tank to immediately catch fire.

By then, all of the *Panthers* had joined in the fray. There were muzzle flashes from twenty-two main guns and twenty-two coaxial machine guns. The enemy started pulling back. Concentrating their fires, the *Panthers* rolled into Hottot.

It was no time for precision movement. *Panthers* slammed into the corners of houses as they tried to take up good firing positions. Walls came tumbling down. Wooden beams were crushed under the churning tracks of the steel behemoths, snapping like oversized matchsticks. The sounds of the main guns firing continued unabated. There was screeching steel and the thunderous roar of detonations; there was the unmitigated cacophony of ready-reserve ammunition exploding.

The afternoon was filled with the sounds of death and destruction. Flames rose from the buildings of Hottot into the skies. The grenadiers followed the tanks into the village and cleared the individual houses—those that were still standing.

A lance of flame showed Markowski the location of an antitank gun that was attempting to take his tank out.

"Turn left!" he ordered.

With a lurch, the *Panther* made a hard turn. The driver then accelerated ten, twenty meters. He then stopped to allow the gunner to fire. The gunner had also slightly traversed his turret. He saw the antitank gun in his optics and depressed the trigger. With a harsh crack, the round left the main gun. It impacted right next to the gun.

At the same moment, there was a flash at the antitank gun's location. The round roared in and slammed into the turret. Markowski felt a hard blow to the side. He heard the cries of his wounded men. Then he smelled gasoline fumes.

"Bail out!" he yelled.

The driver and the loader looked after the badly wounded officer and helped him out of the tank. The radio operator fell over the side; he was dead before he hit the ground. The men, who were relatively unscathed, then helped the gunner and dragged him to the closest covered and concealed position. The commander was able to make it that far before he collapsed.

The remaining tanks penetrated farther into the village. A couple of enemy tanks took up the fight. They were eliminated in the engagement that ensued. The quick and maneuverable *Panthers* blew the enemy tanks apart.

Two of the *Panthers* were immobilized by PIAT's, the British handheld antitank weapon, but the enemy resistance collapsed soon thereafter and *PGLR 902* mopped up. Hottot was once again in German hands. The grenadiers set up defensive positions along the northern edge of the village. Supporting artillery was brought farther forward.

Two hours later, Bayerlein had all of the tanks pulled back from Hottot. Another British attack was underway. Moving along a broad front, they had assaulted across the Tilly–Balleroy road and established positions south of the road. Men of the *PLD* were also there. They sank their fingers into the soil, and they held their positions with heretofore unimagined bravery.

In order to finally break the decisive and determined resistance, naval gunfire was concentrated into an unimaginable barrage. The Allied fleet hammered into Tilly without pause. None of the buildings in Tilly and the surrounding area remained standing. Only rubble and ruins were the hallmarks of what once were the homes and work places of human beings. Debris-filled streets made the roads impassable.

Hauptmann Philipps experienced the cannonade from within his command post, located in a basement at the northern outskirts of the town. It was the worst he had ever experienced in nearly four and one half years of war. A wall of fire, steel and dirt rose to the height of the houses in Tilly. Vehicular dug-outs were literally eradicated upon receiving direct hits. Gigantic craters turned the remaining area into an eerie moonscape. Even tanks fell victim to the onslaught.

When the enemy moved out to attack after two hours of artillery preparation, the men around *Hauptmann* Philipps were back at their posts. Wherever it appeared that no human could survive the barrage, the grenadiers rose out of the ruins. The German defensive fires greeted the first attack waves of the British 49th and 50th Infantry Divisions. The German self-propelled antitank guns moved forward, followed by the remaining tanks of the 1st Battalion. Eventually, the 2nd Battalion also had to be committed. *Oberst* Rudolf Gerhardt, the commander of the *PLR*, eventually had to commit his reserves.

Unteroffizier Job, the gunner in *Oberfeldwebel* Stolz's tank destroyer, knocked out three enemy armored vehicles, as well as two antitank guns. The tank destroyer of *Leutnant* Schönrath, a platoon leader in the 3rd Company, also knocked out three enemy vehicles. *Feldwebel* Dückert's crew was credited with two Cromwells.

The division's combat engineers under *Major* Brandt also distinguished themselves in the fighting.[2] With their commander in the lead, they charged forward with demolition charges and *Panzerfäuste* and took out enemy tanks that had broken through. All of them fought in a battlefield wilderness, and they held Tilly, which meant that Caen was also held. Tilly was the key to the defense of Caen.

Despite a shaky start and a delayed entry onto the battlefield—all caused by senior command indecision and hesitancy—the division had proved itself worthy of the status of an elite formation. All the training, exercises and battle drills had paid off.

On 16 June, the Armed Forces Daily Report announced:

> In fighting against three of the best English infantry divisions, the *Panzer-Lehr-Division*, under the command of *Generalleutnant* Bayerlein, has especially distinguished itself.

2. Author's Note: Brandt was awarded the Knight's Cross for his actions on 18 July 1944.

When the British ground attack lost momentum, the fighter-bombers were sent in again. With howling engines, they swooped down on the German positions in an effort to break all resistance from the air. Despite the punishing blows from above, the German front continued to hold.

During the night of 15–16 June, London was hit for the first time with the *V-1*. Although orders had been issued as early as 6 June for *Oberst* Wachtel's *Flak-Regiment 155* to open fire with its "revenge" weapons, it took another ten days before the new weapon was ready for massed employment, although a test shot took place on 13 June with ten of the rockets. The massed employment saw 224 rockets fired within the space of twenty-four hours.

The soldiers on the ground in Normandy and the other German theaters of war breathed a collective sign of relief. For once, one of the "secret" weapons that had been widely rumored had been employed. The war was being taken to the British once again, and the psychological boost to the German soldier was enormous.

Despite the hopes placed in these weapons, the Allies did not change their overall strategy. On 18 June, Churchill informed Eisenhower that no changes in operational planning needed to occur—some had called for a capture of the launch sites as soon as possible—and that London would hold out for as long as it took for the overall campaign plan to succeed.

CHAPTER 7

A New Major Attack

On 14 June, *Gefreiter* Hoffmann of the 8th Company of the *PLR*, who had been on temporary duty with *Unteroffizier* Nürnberger, arrived in the Caen area. They were stopped by men of the *12. SS-Panzer-Division "Hitlerjugend"* not far from the airport at Carpiquet, along with some other men of the *PLD*. The *SS* soldiers wanted to impress the tankers into their ranks to make up shortages in the *SS* tank regiment.

The *SS* division had been employed in that sector, initially holding up the tanks of the Canadian 2nd Armoured Brigade, before the Allies were able to reach the airfield. The *SS* tankers knocked out twenty-seven Canadian tanks in the engagements there.

Nürnberger and Hoffmann were able to effect a disappearing act and, that evening, finally located a sign pointing them in the direction of the 2nd Battalion of *PLR*. They found their company in a patch of woods, where they reported back for duty. Still wearing their "rear" uniforms, they were forced to seek cover from naval gunfire a short while later.

Since the tank that Nürnberger had been directed to take was leaking oil, the junior noncommissioned officer had to find another one, while Hoffmann remained with the original tank. Hoffmann never saw Nürnberger again. The next day, Nürnberger's tank ran over a mine. The crew had to bail out, whereupon they were taken prisoner.

The next morning, Hoffmann moved out with the original tank, which had been repaired. The new tank commander was *Unteroffizier* Westphal, an experienced tanker. He carried out his duties as a combat outpost, along with four other tanks of the company, with an unflappable demeanor.

Westphal's tank had taken up position at a bend in a hedgerow. One man each from the crew was sent out to either side to establish contact. Both of the men found their neighboring tank. To the left was *Unteroffizier* Schulz; on the right, *Unteroffizier* Pausch. *Hauptmann* Felmer was on the tank farthest to the right. The remaining tanks of the battalion, the 6th and 7th Companies, were located two kilometers farther to the rear.

Two days passed waiting. Then the enemy showed up. Initially, it was just an antitank gun. It was knocked out with high-explosive rounds. A short while later, an artillery observer showed up, followed shortly thereafter by a hail of artillery fire on the one tank that had given away its position. The artillery fire increased to a tempest after the guns had ranged. The tank's sideskirts were peppered with shrapnel. The British forces then started firing smoke. Visibility was reduced, even though a new day was dawning. It was 17 June. The air roared with the thunder of guns. The reports of the guns were mixed with the sound of impacts to one unified crescendo of doom. Despite all that, however, the enemy did not advance.

Leutnant Stöhr's *801* was caught by surprise by the fires. *Oberschütze* Heinz Loewe was in the process of cooking up a big pan of potatoes when the first rounds started impacting. Stöhr's tank had the luxury of a cooked breakfast, because it was about 2,000 meters behind the remaining tanks of the company, serving as the company reserve. At first, everyone looked in horror to the skies. They everyone hit the deck, and the pan and its contents were scattered to the four winds by the force of the concussion of the incoming shells.

The stowage bin on the rear of the tank was split open by a piece of shrapnel. The men crawled under the tank, seeking shelter. The artillery barrage lasted two hours. At noon, a messenger arrived with rations. He had been able to make his way through the mayhem. One of the crew gathered up all of the mess tins and headed towards the other side of the road to get the meal that had been brought forward. He received the crew's share and, as he headed back across the road, it started to howl again.

A heavy naval shell landed twenty-five meters from him. The mess tins rattled and spilled to the ground. Afterwards, the only thing left to enjoy were the cigarettes that had also been distributed. An hour later, the bombers came back. Fortunately for the men of *801*, they laid down a carpet about two kilometers away, where the other tanks were.

Despite the distance, the concussive effect was so strong that it was difficult for the men to catch their breath. A few minutes later, the skies darkened in the distance. Nothing could be made out in the columns of smoke and dirt that had risen skywards. It was another day at the front in Normandy.

Unteroffizier Westphal's tank was in its old positions on the morning of 18 June, when the British started another brutal artillery barrage. When the enemy started firing smoke, the battle-hardened soldier knew that it had to mean an attack this time. His visibility had been reduced to about ten meters.

The enemy soon started to advance, and the four tanks that composed the outpost line began to fire. Main guns and machine guns hammered away as fast as the loaders could keep the hungry beasts fed. The mechanized infantry, which was also scattered along the line, began firing into the thick smoke as well. The sun disappeared under the manmade fog. Once again, however, the enemy had simply launched a feint. No real attack effort was made.

The Germans continued to watch and wait. Westphal's tank was pulled out of the line to assist some infantry in a neighboring sector; their lines had been penetrated. He made his way through the constant artillery fire and tried to disguise his movements from the fighter-bombers that constantly circled overhead, looking for prey.

The tank was soon all on its own and moving down a field path. None of the other tanks of the company could be seen any more. The path was ringed by trees. Westphal had the tank stop and he had Hoffmann dismount to scout ahead. Westphal's combat instincts were on high alert.

Hoffmann got his pistol out and grabbed two hand grenades as he dismounted. He then advanced along a hedgerow, using it to conceal his movements. A few rounds whistled overhead, hitting farther to the rear behind him and then ricocheting. He reached a bend in the road. Hiding, he could see an enemy soldier ahead. The enemy soldier had also apparently taken cover. Perhaps he had seen him? Hoffmann brought his firing arm forward and carefully propped himself up. He was ready to fire, but the Tommy had not moved a muscle in the meantime.

Advancing in a low crawl, Hoffmann approached the enemy soldier. When he guessed he was about ten meters away, he jumped up, pistol at the ready. But the Brit was no longer a danger; he had been dead all along.

Hoffmann continued a bit farther. There was nothing to be seen of the enemy—living enemy, at any rate. There were no hidden tanks or antitank guns. He returned to his tank, reported and mounted up. The tank moved out again. A few hundred meters farther, and the men established contact with the infantry they were to support. Launching an immediate counterattack, the tank and infantry were able to drive back the British forces that had penetrated and advance a few hundred meters. When it turned dark, however, the forces had to pull back to their old positions. At least they had sealed the line.

The ritual repeated itself for fourteen days and nights. On several occasions, things turned deadly serious. In all, four tanks from the 8th Company were knocked out. The rest were spared for the time being, spared for more days of death and destruction.

✠

The divisional air-defense battalion—*HFA 311*—was also integrated into the defensive positions. The guns were employed in a ground-combat role. They fired as traditional artillery, directed by forward observers, and also in an antitank role. The 88 was especially successful in the latter capacity. More than one enemy attack was thwarted by the direct fires of those guns. The battalion soon became an indispensible tool of the division commander and a bulwark of the defense. It was eventually singled out for praise in the Armed Forces Daily Report.

The division command post was moved to Monts. When all of the British VIII Corps attacked on 18 June, the *12. SS-Panzer-Division "Hitlerjugend"* was to the right of the *PLD* on Hill 112. The *16. Luftwaffen-Feld-Division* was north of the Odon.[1] The grenadiers of the *21. Panzer-Division* were positioned in Caen, while that division's tank regiment was in a staging area to the east of the city. The *PLD* continued to hold terrain between Tilly and Cristot. Bayerlein had blocking positions established north of Vendès. That morning, Bayerlein told Kauffmann, his operations officer:

> Our hopes are pegged to the new armor divisions. Our division and the two other armored divisions of the corps have been too weakened. The force ratios have unmistakably turned against us. Our division needs to be pulled out of the line and reconstituted if it does not want to lose all of its combat power. But where are the replacements? We cannot pull out a single man where we are. We are left with no other choice than to remain where we are.

The first British attack on 18 June was turned back. Fighter-bombers then swept over the battlefield and fired on the identified German positions. The second infantry attack got underway. It also collapsed in the face of the German defensive fires. That attack was followed by wings of Flying Fortresses. The ensuing carpet bombing churned up the fields yet one more time.

---

1. Translator's Note: 16th Air Force Field Division. In the latter half of the war, the *Luftwaffe* began fielding ground divisions, since its infrastructure was now too large to support the ever-shrinking aircraft fleet. Rather than transfer the personnel to the Army, Göring initially wanted to form his own divisions. The Army acquiesced, as long as senior command and staff positions were filled by experienced Army personnel. While some of these very well equipped divisions were second rate, many evolved into fine combat formations.

The enemy tanks then collided with the German tanks, which were called forward to counter the armored threat. *Flak* from *Hauptmann* Weinkopf's guns joined in the fray. The grenadiers combated the steel behemoths with improvised antiarmor devices and *Panzerfäuste*.

The fighting lasted from early in the morning that day until the evening. The British employed wave after wave of naval gunfire, field artillery, bombers, fighter-bombers and tanks. It was a battle of attrition, the likes of which have rarely been seen. To the east of Tilly, the men of the *12. SS-Panzer-Division "Hitlerjugend"* brought the enemy onslaught to a halt.

The British were able to achieve partial success, however. Cristot, four kilometers east of Tilly, fell into their hands. The grenadiers of *PGLR 902*, who had been defending there, were buried under the rubble. At 1946 hours on the same day, the lead enemy armor elements also entered Tilly. For the last time, a desperate resistance was offered. Bayerlein knew that further defensive measures with his weakened forces there could only have dire consequences. He ordered both mechanized infantry regiments pulled back. He established a new blocking position south of Tilly.

The general was forced to even commit trains elements into the fighting. *Hauptmann* Hauck's *Panzer-Nachrichten-Lehr-Abteilung 130* fought shoulder-to-shoulder with men of the divisional escort company. Together, they were able to hold back the enemy in their sector. When the divisional artillery delivered its final protective fires, the British attack ran out of steam and was stopped for the day.

The Allies had reached Tilly, but their strength had been sapped. They were not in a position to advance out of Tilly and into the rear area of the *PLD*, thus signaling its fate. By this point in the campaign, the division had lost 160 officers and 5,400 enlisted personnel in dead, wounded, missing and otherwise incapacitated. Of the 190 tanks the division had started out with, only 66 were still operational.

✠

From his command post in the palace west of Fontenay, *Oberst* Scholze defended in the front lines with his grenadiers. For the third time, he saw his regiment slowly bled white in front of his eyes. At the very last minute, his men were finally relieved by *SS* grenadiers from the neighboring *"Hitlerjugend."* They finally were being allowed to march to the rear for some rest. Only 112 men were left in the front lines to make that march with Scholze.

At a fork in the road, the commander had his small column halted. The crosses made of birch wood shimmered in the early summer evening like old silver. The colonel took off his load-bearing equipment and helmet. Around him were his stalwarts from this campaign and previous ones: *Hauptmann* Ehricht (regimental adjutant) and *Leutnants* Schulte and Hinz (regimental liaison officers). The men listened attentively as the small commander spoke: "We cannot take you with us. But that is not important! You will continue to live in our hearts!"

The impromptu prayer ended, the commander told his men to form up and move out. Above the men, Allied bomber formations were streaming towards east—to the homeland.

After returning to the rear, *Oberst* Scholze was informed that he needed to give up his regiment because of his age. He was sixty. For the first time, his grenadiers saw him in a completely unmilitary light: the old man stood in his *Kübelwagen* and waved good-bye to his men until he had departed out of sight.

On 20 June, the U.S. 9th Infantry Division reached the outer defensive ring of Cherbourg. A demand on 21 June to *General* von Schlieben to surrender the city went unanswered. The next day, the Americans launched their attack against the port. Four U.S. divisions attacked concentrically and penetrated the provisional defenses in four places. On the evening of 26 June, they entered the city center, although some fighting continued until 1 July. By that point in the fighting, the Allies had taken some 39,042 prisoners on the Cotentin Peninsula. U.S. forces had buried some 4,000 dead.

On 26 June, British and Canadian divisions moved out for another assault on Caen after a three-hour artillery barrage. They planned on crossing the Odon and advancing as far as the Orne, taking Hill 112 and then Caen in an envelopment. Fontenay was attacked from the direction of St. Pierre and Cristot. Only the *"Hitlerjugend"* was left in position there. Some of the most intense fighting since the start of the invasion ensued. Entire companies were overrun and destroyed. By the afternoon of 27 June, the British were able to establish a bridgehead over the Odon by introducing the fresh forces of the 11th Armoured Division. Hill 112 was lost, only to be recaptured on 30 June by tanks of *SS-Panzer-Regiment 12*, thus saving Caen one more time.

The enemy also attacked in the west in the vicinity of Tilly. Remaining elements of the *PLD* defended against three British divisions. Not a meter of ground was given up. Again and again, the attacks of the 2nd, 49th and 50th Infantry Divisions were turned back.

On 29 June, Rommel recommended to Hitler at Berchtesgaden that Normandy be abandoned and, after a fighting withdrawal, a cohesive defensive position be established by the *7. Armee* in the vicinity of Paris. The German divisions that were still stationed and idle in southern France should also be withdrawn to assist in forming the new defensive lines along the Seine all the way to the Swiss border. Rommel emphasized his point by stating that the British offensive that had been launched on 26 June had only been held back by committing the entire operational reserves of the field army. If the German armed forces did not leave Normandy, the *7. Armee* would be wiped out. The *15. Armee*, which would then be on its own, would be powerless to counter a second Allied landing.

But Rommel was unable to convince Hitler. Both Rommel and Rundstedt, the Commander in Chief West, who was with him, returned to France without anything definitive. On 2 July, Rundstedt was replaced by *Generalfeldmarschall* von Kluge. That same day, *General* von Geyr-Schweppenburg was relieved of command. Taking his place was *SS-Oberstgruppenführer* Sepp Dietrich. The *PLD* was ordered to leave its positions around Tilly and move to the St. Lô area. The movement order took the division completely by surprise. It wasn't the movement aspects of it that were unusual; instead, it was the conditions attached to it. Basically, the division was to leave one third of its tanks, tank destroyers and artillery behind in the Tilly area of operations, where an infantry division was to assume command of the sector, along with tactical command of the *PLD* elements left behind.

Bayerlein immediately went to work to change the orders so that his already battered division would not be split up. All of his efforts were in vain, however. The orders remained in effect.

CHAPTER 8

Westward

On the evening of 2 July 1944, Bayerlein had his commanders assemble at his command post near Monts to discuss the movement of the division into the St. Lô–Coutances area. The general reviewed the lessons learned from the fighting up to that point in the Caen–Tilly area of operations. The last reports had indicated that about sixty tanks were operational. The total number of complete write-offs for the division in armored vehicles was eighty-four. The difference was the number of vehicles that had been battle damaged or had mechanical problems and were being recovered or repaired.

As a result of the fighting along the Odon, the last chance for a German counteroffensive in the direction of Bayeux had disappeared. The advance of the British 2nd Army was tying up all eight of the German armored divisions that had been committed in the Normandy area.

St. Lô in the American sector had assumed the same importance as Caen had in the British sector and was thus subjected to frequent bombing raids. St. Lô was an important traffic hub, with four highways converging there. Also of importance was the bridge over the Vire, which was still intact. The *PLD* was headed west to protect that bridge.

Rommel, looking at the overall situation, drew the proper conclusion that the Americans were preparing a concentric attack in the St. Lô–Coutances area. That was the reason for the precipitous withdrawal of the *PLD* from its previous area of operations and its commitment to a newly threatened sector. It was to be joined by a *Kampfgruppe* from the *2. SS-Panzer-Division "Das Reich,"* which had also been bled white in its area of operations around Raurey. The field marshal had no other armored formations at his disposal.

Montgomery had formulated the overall plan as follows:

We have to preserve such an equilibrium in our division of forces that we will not see ourselves forced in any case to respond to enemy movements or thrusts with counterthrusts; the enemy can do what he wishes, and we will continue to follow our plan. To that end, Bradley will swing around the left wing in the Caumont area to the south in a general line running Caumont–Vire–Mortain–Fougéres with his 1st Army. Once that line is reached, one corps will turn around at Avranches towards the Breton Peninsula, while the rest of the field army advances with a strong right wing in a wide arc south of the *bocage* one after the other with the following objectives:

A. Laval–Mayenne

B. Le Mans–Alencon

The start of the operation is planned for 3 July.[1]

By then, the American forces had grown to four corps with a total of fourteen divisions. Opposing them were six German divisions.

Following the commander's conference at the *PLD* command post, artillery hit it heavily with barrage fire for more than two hours. The command post, which had been carefully camouflaged and had gone twenty days without being hit by artillery or from the air a single time, had been discovered.

The vehicles, some of which had already started to line up for the movement, received their share of the artillery tempest. Two *Kübelwagen* were destroyed; one truck burned out. The men of the division headquarters staff jumped into the dugouts and foxholes that had been prepared for just such an eventuality.

All of the landlines to the division troops and formations were disrupted. Bayerlein was finally able to leave his command post during a short break in the intense fires.

The division staff fell back to an alternate command post in Villers-Bocage. It was there that Bayerlein's driver, *Unteroffizier* Kartheuß, had been killed four weeks earlier. By then, that seemed an eternity, and many men of the division had followed Kartheuß to an early death.

The tanks and mechanized infantry elements were pulled out of the line during the night of 3–4 July and replaced by the airborne troopers of the *5. Fallschirmjäger-Division*. A few kilometers to the rear of the lines, the men started to head west. The vehicles could only be moved at a walking pace.

---

1. Translator's Note: The reader is reminded that this is reverse-translated and the original text may vary somewhat from what is rendered here.

Frequently, the tank commanders had to dismount and guide the vehicles on foot, it was so dark. Despite the additional stress and strain of doing that, it seemed much better than the sheer hell of a daytime movement and its attendant fighter-bomber "escort."

As it started to turn light on 4 July, the air guards were again posted. Orders were received while the units rested:

> The division will continue to march, even if attacked from the air. Disabled vehicles will not be recovered, since they will negatively influence the rate of march. Open fire with all weapons, if attacked from the air. Use main guns on fighter-bomber attacks.

Bayerlein's intent was to expose his marching elements to the enemy's aerial fires for as short a period as possible. The dreary day with the low-level cloud cover seemed to aid and abet the general in his attempt to evade the "street sweepers" from the skies.

After the long hours of the night march, the men started to get drowsy until the hammering of machine guns and automatic cannon awakened them from their dream-like trances. When the fighter-bombers swooped down, the tanks of the 2nd Battalion scattered in order to avoid making a nice target for the attacking aircraft. With a whistle, the first rounds screamed over the tops of the tanks.

The hatches were slammed shut. The machine guns were directed towards the approach route of the fighter-bombers. The first ribbons of fire arced skyward towards the enemy aircraft. The aircraft responded in kind. The tankers were lucky that time. Only one of the vehicles was battle damaged—its main gun was perforated by an automatic cannon round. The tank continued to move with the rest, but it was essentially combat ineffective for the time being.

After the initial air attack, the tankers remained on heightened alert. The air guards constantly scanned the heavens, but there was no repeat of the first attack. It started to rain, and the rain clouds served as a magical cloak to hide the moving armored column.

Somehow, it also got on the men's nerves. After the experiences of the last few weeks, it just didn't seem "normal"—an entire tank battalion on the move during the day and no fighter-bombers. As it turned dusk, the tanks reached their assembly areas in the vicinity of St. Lô. All of the vehicles made it.

In a similar manner, the *PGLR 901* reached its assembly areas almost without incident. Its final elements closed on the St. Lô–Amigny area by 6 July. On that day, however, Bayerlein was strafed on his way to the regiment. Once again, he and his escort were able to escape unscathed, even though he could see burning vehicles farther to the rear. They were not from his division, however.

PGLR 901 established a blocking position in its sector so as to cover the important St. Lô–Caen road. In order to escape the artillery harassing fires of the enemy, the positions had to be moved constantly. As a result, the vehicular losses and personnel casualties could be kept within bounds.

While the *PLD* was on the move towards the west, Montgomery had launched a new major offensive in the Caen area. The fighting raged for days there, and the *16. Luftlande-Division* was essentially wiped out, although individual strongpoints continued to hold out. The *"Hitlerjugend"* was also battered but not broken.

During the evening of 6 July, 467 Lancasters and Halifaxes bombed the northern outskirts of Caen, where the German defense was the stiffest. In a narrow area, 2,560 tons of bombs were dropped, brutally battering the German pockets of resistance. Following the bombing, the Canadian 3rd Infantry Division and the British 3rd and 59th Infantry Divisions moved out during the night of 7–8 July, taking the city. It was only in the suburb of Vaucelles that elements of the *"Hitlerjugend"* continued to hold. As a result, the road to Paris that Montgomery wanted was still blocked.

✠

By 7 July, the *PLD* had completed its reorganization in its new area of operations. Bayerlein held a commander's conference with his leaders in the vicinity of Carontilly, just west of Canisy. He had personally supervised the "broom details" that had been established to clear any signs of the tanks from the road network. When the regimental and battalion commanders arrived, they were directed to park in widely dispersed, concealed positions. Even the route used to walk to the designated meeting place was concealed from aerial observation by a thick canopy of tree tops.

Despite all the care taken, coupled with the continuing bad flying weather, twelve fighter-bombers appeared and showered the officers of the division with a hail of gunfire and bombs. The aircraft continued their strafing runs for nearly half an hour, and the meeting point reverberated with the echoes of machine-gun and automatic-cannon fire. Some of the officers, who had sought cover in a roadside ditch, were caught in a strafing run and killed.

Later on, Bayerlein remarked that not even a mouse would have emerged from that ditch alive. Nine other officers were wounded. The division commander ran over to one of the nearby farm houses. A few of the men followed his example. He reached the house and he succeeded in getting into the basement before the house above him shuddered under the impact of two rockets.

After the enemy had finished his business—more likely, out of ammunition—three houses were burning around Bayerlein and his officers. Some of the vehicles had been destroyed or were still glowing wrecks. After the men had taken stock of the damage, the conference was held. The division had been directed to conduct an attack along the Vire the next day.

The intent of the attack was to drive north far enough to stop the advance of the U.S. forces and divide them in two. If the division succeeded in holding the enemy at the Vire Canal, then the opportunity existed to eliminate the U.S. forces that were already south of it.

On 8 July, the division started its attack, although it did not have all of its forces. What made matters worse was the fact that the Americans were apparently already aware of the attack plan of the division. At 0530 hours, the 2nd Battalion of the *PLR* rolled north in the direction of Pont Hébert with the intent of taking it. It was to serve as a jumping-off point for the main attack. One of the men assigned to the 8th Company of the regiment has provided this firsthand account of the fighting on that day and the three days that followed:

> We were happy that we had reached our march objective. If we then held the hope that we might be able to finally get some real sleep, we had deceived ourselves—as was usually the case. After the necessary work on the tanks, we also received a new attack order. We knew that the enemy had crossed the Vire seven miles north of St. Lô with the XIX Corps and was advancing south to expand his penetration.
>
> Our mission was to take the village [Pont Hébert] that was right in front of our main line of resistance.
>
> We rapidly attacked towards the village. During the advance, we received machine-gun and mortar fire from the right flank, but that did nothing to our steel behemoths. With each meter of advance, however, the defensive fires increased. Despite that, we attempted to reach the village and take it in accordance with our orders. One platoon received orders to attack the enemy in the flank, thus eliminating the threat from there.
>
> While that movement was underway, we identified antitank guns and American infantry in front of us. The enemy was trying everything to stop our attack, but we had to reach the village. From those contrary efforts emerged a strong fight.
>
> The fighting raged back and forth. The garish flames of the main guns firing mixed in with the barking of the enemy antitank guns.

Infantry attacked our tanks. They were held down by machine-gun fire. We then moved into the village. The tanks rolled into the pockets of resistance offered by the enemy. The enemy pulled back. The village was ours. We set up screening elements on the edges of the village, and we hoped to have some peace and quiet.

The night passed quietly. We were alerted at first light. Enemy tanks had broken through and were moving along the main street. We immediately mounted up to hold back the enemy. Suddenly, everything happened very quickly. There was the report of a main gun and an enemy tank was engulfed in flames.

The fight was short and sharp. Tanks engaged tanks. The main guns spit out their deadly rounds. Steel clattered against steel. Flames rose to the heavens. The hard blows from the enemy's main guns blew apart the sideskirts. Rounds hammered against the turret and howled away to the side. The inside of the tank was a hellish cacophony.

After the main gun fired, our tank rocked backwards.

The loader and gunner worked together with the precision of a fine watch. The tank commander issued orders. The driver moved forward, turned to the right and then turned to the left. An enemy tank was hit in the front. The round penetrated its armor. The crew started bailing out. The men were on fire. They ran to the side and then threw themselves on the ground, attempting to extinguish the flames.

"Keep moving . . . keep going!" the tank commander called out.

The remaining tanks followed him. Three . . . four . . . five enemy tanks remained behind. But then our tank was hit. We heard the reports coming in over the headphones several times: "Direct hit . . . bailing out . . . bailing out!"

From those who did not report, we were sure we would no longer see them alive again. We lost seven tanks.

Many of comrades were wounded and dead, but the enemy's tank penetration had been stopped by our fires.

During the days leading up to the attack, all of the division's elements were constantly hit from the air by the Allied air forces. Fighter-bombers attacked divisional artillery positions at Hebecrevon and Amigny with rockets. Rear-area services were bombed at Marigny and St. Gilles. For the first time during stormy weather, aircraft—P-38 Lightnings—appeared over La Chapelle and bombed and strafed logistics elements of the division.

HFL 318, which had been employed to such great effect against ground targets in the area around Tilly, was once again used exclusively for air defense. At that point, no one knew that the division's fateful hour would come in the area around St. Lô.

During the night of 8–9 July, heavy weapons were brought forward to support the attack. An airborne regiment also came forward to support *General der Fallschirmtruppe* Schimpf's *3. Fallschirmjäger-Division* of the *II. Fallschirm-Korps.* Bayerlein saw the airborne regiment march forward. He was amazed at its sloppiness in maintaining operational security. Bayerlein's fears were soon realized. At Les Champs de Losque, the regiment was hit by ten fighter-bombers. Steel rained down on the newly equipped but insufficiently trained regiment. Of the 1,500 men, more than 200 were killed or wounded in the five minutes of death and destruction. That terrible baptism of fire so shook the regiment that it never fully recovered.

But that was just the beginning. Over the next two weeks, after the hell of Tilly, the division would undergo the purgatory of St. Lô.

✠

It had been the U.S. 9th and 30th Infantry Divisions that had crossed the Vire Canal during the dreary morning of 7 July. Before the German forward observers could even ascertain what was going on, the Americans had already crossed the canal. They forced the obstacle with a provisional bridge and, farther to the west, with assault boats. Since the overall situation for the Americans had developed so favorably, Eisenhower also had the U.S. 3rd Armored Division committed. That division was rolling through the grain fields to the north of St. Lô. On 9 July, it was stopped by the *2. SS-Panzer-Division "Das Reich."*

The *SS* division had just arrived from southern France. It advanced on Hill 32, halfway between St. Jean and Pont Hébert. During the afternoon, it reached Chateau de la Mare de Cavigny, where it shattered the 120th Infantry of the U.S. 30th Infantry Division. It was only thanks to massed artillery fires on the part of the Americans that the *SS* division was finally stopped.

On 10 July, General Bradley announced at a conference held at Montgomery's headquarters that he would be unable to continue his offensive until his ammunition stocks had been replenished and he had taken a jumping-off point south of the marshlands. Bradley continued by saying that he would first have to take St. Lô and throw the Germans back to the St.

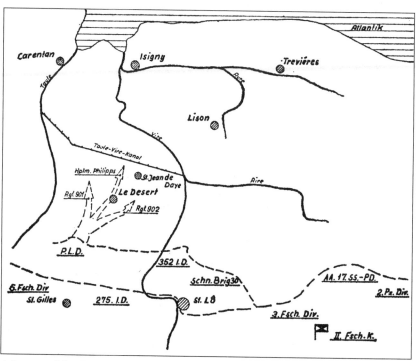

Advance of the *Panzer-Lehr-Division* towards the Taute-Vire Canal on 11 July 1944
Legend: *5. Fsch.Div. = 5. Fallschirmjäger-Division; Schn.Brig 130 = Schnelle Brigade 130;
AA17SS-PD = Reconnaissance Battalion of the 17. SS-Panzer-Grenadier-Division "Götz von
Berlichingen"; II.Fsch.K. = II. Fallschirm-Korps.*

Lô–Périers road. He concluded by saying that those preparations would take at least ten days.

One day later, however, everything took on a new light. A major attack was planned by the *PLD* on 11 July by most of its elements. Bayerlein intended to advance through the enemy forces with two attack wedges and reach the Vire Canal. If the attack succeeded, the Americans' offensive plan would be compromised.

The righthand thrust against the U.S. 30th Infantry Division was led by *Major* Welsch. It consisted of his *PGLR 902* and twenty *Panthers* of the 1st Battalion of the *PLR*. On the left, *Oberst* Scholze was to take the *PGLR 902* into battle. His mechanized infantry were augmented with additional combat power thorough the attachment of twelve tanks from the 2nd Battalion of the *PLR* and a company of tank destroyers under *Hauptmann* Oventrop. It was intended to strike the deep flank of the U.S. 9th Infantry Division with those forces.

The attack started at 0510 hours. By 0630 hours, *Hauptmann* Philipps's men of the 1st Battalion of *PGLR 901* were already three kilometers behind enemy lines. Whenever the mechanized infantry encountered resistance, the tanks were sent forward, eliminating it. An enemy battalion command post was overrun, then another. Prisoners were simply sent back without guards. The Germans could not afford to give up any men for the attack, and the strategy seemed to be working, since the advance was fluid and moved forward rapidly.

One portion of *PGLR 901*, supported by tanks, tank destroyers and divisional reconnaissance elements, fixed enemy forces in Le Désert, while Philipps's men continued pressing to the north. If he could reach the canal, then the American forces to his south would be cut off.

But it turned out that the division was too weak to successfully complete this mission. Even on paper, it only had about half of its authorized strength. It had been bled white at Tilly and its effective combat power had been reduced by almost two-thirds. Once again, the German high command had harbored false illusions about its capabilities and those of the enemy: It had intended for a division one third in its authorized strength to eject two fully equipped and manned U.S. infantry divisions.

The fighting raged back and forth. Tanks encountered enemy counterparts in defiles and fruit orchards. The engagement only ended with the silencing of one of the parties involved. The steel behemoths fired at each other from distances of 150 meters or less.

Leutnant Stöhr, who had been transferred from the 8th to the 7th Company of the *PLR*, was at the front of his tanks that day. He was killed in action. In the middle of an attack, a piece of shrapnel had ripped open his forehead. He was killed instantly, thus sparing him the even worse death of the rest of his crew, who burned to death after a penetration by a main-gun round sent the tank alight.

Leutnant Harning and *Obergefreiter* Borowetz rode forward with the men of Philipps's battalion as well. They were assigned to the regiment's 9th Company—the heavy infantry guns—and acted as forward observers. In that capacity, they were able to assist the Philipps's grenadiers immeasurably. Time and again, they called the guns forward to lend support. They were able to rip holes in the U.S. defenses, through which Philipps's men were able to advance.

That morning, the weather had been dreary and with reduced visibility. In the afternoon, however, it cleared up. With the sun came the fighter-bombers as well. They flew low to the ground over the roads and the fields and hammered away at the advancing companies of *PGLR 901*, forcing them to take cover. The tanks, which were able to advance farther, were unable to hold terrain by themselves. More and more tanks were knocked out. They served as smoke signals along both avenues of attack for the marauding fighter-bombers. In the end, some twenty tanks were immobilized and, in some cases, complete write-offs. Only twelve tanks remained operational at the end of the day of the thirty-two that had moved out in the morning. The losses among the men of the mechanized infantry regiments were also horrendous. More than 500 were killed or wounded that day. Here is another eyewitness to the bitter fighting:

"1st Platoon . . . move out . . . now!" *Oberfeldwebel* Sohlbach yelled as he jumped up and ran forward.

To the left of us, the men of the 1st [Company] were running, and the 3rd was on the right. When I headed out, machine-gun fire whipped towards us. One of my comrades cried out, hit. Then we reached the hedge and dove for cover.

Bucker landed next to me with the machine gun. He crawled into the middle of the hedge. His number 2 followed him. Three seconds later, he was already firing. The tracers arced over towards the enemy. Then the firing started up over on that side that late morning. All of a sudden, an enemy antitank gun began firing. The first high-explosive round tore the hedge apart ten meters off to my side. The second round hit right at the spot where Bücker and his assistant were lying. Everything disappeared in a single ball of fire.

We ran forward again. An enemy tanks was firing off to the left. Then one of our tanks came out of a defile. It fired into the flank of the American. Its ammunition went up with concussive blasts.

The *Oberfeldwebel* called out: "Over to that patch of woods!"

All of the units received the same order at practically the same time. We started running. Rounds whizzed past our ears . . . comrades fell to the ground, to remain there forever.

Sohlbach dove under cover in the middle of a thicket. The enemy started firing from all sides all of a sudden.

"We're surrounded!" one of our comrades yelled out. I think it was Müller. There were muzzle flashes in a large semicircle around us. The tanks were off somewhere to the right of us. We heard their main guns barking and, in between, the somewhat lighter crack of the enemy tank main guns. The enemy approached ever closer.

"There they are!"

The enemy appeared in tight groups on the meadowland in front of us. The soldiers disappeared behind a hedge. When they appeared at the far end, they were greeted by fire from an *MG 42*, which forced those not hit to pull back rapidly. Off to the right, we could hear other sounds of fighting.

"The *Hauptmann* is over there. Looks like they have surrounded the battalion commander."

Sohlbach ran over—bent at the waist—to the side closest to the new scene of fighting. He wanted to see whether he could help. But the Americans started attacking our position again. They were forced to ground by our fires. A few of them surrendered, followed by some more. Among the prisoners we were already dragging along, there were now an additional twenty, making a total of around forty. Over at *Hauptmann* Philipps's position, the firing fell silent. We knew that our comrades had fallen to the superior numbers.

"We need to try to break out, comrades!" Sohlbach informed us.

There were just twelve of us, and we had the forty prisoners on top of that. One after the other, all of the weapons in this sector fell silent. Nothing more could be seen of *Hauptmann* Salzmann's company. We got to a patch of woods and snuck through it. When a group of enemy soldiers that had previously been overrun appeared in front of us, we blasted a way through them. After an hour—perhaps it was really two—we had torn through the encirclement that had placed itself around our battalion like a steel chain. The twelve of us and a handful of others were the only ones who returned to the regiment from that advance.

It was thanks to *Oberfeldwebel* Sohlbach that we did not wind up being taken prisoners by the Americans like *Hauptmann* Philipps and the other survivors. It was shortly thereafter that Sohlbach was

awarded the German Cross in Gold for this operation and the forty
prisoners he brought back.

PGLR 901 was in a difficult situation. If it did not succeed in sealing off
the enemy's penetration, it ran the danger of being surrounded and overrun
itself.

All available units were sent north. *Hauptmann* Hennecke moved forward
with his last six heavy infantry guns and established a blocking position.
The enemy attempted to break through his position again and again, but
was turned back every time. The mechanized infantry, supported by the few
available tanks, clawed its way into the ground and defended with the courage
of desperation. They defied a vast numerical superiority from behind hedges
and earthen walls, in foxholes and along defiles. They were on the edge of
despair. Couldn't they do anything any more? Would they never be on top
again?

Those questions were answered by the Allied bombing attacks that would
follow in the near future, the attack by strong infantry and armored formations
at Le Mesnil on 15 July and the additional attacks against Durandt-Sadot on
16 and 17 July.

Even if Bayerlein's attack, which was conducted with all means available
to him, was not blessed with a decisive victory, the elements of the *PLD*
nevertheless had success in a way that cannot be easily measured. The German
attack was launched in the middle of the American attack preparations
and had delivered a blow to the American command that weighed all the
more heavily: the Americans saw their chances for a rapid breakout of the
Cotentin Peninsula thwarted. The German command had received one more
reprieve.

In fact, the Allied senior leadership in London and Washington feared
that this blow—delivered by a half-destroyed division—was a harbinger
of a swing in fortunes in Normandy. They argued—and not without some
justification—that the Germans had won sufficient time to bring forward their
idle divisions in southern France, commit them to the game and nail down the
Allies in their beachheads. Fall and the onset of winter would reduce Allied
airpower support, which had been the single biggest contributing factor to
their success so far, to a low point.

On the other hand, the senior German leadership still believed that
there would be another landing in northern France, specifically in the area
around the Pas de Calais. Combat-capable infantry and armor divisions were
still positioned there, divisions that might have been able to tip the scales had
they been employed in the Normandy beachheads.

After the abortive attack, there was a short respite. Here is another firsthand account:

In the middle of July, the losses became greater, [but] the 8th Company of *PLR 130* still had seventeen operational tanks. We were supposed to occupy screening positions for a few days and then get some rest. We were all looking forward to it, since we would be able to get our fill of sleep, our dirt-encrusted bodies needed some care and cleaning and we could finally change underwear. *Unteroffizier* Lindstätter wanted to prove his prowess in his [civilian] profession and butcher a pig. The prospects were good. We were already starting to dream about it, and it was soon time to catch a pig, since they were running around in the open countryside. Easier said than done! You'd think we would have done it right away. That's what you think! It was not nearly so easy as we had imagined it. After a wild chase, the hunted pig suddenly disappeared—and the three hunters as well! We all found ourselves at the bottom of a deep bomb crater. Together with our pig.

The promised rest also came, if only for too short a time. On the next day, there were already orders for us. The tanks were repaired as much as time had permitted and most of the battle damage fixed.

The grenadiers of *901* were in their foxholes in front of the assembly area we had occupied. We were expecting a big attack by the Americans. Every sign indicated it. Fighter-bombers had already had us in their sights, but without success.

Then they covered us with artillery fire. Fortunately, no damage was done. A short while later, we saw that the American forces were covering themselves with smoke, which meant we needed to be on a state of heightened alert. The enemy attacked at that point, but the attack bogged down in heavy weapons fire.

In response, their artillery fired into our positions again. During the morning of 16 July, we changed positions. There were already a few tanks in the new positions and they had just received rations.

Towards noon, an aerial observer showed up and flew low over the woods where we were located. We were right in the process of distributing our rations and did not pay too much attention to it. Barely half an hour later—a result of the reconnaissance aircraft— artillery fire commenced on our positions and shook us out of our peace and quiet. We buttoned up and waited for what might come. The first artillery shell slammed into the ground barely five meters in front of our tank, and the second one landed right on it. The crash practically made us deaf, and more shells started landing, of which another two hit our tank. The hatches popped open from the concussive effect—which was good for us. The fighting compartment started to burn, and the gunner, loader and radio operator bailed out.

Unteroffizier Westphal, our tank commander, had not been in the vehicle because he was trying to intercept two vehicles from the 7th Company that had been racing off in the direction of the enemy. When he came back, he saw the mess. There were only three of us; one man was missing. Our driver, *Obergefreiter* Gerbig, had been unable to bail out, since his hatch had been blocked by the turret. Our desperate attempts to get him out of the burning tank went without success. We also knew that the ammunition could go up at any minute and send us heavenward.

Each of us had suffered some burns. Fortunately, they were nothing much to talk about. All of our things were burned up, however. We made our way back to the company. On the way there, we ran into a prime mover, which picked us up.

After about two kilometers, we came to a crossroads that was under artillery fire. Horsedrawn columns scattered. Trucks and staff cars were hit. There was unbelievable chaos, but we had to get back to the company. The driver tried to move through it all. But we were unable to cross the intersection; the fire was too intense. We sought cover in a house in order to wait out the artillery. It wasn't until two hours later that we could move again. Towards evening, we reached the company.

Of course, everyone was sleeping, except for the guards. We immediately looked for a place to sleep in a barn, happy that we had found our company. We immediately fell into a deep sleep.

On the morning of 17 July, *Unteroffizier* Westphal reported to the first sergeant that the crew of *801* was back, but that it was also his unfortunate duty to report that *Obergefreiter* Gerbig had been burned to death in the tank. We received a new issue of clothes and then some rations. We were still somewhat under the effect of all that had happened and we went back to sleep again after a big meal.

We rested for three whole days. It was hard to believe. We were only reminded of the war by the occasional sounds of impacting artillery, which slammed into the earth a ways away.

On the fourth day—it was 20 July—the remnants of the company formed up. As a result of the losses, it was necessary to reorganize the personnel into crews for the remaining vehicles. As a result, some of the crews that had been together for a long time were split up, and we had to get used to one another, which always took a couple of days.

I went to *812*, which received orders to relieve the crew of *Unteroffizier* Schulz, which had already been screening for a few days. I also had some luck inasmuch as the radio operator from *801*, Rudi Weiß, was also assigned to my new crew.

After it had turned dark, we set out. After the days of quiet came the tingly feeling that almost always came before a new operation. We had to go 6 to 7 kilometers to relieve the comrades, who were most certainly already waiting for us. The movement went without difficulty for us, even though we operated without lights. The danger from the air was always there since our opposing numbers also flew at night over the battle areas in order to catch the logistics and relief elements, which could only be brought forward in darkness.

As we got near the tank we were to relieve, we started receiving artillery, but it was unable to thwart our relief-in-place. The tank was in a fruit orchard. I had some reservations about the location, since reconnaissance elements had already identified the location of our predecessor, and it was only a matter of time before we received our "share." As a result, we moved ahead a bit farther and set up to the left of the fruit orchard. Prior to the relieved crew heading back, we discussed the situation with *Unteroffizier* Schulz, who then moved back with his tank.

Our new commander, *Unteroffizier* Fontaine, was on an operation for the first time, and he was a bit jittery. It was planned for another relief-in-place to take place in three days and we already started thinking to ourselves: the three days have already passed. But, as was usually the case, things turned out differently than we had imagined they would.

The hours passed—slowly and monotonously. In the case of a new crew, you initially had something different, until everyone had a chance to say his piece. Then, when everything had been said, it started to become boring. We spent the days in an unchanging rhythm—one after the other.

Four days went that way, and still there was no sign of the relief element. We were promised, however, that we would be relieved the following day.

On that fourth day, *Unteroffizier* Fontaine left the tank to get some fresh air. No one had noticed that the camouflage on the tank had been disturbed in the process, with the result that our location could be identified. It did not take too long before two fighter-bombers suddenly started turning circles in the sky and dove down like lightening all of a sudden.

Highly agitated, *Unteroffizier* Fontaine returned to the tank. We buttoned up and waited for what was to come. We didn't need to wait very long, since one of the fighter-bombers had discovered the tank. The events that followed happened so quickly that you were barely able to follow them. The fighter-bomber dove on us with an eerie howling. A terrible detonation tossed us about. Our tank pitched like a ship at high see under a strong wind. Fortunately for us, the bombed impacted next to the tank, and the tank was not hit.

We had to act. Our driver cranked up the engine, but he was unable to see anything though his hatch. We immediately started being strafed. The intent was to keep us from bailing out. Despite all of that, we moved out, making a sharp right curve, whereupon a large portion of the dirt tossed up onto the tank by the impacting bomb was shaken off. We were then able to open the turret hatches. Standing in his open hatch, the tank commander was able to direct the driver.

But the fighter-bombers had not yet given up on us. They started to make another run on us. In their approach, they strafed in an effort to render us combat ineffective. After about 500 meters, we stopped between three houses along the main road in an effort to at least disappear from the sight of the fighter-bombers.

We then dismounted to see what had been damaged. We had to remove the remaining dirt from the tank with shovels so that we could open all of the hatches. We had barely finished with that, when impacting mortar rounds forced us to take cover. We jumped into the house next to us, thinking that we at least had some safety there.

Enemy artillery fire then started in the fireworks as well, and the firing increased in intensity. We had moved back somewhat, and we were standing next to the decrepit stairwell. In the meantime, a number of other crews from our 8th Company had also entered the house to wait out the firing. Suddenly—no one knew how it had happened—our radio operator, *Obergefreiter* Weiß, was lying on the floor. His face was distorted in pain. He was unable to say a single word. We immediately jumped over to him to help. All of a sudden, *Unteroffizier* Westphal said to me: "You're bleeding as well. You've been wounded in the head!"

I started feeling how blood was running into my right eye. After a received a field dressing, we turned back to our radio operator. We determined that shrapnel had hit him in the upper thigh and had remained stuck there in the vicinity of his testicles. There was not much we could do. Rudi Weiß must have been in terrible pain.

In the meantime, bombers showed up and dropped their deadly cargoes. We had to wait quite a while before we could take the badly wounded man out of the house and bring him to our tank. We were able to get him into the tank with a lot of effort. We then took off immediately to take the fastest route to the aid station.

In our hurry, we had forgotten to lock down the turret. With every crater, the turret jerked a bit. We didn't have any water any more, and the wounded man was terribly thirsty. When he finally reached the aid station, our medics immediately took him inside. He must have suffered terribly. I didn't feel anything at all from my wound, leading to the conclusion that it couldn't have been so bad. But after an hour, I started getting insane headaches.

Rudi Weiß was already in an upper room of the aid station, while I was still below. I was unable to rest, and I wanted to at least see him one more time. While I was climbing the stairs, I ran into a medical NCO, who told me he had just died.

At first, we couldn't believe it. Once again, one of our good comrades was gone, and everyone asked himself: When is it my turn?

During the evening hours, a motorcycle came with our first sergeant, the mail and some special rations. My headaches had become unbearable in the meantime. I lay on three pillows to keep it from getting worse. When it turned dark, an *SPW* came and took us away. We took our dead radio operator with us on a stretcher. The trip to the company area went without any problems.

The next morning, we buried our comrade and took our leave of him.

Two hours later, all hell broke loose. Around 2,000 bombers approached the German positions and dropped their bombs. We saw that they had turned in our direction and that we would be getting a large portion as well. We ran for our puny lives; of course, the bombers caught up with us. The earth opened up around us. The ground swayed and trembled, and we found ourselves in the midst of it. We survived the attack, but our nerves were shot.

I was supposed to be taken by a motorcycle messenger to the main aid station. I protested, but the first sergeant insisted that I get immediate medical attention. Once I arrived there, I only saw men of the *Waffen-SS* and the *Panzertruppe*. After a few hours, we were loaded into ambulances and taken to a rear-area treatment facility. I did not stay there long, since my wound was apparently not too bad. Some hair cut off, some plaster and off I went.

I immediately went back to the company. By then, the Americans had broken through. I no longer found my company where I had left it. I only saw an ammo truck there; I went back with it. After about five kilometers, his unit was reorganizing. To my horror, I discovered that I was running a fever. I lay down in a barn in order to rest a bit. I then lost consciousness. When mortar rounds forced me to leave the barn, I was four days older. I didn't believe my ears when I asked what day it was, but it was true. I had been in the barn with a high fever for four days. I was incredibly thirsty by then and wanted to get something to drink. A *Leutnant* asked me whether I was wounded. It was only then that I started thinking about the recent past. I got something to drink and tried to reach my company on foot. On the way, I accidently ran into a *Gefreiter* who was assigned to the *PLD*. We continued on the same way together.

We took a short break in a village. Suddenly, we heard aircraft, and the low-flying planes were soon strafing the village. After they had turned off, we went farther into the village and saw that a few houses and two trucks were burning. We went past a small aid station. An *Oberstabsarzt* was standing in front of it. When he saw me, he asked whether I was wounded.

Initially, I was not prepared for that question and didn't answer him. It was not until he asked me what I had on my head that I told him about my wound. He immediately took me into the house and took off the dressing.

"My God, your wound is burning!" he said as he took a closer look at it.

Without hesitation, he treated the wounds and applied a new dressing. Then he gave me a pack of cigarettes and took me to the road, where he halted an ambulance, which was instructed to take me to the wounded collection point at Mortain.

On the way there, the ambulance was engaged by fighter-bombers, but it was not hit. As it started to turn dark, we arrived in Mortain. There were a lot of wounded there, who were supposed to be taken farther to the rear. Slightly wounded and badly wounded. I was sent to the fifth floor, where all of the head injuries were.

The next day, I was able to get away from Mortain. We were taken in ambulances to Sèes, where we were given rations. We stayed there one night, until we were taken to the collection point in Paris.

Movements were not allowed by day, so we only went at night. After a long trip, we arrived in Paris, where the German Red Cross received us and immediately placed us in the individual wards.

After a week, we were told we would be going to Germany. We were loaded on to a hospital train at the eastern train station. We were barely inside when there was an air alert. The hospital train departed the station in order not to be caught there in a bombing raid. We then moved via Metz–Saarburg–Karlsruhe–Rastatt and then all the way through Germany to Brünn [Brno] and a hospital there. The trip took eleven days.

✠

On 18 July, U.S. forces reached the St. Lô–Périers road, which would force the Germans out of the important city. They started infiltrating into the ruins along the eastern edge. By 1900 hours on 19 July, elements of the U.S. 29th Infantry Division and the 113th Cavalry Group had basically cleared the city in house-to-house fighting. The headquarters of the *LXXXIV. Armee-Korps* was captured.

The fighting of the previous two weeks had been conducted with unimaginable intensity. In all, it took the Americans forty-four days to take the city from the time they had established their beachheads on 6 June. During the planning of "Overlord," only one week was allotted for its capture.

It then started raining, and the roads and fields were turned into quagmires. Tanks on both sides got bogged down in the muck. The low-lying clouds also did not allow any aerial activity on the part of the Allies. The fronts solidified, and both sides had an opportunity to recover somewhat.

✠

During this period, two individual fighter-bombers scored a success that exceeded that of all of the soldiers employed along the invasion front. During the afternoon of 17 July, *Generalfeldmarschall* Rommel fell victim to their strafing run and was out of commission for a long time. It was just outside the village of Vimoutiers that the two aircraft dove on the vehicle carrying the field marshal. *Unteroffizier* Daniels, Rommel's driver, was hit in the shoulder. The soldier collapsed onto the steering wheel, and the vehicle slammed into a tree trunk. Rommel was tossed out of the car and suffered a fractured skull. Rommel's escort took the stricken general to the ironically named village St. Foy de Montgomery. The Commander in Chief of *Heeresgruppe B*, the man on whom many hopes were pinned, was out of action.

CHAPTER 9

Hell

General Bradley wanted to have his U.S. First Army move out on 20 July after the U.S. 29th Infantry Division had taken St. Lô the previous day. The bad weather forced him to wait, however. His plan called for an intense aerial preparation, followed by breaking through the German lines with armored and motorized formations advancing between Coutances and Bréhal. If the advance succeeded, then the *LXXXIV. Armee-Korps* would be cut off.

Everything remained quiet until 24 July. Up to then, the Germans continued to improve their positions and bring logistics forward. The rain and the low-lying cloud cover allowed for no Allied aerial activity. The only thing not brought forward for the Germans was reinforcements—there weren't any.

On 20 July, the Allies had thirty infantry and thirteen armored divisions ashore. These were augmented by corps and field-army forces such as artillery, engineer and tank destroyer assets. On the German side, there were twenty infantry and eight armored divisions. Due to the constant attrition, their effective combat strengths averaged 40 percent of the authorized numbers. That meant that the Allies had a three-to-one advantage.

✠

"What's the date today, Werncke?"

The division logistics officer, *Major* Bernd Werncke, pointed to the calendar that was on the wall of the division command post at Canisy, south of St. Lô.

"24 July, *Herr General!*"

"What do you think, Kauffmann? Will the Yanks attack us again today?" Bayerlein had turned to his operations officer.

"It can happen any time, *Herr General.* They're ready to attack. No one could miss that. The crappy weather's the only thing holding them up."

"But the 7th Army thinks it won't happen here. The army doesn't think that the Americans will advance in this hedgerow country. Field Marshal von Kluge is convinced that the British will take up their offensive again in the plains around Caen and that this is only a deception operation. They want to withdraw the 2nd Armored from the area around Caumont and commit it in the Orne Valley, since they think the Canadian II Corps will soon move out on both sides of the Caen–Falaise road."

"I'm convinced they're wrong, and . . ."

The telephone in the headquarters rang. Kauffmann picked up the receiver. *Oberst* von Hauser, who had assumed command of *PGLR 901* from *Oberst* Scholze, had his headquarters report.

Kauffmann relayed the message: "Heavy bombing in the sector of the *901, Herr General!*"

"Well, Kauffmann, I think this is it! Put everyone on Alert Level I!"

The alert was sent out via landline. A minute later, the men of the divisions were ready to receive the American attack.

But nothing happened, other than the bombing. Hour after hour passed. Nothing! Messengers were dispatched to the regiments.

A report came in from *PGLR 901*. It didn't make much sense: "Bombing in front of our lines. The Americans are leaving their positions and falling back."

The men in the division headquarters all thought the same thing: a trick?

Bayerlein ordered his men not to pursue and maintain their defensive posture and alert status. As day turned to night, the men increased their readiness posture. But nothing happened. What was going on? Why had the Americans bombed only to then not have their forces attack?

The answer was relatively simple, even if the Germans were not privy to it. Bradley had set the attack day as the morning of 24 July. Since another bad-weather front rolled in, the attack was cancelled, as were the previous ones. Some of the bomber formations, which were already in the air, could not be called back. They approached the German positions, but because of the poor visibility, a large portion of their bombs fell on their own lines, causing considerable casualties. Following that, a number of American commanders pulled back on their own initiative to avoid the risky area.

It was a reprieve of sorts, but what followed on 25 July was hell incarnate.

The *PLD* had established its forward lines in the bend of the Vire northwest of St. Lô. The main line of resistance made a bend to the west and crossed the St. Lô–Périers road. There was another strong *Kampfgruppe* west of the Mesnil–Eury road, while *HFA 311* and the divisional artillery were due north of Canisy. The division rear guard was established southeast of Canisy. There was also a *Kampfgruppe* supported by artillery forward at Le Mesnil Amery. The rear-area services were located in the Cherisy la Salle area along a line running to the east and south in the direction of Percy.

There was cloud cover that day, but it was very high. Around 0700 hours that morning, Bayerlein was in Quibou, when he received a message that had been forwarded from the *PGLR 901*. *Oberleutnant* Möller, *Oberst* von Hauser's signals officer, reported that the American infantry were leaving their positions in a panic in front of the regiment. A short while later, all of the troop elements and formations of the division reported similar sightings. Bayerlein immediately returned to his headquarters.

"Apparently, their heart's not in it," Kauffmann said, as the commander entered the headquarters. "Perhaps the army's right, after all?"

"I'll call and see what they know there."

The *7. Armee* once again confirmed its opinion that nothing would happen around St. Lô. The field army also informed Bayerlein that it had already withdrawn the *2. Panzer-Division* from the front to send it to a new area of operations south of Caen.

"Let's hope for the best, Kauffmann!" Bayerlein still shook his head in a worried manner when he said that. An hour later—it was around 0900 hours—the officers assembled in the division command post could hear the sounds of masses of aircraft approaching. Bayerlein headed outside to an observation post. He could make out bombers in his field glasses—mostly four-engined bombers.

"Damn, that looks like something out of a Party Day Parade!" the general exclaimed.

"Maybe they'll keep on going, *Herr General!*"

"Maybe . . . but now they're turning . . . going into a circle. That means they're waiting for more! Tell the *Flak* to open up!"

A short while later, *HFA 311* opened up with its eighteen 88's. They fired in salvoes at the maximum rate of sustained fire. The rounds exploded in the skies around the bombers, resembling a mosaic of dirty cotton balls. One of the bombers blew up in a mighty explosion and ball of flame.

The bombers started dropping their loads. They targeted the *Flak* positions first. Sixty, perhaps seventy bombers went after the 88's. The earth seemed to come alive where the guns were positioned. Geysers of earth, steel and fire rose wherever the bombs impacted. One gun was lost. Then another. Both lost to the enormous power of a 2,000-pound bomb. The remaining guns continued to fire, and a few more bombers fell victim to the 88's, plummeting to the earth as fiery torches, where they burst apart.

The 2nd Battery of the air defense battalion was especially hard hit. Of the six guns, only two remained intact, with one of them being damaged. Two of the battery's wheeled vehicles—a radio truck and a motorcycle—were able to escape the hellish tempest of dropped bombs. All of the other vehicles of the battery, including those of its trains, went up in flames. *Hauptmann*

Weinkopf had the firing cease. Whenever his men shot down one, another ten flew in to replace it and silence the offending gun.

"Take cover!" the battery commander yelled. There was no defense against that which fell upon them. Airpower proved stronger than air defense.

That was just the prelude, however. The main group of bombers then appeared. No fewer than 2,000 bombers approached the positions of the *PLD*. The waves of bombers appeared overhead as if on a conveyor belt. The positions in and around the *PLD* were transformed into a moonscape within a matter of minutes. The landlines were torn up from the regiments and the division troops to the division headquarters, one after the other. Despite feverish efforts, by 0940 hours, Bayerlein was no longer able to communicate with his subordinate forces, except by radio.

But the reports that were received and entered onto the situation map by the operations officer at the command post during the first half hour of the bombing told their own story. The 2,000 bombers had covered the sector of the *PLD* and those of the neighboring regiments—*Fallschirmjäger-Regiment 13* and *Fallschirmjäger-Regiment 15*—with a carpet bombing the likes of which had heretofore never been experienced. The main line of resistance in an area seven kilometers wide and three kilometers deep was turned into a landscape of death. Every meter of ground was plowed up. The trench lines were covered over; the positions transformed into gigantic craters. Ammo and fuel resupply points were bright points of flame. Ammunition exploded, fueled by untold sympathetic explosions. Hell raged in the sector: man by man, tank by tank.

Whereas there had been 5,000 men of the battered division prior to the start of the attack, there were only 2,500 still alive afterwards. The tanks that had occupied forward assembly areas were disabled, as was the divisional artillery. The 9th Company of *PGLR 901* initially got off the easiest. It was positioned along the edge of the carpet bombing. In the end, however, the infantry-gun company also received its share of the hail of bombs and shrapnel. The men jumped into the slit trenches that had been prepared, but the aerial attack still cost the company seven wounded.

Just after 1000 hours, Bayerlein hopped on a motorcycle driven by an *Oberfeldwebel* and made his way forward. The motorcycle bounced along small field paths. It then reached the cratered landscape around Le Mesnil Amey. The regimental command post of *PGLR 901* was still intact, but the surrounding fields were burning. There was thick smoke over the battlefield.

"There's the observation post, *Herr General!*"

"Head that way!"

They stopped by a tower constructed of stone. While the driver parked the motorcycle in a concealed position, Bayerlein climbed the tower. From there, he was able to observe the next wave of attacks by the Americans. He was able to make out Amigny through his binoculars. It was on the U.S. side of the battlefield. From there, he could see the 400 fighter-bombers and medium bombers that then put down their own carpet bombing.

The general observed for one and a half hours. Around 1200 hours, Bayerlein was no longer able to observe because the smoke, clouds of dust and flames had become so thick.

The general dispatched motorcycle messengers to the individual regiments. A short while later, the first artillery fire started to come in. The reports that started filtering back demonstrated that almost all of the formations had been badly battered and that the men were either dead, buried, wounded or out of their heads in the main lines of resistance.

The forty tanks that had been positioned forward in the main line of resistance were either eliminated or badly damaged. A few of them were found completely flipped over. Others were in the craters, incapable of getting out under their own power. To the south of Hebecrevon, a messenger found the company command post of the 4th Company of *PGLR 902* completely destroyed. The regimental command post, which was not far away, had also been hit hard. The regiment had been in the center of the maelstrom.

It was starting to turn dark when the assault divisions of the U.S. VII Corps moved out. The U.S. 9th Infantry Division was on the right side of the assault wedge. The U.S. 4th Infantry Division was in the center, and the U.S. 30th Infantry Division on the left. The U.S. 2nd Armored Division moved to the right and succeeded in making a break through all the way to St. Gilles. The U.S. 1st Infantry Division and the U.S. 3rd Armored Division followed on its heels.

The remaining battle groups of the *PLD* offered resistance until they were overrun. Even the officers and men of *HFA 311* were employed as infantry since they no longer had any heavy weaponry. The pockets of resistance were scattered, and it often took several days before what was left could be reformed. When, for instance, the 2nd Battery of the *Flak* battalion regrouped several days later at an inn in the rear area, there were only twenty men on hand. Although a few more men joined their band of brothers over the course of the next few days, the entire battalion effectively ceased to exist.

On the way to the command post of *PGLR 901*, which was located in the basement of a massive stone house, Bayerlein discovered that the regiment also effectively ceased to exist. On his way to *Oberst* von Hauser, Bayerlein only saw dead soldiers.

Thanks to Bayerlein's tireless efforts, the division rallied in the vicinity of Marigny. The U.S. 1st Infantry Division was stopped there by a *Kampfgruppe* from *PGLR 902*. It was supported by the tank regiment, which had seven operational tanks. It was only after Marigny was attacked by forty medium bombers that the U.S. 2nd Armored Division was able to continue its advance on Canisy. The division command post was surrounded on three sides, but it managed to break out and move five kilometers farther south in the vicinity of Dangy.

The American tanks continued rolling through the gap in the lines. They reached the high ground at Le Mesnil Herman and occupied it. It was from that point that Bradley wanted to cover the attack launched from the line running Marigny–St. Gilles the next day.

That night, Bayerlein reorganized and committed his final reserves into the contested front lines. The night offered a bit of a reprieve at the gallows, and he wanted to exploit it as much as he could. All of the men in the command post worked like demons possessed. Nine tanks were made operational again by their crews. A few more were released by the maintenance facility that night and also sent forward.

Radio contact was re-established between the division and the regiments and battalions. No reports were received from the corps, however.

The road north of St. Gilles, which was the division's main supply route, had been rendered untrafficable by the bombing. A new route had to be found, and the detours made resupply even more difficult than it normally was.

✠

At 0900 hours on 26 July, the game started anew. Flying Fortresses and Liberators flew over the German lines for nearly four hours, dropping their deadly cargoes. The air raid was followed by an artillery preparation.

At 1300 hours, the U.S. infantry stormed ahead, supported by fighter-bombers and fighters. They moved in narrow attack sectors and hunted down everything in their way. The linear attack sectors ran from the south to the west. The eastern sector was Canisy and Soulles; the western Marigny and Erist la Salle. Later on, Bayerlein commented on the initial assault: "There wasn't a single second where the skies were not filled with the roar of bomber and fighter engines."

Although the St. Lô–Coutances road was completely in U.S. hands by 1800 hours, an *Oberstleutnant* from von Kluge's field army headquarters was able to make it through to the division command post. He brought orders with him from the Commander in Chief West that the St. Lô–Périers line was to be held under all circumstances. It was a line that no longer existed. Bayerlein himself later commented on the strange spectacle:

We were in our command post in Dangy, hungry. I sat in my room with my operations officer, *Oberstleutnant* Kauffmann, and a liaison officer. Outside, the hot July sun of 26 July beat down mercilessly on the blood-soaked, hotly contested soil. Suddenly, a vehicle pulled up outside. The driver was looking for the staff of the *PLD*. He was visibly happy to have found it here. An *Oberstleutnant* climbed out of the vehicle in a clean, magnificently fitting uniform. He had come from the headquarters of the Commander in Chief West, from *Generalfeldmarschall* von Kluge.

For a second, I thought the *Oberstleutnant* might be bringing help or at least say that he would. He wanted nothing of the sort! The *Oberstleutnant* only brought new orders. He was visibly uncomfortable when he stood in front of the men who had been in action for days and whose faces registered the hard fighting. Perhaps he realized that the men there only had recollections of warm meals, the kind he had every day.

The *Oberstleutnant* stood at attention to report: "*Herr General, Feldmarschall* von Kluge demands that the St. Lô–Périers line be held!"

There was an uncanny silence all around, which became all the more oppressive by the second. *Major* Wrede, the division adjutant, stared through the window. *Oberstleutnant* Kauffmann looked at me.

"So, the St. Lô–Périers line is to be held," I said, repeating the order. "May I ask: With what?"

The *Oberstleutnant* deliberately ignored the question. He simply continued to speak: "That is the order that I was to bring to you, *Herr General!* You must hold . . . no man of the *PLD* may leave his positions."

And, as if he also had to report something good, he continued: "A *Panther* battalion of the *SS* will conduct a flank attack against the Americans, thus relieving your front."

I stared at the man.

No man may leave his position!

I rested my fists on the table. I had gone through all the stations of the war. I had experienced Russia and the death knell of the *Afrikakorps*. But this was worse. This completely senseless order after the horrific bloodbath in which my division had been lost.

My words were more likely soft than loud, but it appeared they grew to mountains in the room when I answered: "Everyone's holding up front, *Herr Oberstleutnant*. Everything! My grenadiers, my engineers, my tanks, and all of the others. Every man is holding.

No one is leaving his position, since they are all lying in their holes. Buried and silent—dead!"

I took three steps up to the officer. I stopped right in front of the emissary.

"Tell the field marshal that the *Panzer-Lehr-Division* is destroyed. Only the dead can continue to hold up front. But I—I will remain here, if that's what's ordered."

Just then, an intense detonation relieved the general from having to say anything else and the staff officer from answering. The large ammunition dump at Dingy flew into the air after being hit by rocket salvoes from fighter-bombers. Thousands of artillery shells and rockets flew skyward and transformed it into a sea of flame. What remained of the windows in the building housing the division command post flew out of their frames from the concussion. Doors were flung open.

The earth seemed to spin drunkenly on its axis. Mines, shells, tracer elements, machine-gun ammunition and a seemingly unending stream of rockets signaled their demise with fiery trials. The field army staff officer took off. Bayerlein waited for the *Panther* battalion that had been promised. Instead of the forty tanks, only five eventually showed up. The remnants of the division that had survived the hell of St. Lô assembled in the Canisy area. In all, some fourteen divisional tanks eventually showed up.

On 26 July, *PGLR 901* was relieved by *General Graf* von Schwerin's *116. Panzer-Division*. The regiment marched to Senlis by way of St. Just, Clermont and Creil. The battered 1st Battalion was reorganized and *Hauptmann* Hennecke was given command. Hennecke, who had commanded the infantry-gun company, turned over command of the two remaining self-propelled guns to *Feldwebel* Kanzelsberger. All elements of the regiment that were no longer combat capable were sent to Pancy (near Laon). It was intended to reconstitute the regiment there. But the enemy didn't sit idle. Bombers appeared over Laon, and the city went up in flames. The regiment was then moved to Sedan.

Bayerlein then attempted to regroup his division around Dangy, Soulles and Garanantilly to the east of Pont Brocard, with the intent of pulling it farther south. That opened the way for the U.S. 2nd Armored Division. On the night of 26–27 July, it advanced another six kilometers. The 27th of July would prove to be the decisive day for that sector of the front.

At 0900 hours on 27 July, the American attack started without artillery preparation. The lead elements of the U.S. 2nd Armored Division turned south in the direction of the Bréhel–Tessy road. The U.S. 1st Infantry Division and the U.S. 3rd Armored Division attacked in the direction of Coutances. The

U.S. intent was to surround the *LXXXIV. Armee-Korps*, which was attempting to pull back from the Périers–Lessay area.

Just before the American operations started, fourteen repaired tanks had returned to the *PLD*. That boosted Bayerlein's morale, and he headed forward to the front lines. Around Pont Brocard, his vehicle was attacked by fighter-bombers, which were again swarming over the battlefield by the dozens. Bayerlein had just climbed out of the vehicle to inspect a defensive position when rockets scored direct hits on the staff car. The driver was killed; it was Bayerlein's fifth driver since the start of operations in Normandy. Although the general was not far from the vehicle, he once again miraculously escaped death or being wounded.

Bayerlein returned to the new division command post location at Garanantilly along Soulles Creek in a borrowed *Kübelwagen*. His headquarters had been established in a farmer's house. In all, there were seven officers and about fifteen enlisted personnel. Most of the latter were messengers and radio operators.

Efforts were made to assemble the scattered elements of the division. At 1630 hours, a messenger stormed into the command post and announced that American tanks were 300 meters away on the far side of the creek bed. The aerial attacks, which had continued without pause up to that point, let up. The American air-ground coordination was superb.

The tanks started firing into the building.

"*Herr General*, the windows on the far side leading into the courtyard have iron-bar grates. We have to exit out the front!"

With two long strides, Bayerlein was at the window. He could see the squat silhouettes of the Shermans on the far side of the creek. He could also seer the muzzle flashes as they started firing again.

"Pack up the secret items and get out of here!"

The officers and enlisted personnel left the house individually. They ran like rabbits, looking for cover—followed by main-gun rounds and machine-gun bullets—and then disappearing. The next-to-last to leave the command post was *Major* Wrede. He reached a tree about fifteen meters from the house and then looked to see where the tanks were. After they had fired, he waved to the general.

Bayerlein jumped up and ran out into the open. A main-gun round screamed past him only a few meters away. He had reached a potato patch when there were the reports of main guns again across the creek. The general dove for cover and pressed his face into the soft ground. The rounds whizzed overhead.

"Let's go . . . keep going!"

And they ran. Pursued by death-bringing steel, they ran for their lives, the division commander and his staff.

✠

It was already turning dark by the time Bayerlein reached the new blocking position at Percy. He was by himself. He had become separated from the other men. A general without soldiers. He was on foot, the man who had commanded the most powerful German armored division only a few weeks previously. It was the division that Guderian hoped would push the Allies into the sea.

Oberstleutnant Welsch had had his *PGLR 902*—at least what was left of it— dig in. A couple of *Jagdpanzer IV* tank destroyers from *Hauptmann* Oventrop's battalion were in support. Right behind them were two batteries of heavy field artillery, which *Oberstleutnant* Zeißler had been able to save from the hell of St. Lô.

The grenadiers were in position in their trenches and foxholes. They still had a few *Panzerfäuste* and *Panzerschrecks*. Integrated into the weak defense were two heavy mortars and a 7.5-centimeter antitank gun. Everyone was waiting for the next wave of fire. When it came, it thinned out the ranks of the soldiers even more. When it was over, *Major* Welsch had joined many of the soldiers of his command in death. He had commanded the regiment barely two months. *Major* Kuhnow assumed acting command.

Fortunately for Bayerlein, he ran into a radio truck at Percy. That put him in the position of reporting the demise of his division to the Commander in Chief West. Almost all of his tanks were gone or non-operational; most of his ground soldiers dead, wounded, missing, scattered or captured.

The headquarters had lost all of its command and control measures: documents, codes, maps and radio equipment. Although the general had escaped, he only had what he carried on his back.

The 2nd Battalion of *PGLR 901* bore the brunt of the attack, but it held firm.

Bayerlein had been there when sixty tanks had attacked. They rolled towards the positions of the division in a broad semicircle. The howitzers fired over open sights. The antitank gun took the closest Sherman under fire. The tank's turret was dislodged from its race with the first round, and it started to burn.

Infantry had followed the tanks in halftracks. The German mortars opened their fire, and they were soon joined by hectic bursts of machine-gun fire. The tanks and tank destroyers held in reserve were called forward. They joined in the fray, firing as fast as they could. The turrets traversed the battlefield; flames shot from muzzles. The closest Shermans, which were right in front of the German infantry at this point, began to be engaged by the *Panzerfäuste*. The rockets couldn't miss at that range—as long as the gunner had a steady hand and nerves—and several were knocked out or at least rendered combat-ineffective.

By then, the U.S. infantry had dismounted. They were caught by the German machine guns and forced to earth. It was a murderous struggle and conducted with the courage of desperation. The men won out. If ever courage and determination were determinants of a battle's outcome, it was there.

The American attack was turned back. In the 2nd Battalion's command post, Bayerlein shared some bread and a bottle of wine with an *Obergefreiter*. When it came time to take his leave and return to the re-established division command post, Bayerlein wanted to say something. Try as he might, he could not come up with fitting words. Mere words were insufficient in expressing what he felt. The only thing left was to shake hands with all the soldiers he could.

They were the men whose bravery and actions had been reflected in the general's award of the Swords to the Oak Leaves to the Knight's Cross of the Iron Cross on 20 July.

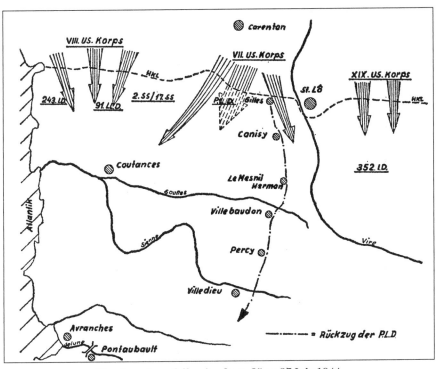

The American Offensive from 25 to 27 July 1944.
Legend: *Rückzug der PLD* = Withdrawal of the *Panzer-Lehr-Division*

CHAPTER 10

Retreat

The *2. Panzer-Division* and the *17. SS-Panzer-Grenadier-Division "Götz von Berlichingen"* were positioned on 28 July by the *LXXXIV. Armee-Korps* oriented west. It was intended for them to block the enemy advancing on Coutances. On the morning of 28 July, they succeeded in stopping the U.S. VII Corps.

During the night of 28–29 July, *Panzergrenadier-Regiment 304* of the *2. Panzer-Division* reached the crossroads at Le Denisière, thus blocking the main artery between St. Lô and Percy. More than thirty enemy tanks were knocked out in front of the regiment's positions.

While both of those divisions were still engaging the eastern wing of the U.S. attack, the U.S. VIII Corps had already started a new attack from the Périers–Coutances area. The corps' attack encountered little resistance and reached Coutances, which fell to the Americans during the afternoon.

As it started to turn evening on 28 July, American forces were rolling along all of the major rounds between the Vire and Coutances. A few of the assault forces reached objectives that were twenty-five kilometers beyond the original start point. A cohesive German front line no longer existed, and the *LXXXIV. Armee-Korps* had been torn apart. One thing was certain: the U.S. First Army had broken out of its beachhead and was in open terrain.

On the evening of 30 July, the U.S. 4th Armored Division reached Avranches. General Collins, the commanding general of the VII Corps, pushed his forces ever onward. The next day, Pontaubault was taken, thus giving the Americans a bridgehead over the Sélune. The door to the heart of France had been kicked open. The German Armed Forces announced the establishment of this bridgehead in its daily communiqué on 1 August:

> The enemy, who had penetrated deeply into our positions along the west wing, was stopped just south of Avranches in an immediate counterattack. During the night, heavy bombers conducted effective raids against enemy troop concentrations and assembly areas in the area northwest of Avranches.

Force reorganizations were initiated on both sides. Commanding the U.S. 12th Army group was General Bradley. Reporting to him were General Hodges (First Army) and General Patton (Third Army). The First Army received orders to advance east in the direction of Vire–Mortain. The U.S. Third Army formed an enveloping wing, which spread out and advanced into the open area to the west, south and southeast.

German reorganizational efforts saw the allocation of the forces of the southern front to *General der Panzertruppen* Eberbach, who had succeeded *General* von Geyr as the Commander in Chief of *Panzergruppe West* on 5 July, with the resulting force referred to as *Panzergruppe Eberbach.* Succeeding Eberbach in command of the area of operations around Caen and the *5. Panzer-Armee* (the former *Panzergruppe West*) was *SS-Oberstgruppenführer* "Sepp" Dietrich, who was previously the commanding general of the *I. SS-Panzer-Korps.*

The *7. Armee* remained the lefthand neighbor of the *5. Panzer-Armee.* Within the *7. Armee, General der Fallschirmtruppen* Meindl's *II. Fallschirmjäger-Korps* was assigned the sector referred to as *Nahtstelle Vire* ("Nodal Point Vire"). The *LXXXIV. Armee-Korps,* commanded by *Generalleutnant* Elfeldt ever since 29 July, when *General* von Choltitz was relieved, adjoined it.

On 7 August, the new German main line of resistance ran as follows: Vire–Champ du Boult–St. Sévere–Calvados–St. Pois–Sée Valley (near Le Mesnil)–Guilbert.

By 2 August, *General* Warlimont from the Armed Forces command staff appeared at *Generalfeldmarschall* von Kluge's headquarters with new orders from the *Führer.* Hitler wanted an operational-level thrust launched from the area around Mortain in the direction of Avranches and then on to the coast. The German counteroffensive was dubbed *Operation "Lüttich."* The operation necessitated the formation of a new armored command, which was placed under the commanding general of the *XXXXVII. Panzer-Korps, General Freiherr* von Funck. Funck's forces were considerable, considering the overall German situation: the *2. Panzer-Division;* the *116. Panzer-Division;* elements of the *1. SS-Panzer-Division "Leibstandarte SS Adolf Hitler";* the *2. SS-Panzer-Division "Das Reich";* the *17. SS-Panzer-Grenadier-Division "Götz von Berlichingen";* the *9. SS-Panzer-Division "Hohenstaufen";* the *10. SS-Panzer-Division "Frundsberg";* and the remnants of the *PLD.* The operation was to start on the night of 6–7 August, and high hopes were placed in its successful outcome.

By the evening of 6 August, Patton's forces had reached Le Mans. What was left of the *PLD* had assembled some fifty kilometers behind the front around Domfront. In the early-morning hours of 7 August, *Operation "Lüttich"* was launched. Four hundred German tanks rumbled off in the direction of Avranches in an effort to prevent the German field army from being encircled.

The 2. *Panzer-Division* succeeded in making a twenty-kilometer-deep penetration. By then, however, the Americans had recovered from their initial shock and the waves of bombers and fighter-bombers started to arrive. By 9 August, the offensive was over. On the battlefield at Mortain, the Germans left behind forty-three tanks and 800 soldiers. Among them were also tanks and soldiers from the *PLD*.

✠

A firsthand account from a tanker in the 8th Company of the *PLR* during this time period:

> When I returned back to my company about eight days after I had become separated from it and reported back to our top sergeant, *Feldwebel* Bischoff, I discovered that I had already been turned in as missing-in-action. I asked him right away to be assigned to another crew. As a result, I went to *Unteroffizier* Schulz, who was one of the old hands and in command of *806*. The loader was *Gefreiter* Schäfer, the driver *Gefreiter* Kordas and the gunner *Obergefreiter* Noack. I was the radio operator.
>
> It didn't take too long before we heard: *"Panzer maaarsch!"* But instead of moving to the front, we headed to the rear. Our vehicle was responsible for providing rearguard. We were the last ones to move. We headed out with the turret at six o'clock. Rumors concerning relief and reconstitution were rife. Unfortunately, none came to pass. During the counterattack of 7 August, we slipped from one pocket to the next. We were always the tail light [rearguard]. On the map, the broad outlines of the Falaise Pocket could already be seen.
>
> On 5 August, *Major* Walter Brandt was awarded the Knight's Cross to the Iron Cross. He was the commander of our engineers, and he had often helped us out of a difficult situation. But right after that, he was reassigned as an instructor at the engineer school in Dessau. Assuming command of the engineer battalion from him was *Hauptmann* Oskar Kunze, a brave and experienced officer.
>
> On 10 August, we received orders to occupy a screening position. We moved out. We looked for a covered position at the crossroads and then set up. We had a clear field of fire to three sides. To our right

were comrades from the *Waffen-SS* with an *SPW* and a 5-centimeter [antitank gun].

The days passed quietly. On 12 August, we had visitors from the air for the first time at our location. A German truck column, which was rolling along the road, had been spotted and attacked a short while later by fighter-bombers. Several vehicles were hit by the rockets and went up in flames.

An hour later, there was the sound of fighting behind us. Rifle and machine-gun fire told us that something was afoot. We occupied our ready position and waited. Then we also heard the sound of fighting to our right. Since our position was not well suited to conducting a defense from two or even three sides, *Unteroffizier* Schulz decided to pull back.

Schulz had the vehicle roll forward. When we reached the road, the engine on our tank started to cough. Then our crate stopped. Kordas was able to get it going again a few times, but only for a few meters at a time. Then nothing.

The gunner was the first to dismount. He was followed by the loader. *Unteroffizier* Schulz then ordered the others to dismount.

"Schulz, traverse the turret so we can get out," Kordas shouted out to the tank commander.

The turret, still positioned at six o'clock, was blocking the hatches of the driver and the radio operator. *Unteroffizier* Schulz then turned the turret. But he only traversed far enough that the driver could get out. My hatch was still blocked and would not open. I only had one way: climb back into the fighting compartment and dismount through a turret hatch. I struggled through with some difficulty, and when I finally got out to the mudguard, a Sherman tank appeared from behind the curve to our rear. I felt like everything had frozen inside me.

I jumped down and fell and then fell over again. Once down there, I found out that our tank was on an elevated road and that I had fallen down the embankment. All of my bones were hurting. To add insult to injury, I had landed right on top of *Unteroffizier* Schulz.

Before we could come to our senses, we heard the report of the main gun on the Sherman. The round slammed into our tank. The tank started burning after the second round.

We ran towards a patch of woods. Our driver joined us. All three of us snuck through the woods. After an hour, we reached an infantry unit, which had set up there to conduct an immediate counterattack. It was an *ad hoc* formation, and we went with it so as not to lose contact with friendly forces again. We found a couple of comrades from the *901* and *902*. Altogether, there were fifteen of us from the *PLD*.

When it turned dark, we attacked. We worked our way forward through the patch of woods. We soon bogged down in the face of the enemy's heavy fires. Many comrades paid for this attack with their lives. We then tried at another location. Finally, at a third. But it was always the same. We were greeted everywhere by heavy machine-gun and rifle fire. The enemy had surrounded us.

We wanted to try one more time in the morning, and tried to get a short rest in a barn. Towards 2330 hours, there was a knock on the barn door. We took the safeties off our weapons and opened the door. It was a French farmer, who brought us potatoes and cream.

Was that a trick to lull us? We set up four men as guards. But, in the morning, the farmer brought us something to eat again and a carafe of coffee.

The next day, we continued on our way—always prepared to fight our way through, if need be. We saw our burnt-out tank one more time. But it was empty and no longer capable of moving.

A short while later, we were finally captured and taken to Carrouches. The next day, additional prisoners arrived. Among them were approximately twenty *Landser* from the *PLD*. The tallest of them was *Obergefreiter* Kirchhoff of *902*. He was 1.85 meters.[1] The shortest one, *Gefreiter* Pfaff, also from the *902*, was almost half a meter shorter. The men were sent to a corner of the courtyard and patted down by partisans with red-white-blue armbands. Following that, one of the partisans approached the men with a helmet in hand and hit every one of them on the head with it, all the while uttering the word *boches*. It was one of those old French helmets with the comb along the crown: a dangerous weapon.

Once he made his pass, he started up again from the rear. We had to contain ourselves not to jump on that poor excuse for a man. But any movement would have cost us our lives. The partisans were waiting for an excuse to open up. When an *SS* man was led into the courtyard, the partisans fell upon him, and one of them hit him in the face with his carbine with so much force that the rifle stock went between the upper lip and upper jaw and came out on the upper side of the nose. The fact that the unfortunate man did not bleed to death

---

1. Translator's Note: About 6'1". The reader is reminded that soldiers of all armies were considerably smaller than today and Kirchhoff was considered relatively tall by World War II standards.

was thanks to a medic who fortunately still had his field dressings with him.

The next day—and that was our good fortune—an American MP patrol arrived. It was under the command of an officer. A *Leutnant* reported to him what had happened and also the fact that we had not had anything to eat for the last forty-eight hours. The American officer was enraged. He immediately got some rations, and two MP's led the sadist away. We were picked up by an American detail and landed in a collection point. The war was over for me.

✠

Early on 13 August, *Kampfgruppe Panzer-Lehr* was in the vicinity of Habloville, about ten kilometers northwest of Argentan. It was a Sunday. Motorized elements wormed their way along a road. Bayerlein had established his command post on the edge of the village. It was chaotic everywhere. It was only to the north and east that small corridors remained open that the Germans could use to escape from the Falaise Pocket.

A few vehicles of the *PLD* were parked in the woods and fruit orchards. The past night, they had had to endure a heavy bombardment of the road network east of Habloville. The confusion that had reigned quickly devolved into chaos. It was 0900 hours when the fighter-bombers appeared over the front again. You could almost set your watch by them. Flying at low altitude, they flitted over the 250 trucks, guns and rocket launchers that were in and around the village. Some of the drivers attempted to move out to the surrounding fields and fruit orchards, fully aware of what might happen to them if they remained on the roads in and around the built-up area. The rockets of the fighter-bombers first hit an ammunition column that was carrying rockets for a launcher unit. Once one of the vehicles went up, the sympathetic explosions moved down the line, successively blowing up the remaining ammunition trucks. Observed from the ground, the rockets seemed to jump off the wings of the aircraft carrying them—almost like starters at a race—scurrying towards targets and crisscrossing the heavens on their way to houses and vehicles.

Within a minute, the streets were saturated with burning vehicles of all types. The command post of the *PLD* was also hit, going up in flames. Bayerlein ran with the men of his staff towards the slit trenches that had been dug on the edge of the fruit orchard. A minute after the first hit on the command post, another fighter-bomber approached. It zoomed overhead, barely clearing the crowns of the apple trees. It described a large circle, and the pilot turned to see what other targets might present themselves.

To Bayerlein on the ground, it seemed as if the pilot had spotted him in the slit trench and was peering into his eyes. It seemed as if the pilot's face registered triumph and also a promise: "I'll be coming right back!"

The men certainly did not have to wait long for the fighter-bomber to return. After a sharp turn, the pilot was in position. He raked the trench with rounds from his 2-centimeter automatic cannon. He then released two bombs. They howled on their way to the earth, and the men in the trenches tried to press themselves even farther into the ground.

With two mighty blows, the bombs detonated just beyond the slit trench. Dirt, tree limbs and rocks rained down on Bayerlein and his men. Some of the men were hit by shrapnel and cried out in pain; three were killed. Hardly anyone emerged unscathed.

The fighter-bombers continued their attacks until 1300 hours. Immediately after the attacks ended, Bayerlein attempted to re-establish contact with the flanking friendly forces and his subordinate commands. It was a difficult task, since all of the landlines were gone and most of the radios did not work.

The fighter-bombers returned at 1400 hours. When he jumped into the slit trench this time, Bayerlein severely sprained his ankle. Four more fighter-bombers followed in the wake of the first one. They bombed and strafed the slit trench as if they knew there was a general officer in it. As soon as they were gone, the survivors crawled out of the trench and looked after the wounded. Bayerlein hobbled out into the fruit orchard in excruciating pain. Completely exhausted, he collapsed and fell into a deep sleep. Later on, after being taken prisoner in the Ruhr Pocket in April 1945, he informed his U.S. interrogation officer about the incident: "I didn't care whether I lived or died."

The roads were filled with craters and completely impassable. Nonetheless, the fighter-bombers continued to bomb and strafe until it turned dark. They were followed by medium two-engined bombers, which continued the aerial assault through the night. No one stopped their bombing. There were no more German fighters to oppose them, no more fighters that could have been committed against them. The bombing continued unabated, and the men of the battered *PLD* had to endure hell.

Bayerlein made every effort he could to get his remaining elements through the narrow corridors and out of the pocket. He and his staff were successful in eluding the Allied net. He seemed to attract fighters and fighter-bombers, however. At Senlis, east of Paris, his vehicle was attacked by a fighter. Because his foot was still badly swollen, Bayerlein did not get out of the vehicle fast enough. The bombs were already falling, as he made it to the roadside ditch. He was wounded in the foot by bomb shrapnel.

Coupled with his injury, Bayerlein was out of action for three weeks and hospitalized. He was gone when the orders relieving the division finally arrived. It was directed to be reconstituted and the men given some rest. Approximately 5,000 men of the rear-area services of the *PLD* had assembled in the area around Fontainebleau at that point. They were joined by about 1,000 combat soldiers, some of them replacements. Some repaired tanks were returned from the divisional maintenance facility and workshop; some new tanks arrived as well. Within a few days, the *PLD* had more than twenty tanks, four batteries of artillery and half of a *Flak* battalion. The division was ordered to form a *Kampfgruppe*, defend the northern crossings of the Aisne and pull back slowly. The division was ordered to form yet another *Kampfgruppe*, which consisted of the divisional engineers (*Hauptmann* Kunze) and the 1st Battalion of *PGLR 901*. It was sent to Paris, where it was employed against the partisan uprising there and assisted in freeing the beleaguered city garrison.

The *Kampfgruppe* reached the outskirts of Paris at first light on 25 August. There was unbelievable confusion along the roads leading into the city. The battle group was only able to move with difficulty. The military administration and city garrison were attempting to vacate the city in advance of the approaching Americans. Panicky garrison troopers had packed vehicles to the gills and were heading in the direction of Germany. Everything appeared to be happening in slow motion, however.

The *Kampfgruppe* gradually made its way into the city interior. At the Gare du Nord, an encircled group of soldiers was freed, who had been fighting the rebels and partisans. Approximately 2,000 men were spared an uncertain fate at the hands of the "Free French."

Six days earlier—on 19 August—some 3,000 *gendarmes* of the Paris police prefecture had pounced, seizing the Ile de la Cité. Seizing upon the bold move, the city hall, the ministry of justice and the war department were also seized the next day.

On 20 August, *General* von Choltitz was able to achieve a three-day ceasefire, but only upon the condition of recognizing "Free French" forces as legal combatants. The French failed to live up to their end of the bargain, continuing to ambush German soldiers wherever they found them.

Bradley directed the U.S. V Corps of Lieutenant General Gerow to enter Paris with the French 2nd Armored Division and the U.S. 4th Infantry Division. The mission of the *Kampfgruppe* from the *PLD* was to hold out long enough from those forces—within and without—long enough that the garrison and all other German forces in the city could be evacuated. The *Kampfgruppe* was much too small, of course, to offer significant resistance. It soon had to pull back to Villeparisies. The situation soon turned critical there as well, and the battle group started pulling back slowly.

On 26 August, the high point of the fighting was reached; the battle group was surrounded. A desperate breakout attempt was launched. The individual companies assaulted the encircling forces again and again. A few determined elements fought their way through two Allied divisions. The 6th Company of *PGLR 901* was hit the worst, with many if its soldiers being lost in close combat. By the time it was all over, only eight men under *Unteroffizier* Junge broke out. Almost all of the rest remained on the battlefield—wounded and captured or dead.

What remained of the battle group then withdrew in the direction of Reims and set up quarters in Neufchâteau. Morale was at rock bottom and there were signs of dissolution within the German armed forces. The members of the battle group witnessed a recently formed infantry regiment march past it and straight into captivity.

On 28 August, *Major* Schöne absorbed what remained of the 1st Battalion into his 2nd Battalion of *PGLR 901*. The *Kampfgruppe* rejoined the division, participating in the general retreat. The withdrawal took the division through the Ardennes, where it would be employed again in a few short months. On 18 and 19 September, *Kampfgruppe Panzer-Lehr* was involved in bitter defensive fighting in the Bitburg area. On the morning of 19 September, there were the glowing wrecks of sixty U.S. tanks on the battlefield. Among them were the remaining twenty-four tanks of the *PLD*. While the Allies could quickly replace those losses, it would take the Germans a considerable amount of time. More important for the overall perspective, however, is the fact that the *PLD* was able to temporarily halt the U.S. advance—which had a four-to-one force ratio advantage—and even force it back across the Our.

The 6th Company, *Panzer-Lehr-Regiment*, in Tucheler Heide, 1939.

General der Panzertruppe Heinz Guderian, creator of the *Panzertruppe*.

The Russian campaign. *Lehr Brigade 900* at the Dneiper.

Generaloberst Hermann Hoth visits the brigade during the first summer of the Russian campaign.

Oberfeldwebel Reetz briging supplies to the 3rd Company *Panzergrenadier-Lehr-Regiment 901.*

Brigade staff of the *Panzergrenadier-Lehr-Regiment 901* in Russia, autumn 1941.

The bridge over the Volga near Kalinin.

The retreat begins, 15 January 1942. *Panzerjager 4.7-cm Pak(t) auf Panzerkampfwagen 1 Ausf B.*

Kampgruppe headquarters group, March 1942. *Oberleutnant* Philipps and *Hauptmann* Kahn consult their maps.

The grave of *Oberfeldwebel* Fritz Neubauer in the cemetery at Gschatsk.

Medical *Oberfeldwebel* Kiefer and *Unteroffizer* Heinzmann delivering wounded to a field hospital.

The *2./901* in their jump-off positions for an attack on Starobjelsk.

Soldiers of *Lehr Brigade 900*. *Hauptfeldwebel* Rau and *Oberfeldwebel* Pinger returning home.

Anti-partisan actions in Dalmatia—a mobile quick reaction force.

Fallingböstel training grounds. *Marder III* tank hunters with the 7.5-cm *PaK 40/3* main gun.

The 3rd and 12th Companies of *Panzer-Lehr-Abteilung 130* at Wünsdorf.

Russian 7.62-cm antitank gun on the chassis of the *Panzer II* at Wünsdorf.

The *Unteroffizier* group of the 6th Company of the *Panzer-Lehr-Regiment* at Wünsdorf.

The 9th Self-propelled Artillery Company near Scharf Schiessen. The vehicle is a *"Grille"* (cricket) mounting a 15-cm howitzer on the chassis of the *Pz.Kpfw. 38(t)*.

Oberst Helmut Ritgen with his adjutant *Leutnant* Meyer and an unidentified officer. In the foregound is *Oberst* Ritgen's command pennant.

Regimental staff of *Panzer-Lehr-Regiment 130.* Sixth from the right is *Oberst* Gerhardt.

Oberleutnant Rahnberg, commander of the 5th Company, *Panzergrenadier-Lehr-Regiment 902.*

Generalleutnant Fritz Bayerlein, commander of the *Panzer-Lehr-Division*.

Generalmajor Horst Niemack, the last commander of the *Panzer-Lehr-Division*, shown here as an *Oberst*.

The invasion has begun—bombers and fighter-bombers attack incessantly. Here the first gliders land.

Villers-Bocage: M3 half-tracks destroyed by Michael Wittmann's *Tiger*.

Generalleutnant Bayerlein with *Oberst* Scholze, commander of the *Panzergrenadier-Lehr-Regiment 901*, and *Oberst* Gutmann, commander of the *Panzergrenadier-Lehr-Regiment 902*

Oberstleutnant Prinz von Schönberg-Waldenburg, shown here as a *Hauptmann.* Commander of the 2nd Battalion, *Panzer-Lehr-Regiment 130.* Killed in action on 11 June 1944.

A *Panther* moves to the front in Normandy.

The last orders conference for the *I./6. Panzer-Regiment* before an attack.

The 2nd Battalion, *902 Regiment*, June 1944, on the invasion front. Left to right: *Hauptfeldwebel* Janasch (*8./902*), *Hauptfeldwebel* Dascwald (*7./902*), *Hauptfeldwebel*? (*6./902*), *Hauptfeldwebel* Rotau (*V.-kpn /902*), *Hauptfeldwebel* Mäurer (*5./902*).

Headquarters of the *Panzer-Lehr-Division* in July 1944 at the Chateau le Mesnil Amey.

Panzer-Lehr-Regiment 902 in Luneville. Left to right: *Oberfeldwebel* Ratke, *Oberfeldwebel* Köster, *Oberfunkmeister* Beck and Meyer.

The destruction of St. Lô by massive air and artillery bombardment.

A machine-gun team holds up a British attack.

British Churchill tanks, heavily armored but relatively slow. Used primarily for infantry support, these are AVRE variants armed with a 29-cm mortar for demolishing bunkers and other heavy fortifications.

An M36 tank destroyer armed with a 90-mm high-velocity gun. Operational in Europe in late 1944. The armor was relatively thin at 50 mm maximum.

A heavily camouflaged self-propelled anti-aircraft gun lies in wait for an unsuspecting Allied fighter-bomber. In this instance, it is what appears to be a *2-cm Flakvierling 38* on a *Zugkraftwagen 8 tonne* half-track.

The last great attack of the *Panzer-Lehr-Division* in the Ardennes offensive. The division was one of the spearheads of the attack.

A convoy of Type 166 *Schwimmwagen* amphibious light personnel vehicles.

Remote-controlled *"Goliath"* demolition vehicles being prepared for action. Slow and vulnerable to small-arms fire, these ingenious vehicles were not very successful in action.

A fine study of a *Landser* taking a break from the stress of combat. He is holding what appears to be some sort of journal, perhaps a daily diary.

A late-model *Panzer IV Ausf. H*, fitted with *Oskette* track extensions, passes a somewhat less mechanized form of transport.

This *Panzer IV Ausf. H* has supplemented its frontal armor with what appear to be Russian T-34 tracks.

A 1*5-cm schwere Feldhaubitze 18*, the standard German heavy field gun of World War II.

Panther Ausf. G on the attack. The high-velocity 7.5-cm main gun could destroy any Allied tank at long range.

Another view of a *15-cm schwere Feldhaubitze 18* at the moment of firing.

An armored *Panzergrenadiere* squad on the move.

The *Jagdpanzer IV L/48*, and later the *L/70* version, equipped two companies of *Panzerjäger-Lehr-Abteilung 130.*

The deadly *Jagdpanther* with its L/71 8.8-cm gun. Thirty-five of these vehicles equipped *II./PLR 130* in March and April 1945.

A well-camouflaged *Panzergrenadier* in Normandy armed with a *Kar 98K* rifle and a *Panzerfaust* one-shot, rocket propelled, antitank weapon that could penetrate the armor of any Allied tank at short ranges of 100 meters or less.

Fast, maneuverable, well armored and heavily armed, the *Panther* was more than a match for any Allied tank in Normandy.

An *Sd.Kfz. 234/2 Puma* heavy armored car. This vehicle mounted a *5-cm KwK 39/1* in a fully rotating turret. Usually issued to the reconnaissance battalions of *Panzer* divisions.

Infantry anxiously watch the skies for the dreaded, and ever-present, Allied *"Jabos"*— fighter-bombers that shot up everything that moved behind the German lines in Normandy.

An orders conference between a *Panther* commander and the crew of an *Sd.Kfz. 251 Ausf D.*

An *Sd.Kfz. 251/6* command vehicle of a *Panzer* unit.

An *MG 42* machine gun used in the heavy machine-gun role.

An *Sd.Kfz. 251* half-track being used as an ambulance. Despite the prominent red crosses, German medical vehicles were frequently attacked by Allied aircraft.

Infantry attack under cover of smoke.

Infantry training with *Sd.Kfz. 251* armored personnel carriers.

CHAPTER 11

At the *Westwall* and Beyond

Initially, the *PLD* was directed to take up positions in the *Westwall*, popularly referred to as the "Siegfried Line." *Oberst* Rudolf Gerhardt, the commander of the *PLR*, later recounted that chapter in the division's operations from his perspective as a regimental commander:

> The "Atlantic Wall," which was often cited and put on display, was nothing more than a phantom, at least in the area of the *PLD*. The forces employed there—garrison-type forces incapable of moving— were not up to the task assigned them, with a few exceptions, that fought with the courage of desperation. They had become a rabbit-raising society. When the invasion arrived there, they ran away. By the end of the first day, the garrison forces were no longer there. The ready-reserve forces only got to the front in battered condition due to the constant air attacks. Once there, they found themselves hopelessly outnumbered.
>
> The *Luftwaffe* did not appear, either to defend or conduct reconnaissance. Of its highly vaunted striking power, there was nothing left but the good intentions of the flight crews.
>
> As a result, the only thing we could do was slow down the advance of the enemy and, by doing so, create the prerequisite for the completion of the *Westwall*.
>
> But when we got to the *Westwall* after ten weeks of murderous fighting, we found out that not the slightest thing had been done there. No troops in the line. The bunkers barricaded. Signals means and weapons removed; the local populace not in any way prepared for the [coming] battle, let alone evacuated.
>
> The forces coming from the front—decimated and on the edge of exhaustion, with my regiment, for instance, having only 12 operational tanks out of an authorized 160—now had to take over the defense of the *Westwall* as well.
>
> Then, however, *Panzer-Lehr-Regiment 130* was pulled out of the line and sent to the Neckar, north of Stuttgart. While there, we had our hands full with the party functionaries, who fancied themselves

as "Commissars for the Defense of the *Reich*" and who did nothing to properly and doctrinally take care of the regiment with regard to equipment and replacements.

We were not given enough time to even make a small *Kampfgruppe* out of the battered division. In the space of ten weeks, we changed locations four times. We moved from the Neckar to Camp Senne at Paderborn. From there, we went to the Hunsrück and then back again to the Eifel.

✠

By the end of September, the division had 6,000 soldiers on its books. Most of them were in rear-area services or new replacements. That was what was left of an original overall strength of 17,450 men. Of that number, approximately 1,000 men were from the *Kampfgruppen*, which had started the campaign with more than 8,000 men in their ranks.

The division was sent to the Heilbronn area for its reconstitution. Before leaving the Eifel, it had transferred all of its remaining heavy weapons to other formations. Bayerlein was informed that his forces would be completely rebuilt with the most modern of equipment. Bayerlein did not place much stock in the promise; he knew the sad state of Germany's ability to regenerate its forces.

From Heilbronn, the division was moved to the Paderborn–Detmold area. The rail movement took eight days instead of the usual three. At Paderborn, the *PLR* was issued sixty tanks. In additional, lost artillery pieces were replaced, as well as *Flak* and antitank guns. Training was initiated for all of the division troops and formations.

Bayerlein was tireless in his efforts to restore the division's combat power and abilities. He visited his troops on a daily basis. He also made a trip to Berlin to personally argue for more *Flak* for his division. There was no denying his ability to speak on the matter after his experiences at the hands of Allied airpower in both North Africa and Normandy. The general wanted every company to have at least two *Flak*—a quad 2-centimeter and a single-barrel 3.7-centimeter. But his wishes were not granted. For the entire division, he received four quad guns, a few 88's and four 3.7-centimeter guns.

He emphasized air defense over and over again. He pressed upon the unit commanders the need for every weapon to be used when conducting active air defense. Once again, night attacks were practiced. The general also placed special emphasis on camouflage, which had been a matter of life or death in Normandy on numerous occasions.

He was hampered in his efforts at unit-level training by the lack of fuel. Large exercises proved impossible, and the division was unable to turn into a cohesive whole brought about by shared experiences and lessons learned through practice. Despite his best efforts and his high-level connections, Bayerlein was never able to get enough fuel for proper training.

✠

On 9 November, the division was moved into the Hunsrück region. The individual units were housed in Kastellaun, Morbach, Büchen and Beuren.

At the time, Bayerlein submitted his periodic report on the condition of his division and its current combat rating. Three copies of the report were prepared. One of the reports remained in the division headquarters, the remaining two went to the responsible field-army group at the time and to the *Führer* headquarters. The readiness report closed with the words:

> The condition of the division in terms of equipment and personnel for new operations is not sufficient. Air defense weapons, in particular, are lacking, which are needed to protect the advance of the division in the face of the enemy's air superiority. The equipment levels in the tank regiment, as well as the *PJLA* and the artillery regiment, are insufficient.

Six weeks later, Bayerlein heard his exact words spoken on the Calais station, a propaganda outlet for the Allies directed towards German forces. It was a literal quote of several paragraphs from the secret report. Bayerlein knew that the copy he had was not the source of the leak. But which one of the other two? Who was conducting that betrayal? Or was it possible that the betrayal was being conducted elsewhere? Had orders fallen into the hands of the enemy? If so, how many German soldiers had ridden into combat, their plans and intentions already known?[1]

✠

By the evening of 18 November, the reconstituted *PLD* had finished assembling in the new area. On 22 November, orders were issued for the

---

1. Translator's Note: At the time the author originally wrote this, it was still not known how important the cracking of the "Enigma" code was for the Allies. In addition, the nature and extent of Soviet infiltration into command and control entities was barely realized. It is interesting to note how Bayerlein, among countless other senior German field commanders, had the dark feeling that some, if not all, of their plans were being betrayed to the enemy.

division to move into the Saargemünd area, where it had been directed to participate in the fighting around Saarluckenheim. That same evening, the initial elements of the division moved out.

Although the division theoretically did not have the fuel needed to complete the march, there were numerous fuel depots in the new area of operations, from which the division could help itself.

Before it turned light, Allied aircraft were already appearing over the march route of Bayerlein's men. They showered the lead columns with bombs, and the commander estimated that some 200 twin-engined bombers were involved. The crossroads in the division's attack sector had been targeted as well. Despite all the fireworks, there was no great damage. What worried the general greatly was the fact that the enemy seemed to know all of his division's movements in advance.

Bayerlein had his men continue to march at the greatest possible speed at night. The men, who had just completed a major movement, were still tired from the first one. The general's ears certainly must have been ringing that night and the next two nights. Bayerlein knew how unpopular the nighttime marching was, but he also knew that marching under the cover of darkness would save the lives of hundreds of his men. That was the only thing that carried weight in his mind.

Part of the reason for the shifting of the division to a new area of operations was the Allies' attempt to quickly establish a bridgehead over the Rhine. That subject had been discussed by Montgomery and Eisenhower at a conference in Brussels on 18 October. The one unanimous decision to result from the discussions was that the greatest effort must be made to establish that bridgehead before the onset of winter. A plan that was hammered out during the conference envisioned an advance to the Rhine through Aachen by the U.S. First and Ninth Armies.

After crossing the Roer, the First Army was to pivot east and head for Bonn and Cologne, while the Ninth Army would turn north and advance on Krefeld. To support the operation, the British Second Army would move out to attack from the Nijmegen area sometime around 10 November in the direction of the Reichswald. It would break through the German defensive lines and head south between the Rhine and the Meuse.

When they realized this plan, the Allies hoped to reach the Rhine along a front of some 160 kilometers from Arnhem to Bonn. It was then intended for the First Army to cross the major river to the south of Cologne, while the Ninth Army would do the same north of Düsseldorf. That envelopment movement would lead to the capture of the Ruhr industrial area, which both Eisenhower and Montgomery considered to be the most important objective of the Western Allies.

General Patton, the Commander in Chief of the Third Army was directed to resume his offensive as soon as his logistics situation permitted it. It was intended for him to support the main operations being conducted to the north.

The U.S. First and Ninth Armies moved out on 5 November. Patton was directed to start his attack five days later. Patton had informed Bradley that he thought he could advance to the Saar in three days and easily break through the *Westwall* there. His field army had grown to six infantry and three armored divisions, as well as two motorized brigades. In all, he had some 250,000 men under his command.

The *1. Armee*, which faced Patton's formations, had all of 86,000 men at its disposal. The German field army's forces—seven infantry divisions—were spread out over a sector running 108 kilometers. There was one operational reserve, the *11. Panzer-Division*, with its sixty-nine operational tanks. Patton, on the other hand, was able to concentrate his main effort just about anywhere along that frontage, thanks to the Allied air supremacy and the great mobility of his forces.

The force ratios were telling in favor of the Americans: three to one in infantry, eight to one in tanks and armored vehicles and three to one in artillery. Supporting Patton's ground forces were some 1,300 Flying Fortresses and Liberators. With all those forces, Patton had reasons to be optimistic. His plan called for the XII Corps of Major General Eddy to conduct the main offensive effort to the Saar from the area to the northwest of it. One day later, Major General Walker's XX Corps would move out to encircle Metz, take it and thus clear the left wing of the U.S. First Army all the way to the *Westwall* north of the Saar.

Patton wanted to start his offensive on 8 November. After a full day of rain on 7 November brought high water to all of the rivers in his sector, Major General Eddy went to the Commander in Chief and asked to postpone the attack. Patton's answer was typical: "Recommend your successor to me, if you don't want to start the attack!"

Eddy attacked the next day. The three infantry divisions of the corps made slow progress, but the two armored divisions got stuck in the mud. The corps' attack literally bogged down. The German divisions bent, but they did not break. It was not until ten days later, on 18 November, that Patton's forces were able to secure a ring around Metz and continue their attack in the direction of the Saar.

On 22 November, Lieutenant General Haislip's U.S. XV Corps gained the approaches to the Zabern Depression. Not encountering much resistance, he advanced in the direction of Straßburg, with the French 2nd Armored Division in the lead. The breakthrough split the German front between the *1.*

Armee and the *19. Armee*. As it turned out, the only mechanized force available to stop the advance was the *PLD*.

During the evening of 22 November, the *PLD* reached the area around Sarreguemines, where Bayerlein received a telegram from the field-army group with the following content:

> The *PLD* launches an immediate counterattack into the enemy. The fate of all of Alsace rests with you. Forward! Start of the attack for your division is first light on 29 November.

Bayerlein knew what was in store for his division if he had his forces roll into the sack that had been formed by the Americans in Alsace. Later on, he commented:

> The Americans would have considered me crazy if I had rolled into this open sack. But orders were orders. I had to obey them. On the other hand, if I took Rauwiler and Schalbach in advance, then I had a chance.

At 1600 hours on 24 November, the division moved out. The next morning, Rauwiler was reached. The Americans, who were completely surprised by the presence of a German armored division, were ejected after a sharp skirmish. An entire U.S. infantry battalion was taken prisoner. The divisional engineers particularly distinguished themselves. A surprise American immediate counterattack from the direction of Bärendorf caught antitank assets by surprise and, after a sharp engagement, the guns were captured by the Americans.

The next day—26 November—*PLR 130* launched an attack on Schalbach. Grenadiers from *PGLR 901* and *PGLR 902* rode on the tanks. The attack did not make any progress, however, since there were strong U.S. armored elements in the village and a number of German tanks were knocked out.

Major Kuhnow, who had assumed acting command of *PGLR 902* after the death of *Major* Welsch at Canisy, was up front with his forces when they were attacked by strong U.S. armored and infantry forces. In the ensuing skirmish, he went missing and presumed dead. It was not until after the war that his fate was discovered: he was taken prisoner during the fighting. *Oberstleutnant* Joachim *Ritter* von Poschinger assumed command of the orphaned regiment.

By the morning of 27 November, the Americans had gained the initiative and started attacking. The division was too weak to hold them up for long. When the thick cloud cover lifted on the afternoon of the same day, the fighter-bombers began their merciless attacks against the division again.

Bayerlein was at the command post of *PGLR 902* in Wolsthof, when a group of aircraft conducted a run on the headquarters and dropped its bombs. There were heavy losses. The divisional artillery, which was located in the woods north of Eywiler, was also identified and attacked. The *PLD* was forced back, step by step. The division moved through Mackwiler and Domfessel, aided by the inclement weather conditions, which slowed down the bombing runs by restricting flying weather.

On 30 November, *Generalfeldmarschall* von Rundstedt ordered the division pulled out of the line and retained as an operational reserve. The aged field marshal, who had been relieved by Hitler as the Commander in Chief West as a result of a difference of opinions during the previous summer, had been reinstated in the same capacity after the suicide of *Generalfeldmarschall* von Kluge on 18 August. He intended to have the division reconstituted for a new large-scale offensive.

Von Rundstedt directed the division be returned to the Eifel area, where it was to reorganize. Once again, Bayerlein was forced to give up his tanks, this time to the *11. Panzer-Division*. Despite the intent of pulling the division out of combat, it was constantly entangled in defensive skirmishes until 6 December, when it reached Lauterecken. There, however, the division was hit by medium bombers and fighter-bombers. Two long columns of vehicles that were parallel to the railway line were hit and suffered extensive damage. The rail station was essentially plowed under.

From there, the division was able to make it to Cochem (on the Mosel), where it enjoyed a short period of rest and efforts were made to reconstitute it. Even at that relatively late date, Bayerlein was still unaware of Hitler's plan to conduct an offensive in the Ardennes, even though Rundstedt and Model were privy to it as early as late October. By the beginning of December, the German High Command had earmarked twenty-eight divisions for the offensive, the *PLD* being one of them.

During a commanders' conference at the headquarters of *General-feldmarschall* Model on 3 November—where the Commander in Chief West and the Commanders in Chief of *Heeresgruppe B* and the *5. Panzer-Armee* participated—*Generaloberst* Jodl spoke on behalf of Hitler. Jodl stated that the attack was to take place in a sector where the forces assembled could obtain a breakthrough with certainty. He stated:

The Supreme Command considered the Monschau (Eifel)– Echternach sector as the best suited one due to its being thinly held by the enemy. The attrition to the enemy forces in the previous offensive fighting had been considerable; he had tied up his reserves near the front and his logistical situation was tense. Consequently, as a result of the thin occupation of the front and the fact that the enemy was not expecting a German attack and certainly not in that area, then a rapid breakthrough of friendly forces could be expected, if complete surprise were maintained and it was executed under weather conditions unfavorable for the enemy air forces.

As a result, the freedom of movement for armored formations would be forced. They would take bridgeheads over the Meuse between Lüttich [Liége] and Namur so as to then advance without stopping to the west, bypassing Brussels to the east, and reaching Antwerp.

It was to be assumed that the attack would cut the rearward lines of communication for the U.S. First Army, which most likely ran along the Meuse Valley. As soon as the Brussels–Antwerp area had been reached, the British 21st Army Group would also see its rearward lines of communication threatened and, if Antwerp were taken, then also cut off.

Up to this point, the enemy had been unable to fully exploit that harbor, which had a high capacity and was essential to him. He would soon be at that point and then he would be able to overwhelm us with forces and logistics of all types, most of which would be landed at Antwerp. If the German objective were reached, then the prerequisites would be met to take up the fight from all sides against the forces of the U.S. First Army, which had been cut off from its logistics, and against the British 21st Army Group. That would put an end to twenty to thirty divisions, and a successful attack would additionally lead to the capture or destruction of huge quantities of materiel of all types that had been stockpiled in the cut-off area, not only in general but specifically for the Allied offensive expected in the middle of December through the *Westwall* to the Rhine.

It was intended for the breakthrough along the entire front to be conducted by the divisions already in place. The conduct of the attack had to be in such a manner that the penetration of the enemy positions took place quickly, so that the armored forces could be committed in a timely manner. It was intended for them to exploit the shock effect on the enemy and immediately move west.

For the armored divisions, it was imperative that they did not allow themselves to be held up during their thrust to the Meuse. They were to bypass built-up areas and positions that could not be collapsed right away and also not stop due to open flanks—a course of action that we had employed to great success during the campaign in the East in 1941. Bastogne was to be taken, however, on express orders from Hitler.

During the briefing for the three commanders in chief, Jodl indicated the attack start date would be 25 November. Jodl let there be no doubt that Hitler was adamant about the order of battle that had been determined and the employment of the forces for the long-range objective.[2]

In Cochem, the *PLD* received twenty-five tanks, a battalion's worth of artillery, reinforcements for the *Flak* battalion and 2,000 grenadier replacements for the two mechanized infantry regiments. What the division was still lacking was transportation and evacuation means, particularly eighteen-ton prime movers for immobilized tanks (*Sd.Kfz. 9 FAMO*). The vehicles had been manufactured in Breslau; by then, the Soviets were advancing towards the metropolis and had already bombed and destroyed the factory

Bayerlein used every spare moment available to him during the short rest and reconstitution period to get more equipment and heavy weapons for his forces. He also strove to replace the trucks that were in increasingly short supply as a result of Allied air attacks.

On 10 December, he was summoned to the headquarters of the *XXXXVII. Panzer-Korps* at Kyllburg. The ostensible purpose of the meeting was to discuss a possible attack on Meuse. Once there, he was soon asked whether his division was in a position to take Bastogne.

Bayerlein answered in the affirmative, but added the caveats that only a surprise attack had a chance to succeed and that the attack had to be well planned and executed. He was told that he was not being aggressive enough! Bayerlein received the impression that the taking of Bastogne was considered to be a step beyond a Sunday stroll. Despite the questions, Bayerlein was still not fully briefed on the impending operation.

When Bayerlein returned to the division that day, he redoubled his efforts to get fuel. Although he had not been told directly, he knew that something was up. Everything that he could acquire in the way of petroleum products was carefully stored in the large railway tunnel west of Cochem.

2. Author's Note: Quoted with friendly permission from *General der Panzertruppen* Hasso von Manteuffel's book *Die Schlacht in den Ardennen, 1944–1945* (*The Battle in the Ardennes, 1944–1945*). Translator's Note: Most of the passage is written in the subjunctive in German, indicating that von Manteuffel is paraphrasing Jodl.

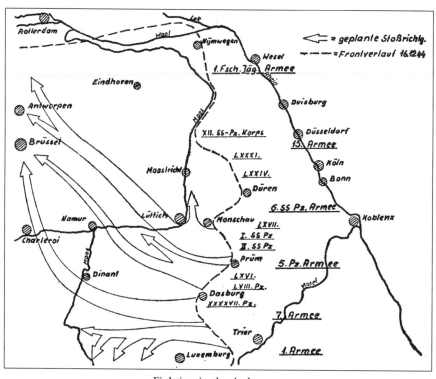

Fighting in the Ardennes
Legend: *geplante Stoßrichtung* = Planned Avenue of Advance;
Frontverlauf 16.12.44 = Frontline trace on 16 December 1944

CHAPTER 12

Victory Lost:
The Fighting in the Ardennes

At noon on 12 December, a message arrived at the headquarters of the division instructing Bayerlein to report to the headquarters of the Commander in Chief West at 1600 that same day. He was not to take a vehicle near the latter headquarters, and he was not to be accompanied by anyone. Bayerlein had himself immediately driven to Ziegenberg, where the senior command was located in a medieval castle.

Commanders from division on up were assembled there. They ate together and were then sent to a cloakroom, where they were ordered to leave their side arms and their briefcases and then proceed to a bus that was already waiting for them outside. They were going to an undisclosed location to receive special orders and missions.

Looking at his watch, Bayerlein saw that it was 1700 hours. It had already turned dark. There was deep cloud cover, and it started to rain. After driving for half an hour—a trip that seemed to go in circles, according to Bayerlein and many of the others present—the bus halted in front of the *Führer* Headquarters in the west.

As the generals left the bus, they had to pass through a corridor flanked by grim-looking *SS* men. They then entered a long hallway that led to a large underground bunker. In the main room of the bunker, the generals again saw *SS* men. They sat down across from the bodyguards, who were spaced approximately one meter apart. The head of the table was empty.

A short while later, Hitler entered from a back door. He was accompanied by *Generaloberst* Jodl and *Generalfeldmarschall* Keitel. Two more officers with document portfolios followed.

Bayerlein could tell at a glance that Hitler looked old and broken. His party sat itself at the one end of the table. Hitler's hands shook when he held the prepared remarks and read from them. Prior to starting, he put on a pair of glasses. Bayerlein had never seen him wear glasses before.

Hitler's comments started out with a detailed history of the party and the good deeds it had done for Germany. All of the generals had heard similar remarks before. But none of them showed any impatience. They all sat rigidly in their chairs. Bayerlein later commented:

> The *SS* observers literally watched every movement of every individual. One did not dare to even reach into one's pocket and extract a handkerchief for fear of being seen as a Pharisee and being shot.[1]

After a good hour, Hitler finally came to the point of the commanders' conference. Bayerlein had read the tea leaves correctly: there was going to be a big offensive in the Ardennes.

Hitler stated that he had assembled everything necessary to assure success. In the event that the attack went without success, then Germany was lost.

It was intended for *General der Panzertruppen* Hasso von Manteuffel's 5. *Panzer-Armee* to take Antwerp. *SS-Oberstgruppenführer* Josef "Sepp" Dietrich's 6. *Panzer-Armee* was to take Lüttich (Liége).[2] The resulting effort would encircle the British 21st Army Group. As a political consequence of such a success, Canada would withdraw from the war. After the loss of an entire field-army group, the U.S. would be demoralized and then only play a subordinate role. Hitler added, in conclusion, that a big blow would be delivered when the *Luftwaffe* launched a surprise attack with 3,000 fighters, which would remove Allied airpower from the skies.

Hitler then departed. The generals remained behind a short while longer to celebrate the seventieth birthday of *Generalfeldmarschall* von Rundstedt. *Generalfeldmarschall* Model gave the chief address. Bayerlein departed as early as decorum would allow. He wanted to get back to his division, stopping along the way to visit his family in Würzburg for an hour. He felt that it might be his last opportunity to do so.

On 13 December, Bayerlein returned to the division and started preparations for what he privately considered to be a "crazy attack." That same day, the division received more tanks and additional allotments of fuel. The additional allotments were not enough to cover all the division's needs, however. Instead of a projected requirement for enough fuel to cover 500 kilometers, the division only received enough for 200 kilometers. Given the poor road network in the Ardennes, some calculated it might not even be enough for 100 kilometers.

Moving at night, the division advanced its wheeled elements to its staging area around Kyllburg. The remaining units of *PGLR 901*—minus

---

1. Author's Note: It should be noted that other commanders who were present at the conference did not come away with that impression.

2. Translator's Note: Most accounts designate Dietrich's field army as the 6. *SS-Panzer-Armee*, but it was never officially designated that.

the 9th Company, whose self-propelled infantry guns were still stuck in Hellertshausen—arrived there during the night of 15–16 December. Bayerlein had the tracked elements moved by rail to the staging area, where they detrained at Bensborn and Birresborn. Some of the trains had been attacked by medium bombers, but little damage resulted.

On the morning of 16 December—a Saturday—Eisenhower received a letter from Montgomery reminding him that he (Eisenhower) had made a bet a year ago that the war would be over by Christmas 1944. Eisenhower sent back a reply that he would pay on Christmas Day and not a day earlier: "After all, I still have nine days." But in those nine days, the victory of the Allies, which had seemed palpably near, yielded to a situation that caused great worry.

Wacht am Rhein—"Watch on the Rhine"—was about to be launched in the Ardennes. No fewer than twenty divisions had been earmarked for the offensive. More than 250,000 German soldiers were positioned along 140 kilometers of "quiet front." Just before midnight on the night of 15–16 December, the operations officer of the *PLD* read aloud the attack order that had been issued by *Generalfeldmarschall* von Rundstedt to the assembled men of the division staff:

Soldiers of the Western Front!
Your hour of greatness has arrived. Strong offensive armies are marching towards the Anglo-Americans. I do not need to say anything else to you. We're betting everything on one card! You have the holy duty to do your best and perform herculean tasks for the *Führer* and the fatherland.

Midnight passed. The morning of 16 December was greeted by an eerie calm.

In a few hours, at 0530 hours, fire spewed forth along the "quiet front" of the Ardennes, where the German divisions had approached unnoticed by the enemy. Rockets, mortar rounds and artillery shells screamed towards the unsuspecting American positions along the 140 kilometers of the attack zone. The earth trembled under the impact of untold numbers of detonating munitions. From the rear, the preparation was even supported by railway guns of 28- and 38-centimeter caliber.

The artillery preparation lasted for an hour and was conducted with an intensity such as the Germans had not seen for years. As suddenly as it had started, the artillery preparation stopped.

A few seconds later, German grenadiers, camouflaged by white winter overgarments, started moving forward. Engines roared to life from hundreds of tanks, assault guns, self-propelled guns, tank destroyers and half-tracks. Von Manteuffel's tanks rolled across the bridge at Dasberg in the direction of Clervaux. The small, wiry general officer—one of the youngest in the German army—personally directed traffic across the bridge over the Our.

Within the *PLD*, *Hauptmann* Kunze's engineers had constructed bridges over the Our at Gemünd, Dasberg and Vianden during the night of 15–16 December. The formations crossed the Our eleven kilometers to the south of von Manteuffel's forces the next day, 17 December. It had not been possible to cross the river the previous day, since the long columns of the division were being held up by roads completely jammed with horse-drawn transport.

The division's objective was Bastogne. Prior to the start of the attack, Bayerlein had said only a few words to his men, but they were words that stuck: "Our objective is the Meuse! This is the decisive battle of the war, and I expect sacrifice and devotion to duty from everyone."

The general had moved ahead to his advance guard and moved with the lead elements of his division. When his headquarters personnel attempted to hold him back, he replied: "It is not important whether I am killed."

Spurred by his personal example, the men of the division were filled with an iron will to win. They wanted to emerge victorious from the fight. This time, there were no aircraft hovering in the skies to disrupt their approach march. Although the men did not have the numbers of equipment they had initially enjoyed on the invasion front, they were still filled with the same spirit.

With no more than nominal resistance, the *PLD* moved through Draufeld on 17 December. Around 1400 hours on 18 December, Eschweiler was reached. At 1900 hours, the division's lead elements were around the Upper and Lower Wampach.

Along with the *PLD*, the other divisions of *General Freiherr* von Lüttwitz's *XXXXVII. Panzer-Korps* had advanced twenty kilometers. On 18 December, the *116. Panzer-Division* advanced on Houffalize and the *2. Panzer-Division* and the *26. Volks-Grenadier-Division* also had their sights set on Bastogne.

The division was northeast of Wiltz when it received orders from the commanding general to take the villages of Wiltz and Wilerwiltz. It was only then to continue its advance on Bastogne.

Let us once again allow *Unteroffizier* Eduard Job, a gunner on a *Jagdpanzer* in the 3rd Company of *PJLA 130*, commanded by *Oberleutnant* Wagner, to comment on the fighting. Job's tank gun commander in the attack on Wiltz was still *Oberfeldwebel* Erich Stolz:

> We received orders to join the column, which had been directed to take Wiltz (under the orders of the commander [meaning Bayerlein]). One battalion from *901*, our engineers and elements of the 2nd Battalion of *PLR 130* under *Hauptmann* Ritgen headed southwest, along with some artillery. The commander moved at the head of the battle group in a command and control *SPW*.
>
> We reached the village late in the afternoon. The roar of enemy antitank guns could be heard firing at us from the edge of the built-up area. There was a tank obstacle in front of us.
>
> We were radioed orders: "*Jagdpanzer*, bypass the obstacle and advance against the southern outskirts of Wiltz."
>
> *Leutnant* Schönrath's orders were immediately executed. He was in the lead tank destroyer.
>
> "Ömmes [the nickname for the driver], cut a path to the right!"
>
> Krenstedt pivoted. We lumbered past the obstacle, and Ömmes picked up the pace, since we were also being engaged. Small-caliber rounds were smacking into the sideskirts. The fighting compartment was ringing like a bell. We then reached a defile, which offered us some cover and concealment. Our four fighting vehicles rolled through it. At the end of the defile, which leads into a patch of woods, we turned back in the direction of the outskirts.
>
> "Guns 1 and 3: ten o'clock . . . Guns 2 and 4: two o'clock!"
>
> The tank destroyers pivoted in the designated directions. Our vehicle gave a jolt when it moved through a ditch. A few lances of flames were visible straight ahead coming from a low hedge.
>
> "500 . . . twelve o'clock . . . AT!"
>
> "Identified!" I announced when I saw the second muzzle flash. I aimed and did not wait for the gun commander to issue an order to fire. The *Jagdpanzer* rocked backwards as the high-velocity round left the barrel on its way to the target.
>
> "Target!" Stolz announced, using the tanker shorthand to indicate a hit.
>
> "Move forward!" Schönrath ordered.
>
> With a jolt, the *Jagdpanzer* lurched forward. My loader, "Jupp" Heller, had already rammed home a round. When I saw the trail of flames revealing the location of a bazooka that had just fired from the vicinity of one of the first houses, I had Ömmes pivot a bit. When I fired, the round tore a big chunk out of the masonry building,

showering the area where the bazooka had been with rubble and concrete dust. There was no more enemy firing from that location.

We then rolled into the southern end of the village. All four of the tank destroyers were firing as fast as they could. A fence disappeared under our vehicle's tracks. We slammed into the wall of a house, and the edifice collapsed. Off to the right, where the fourth *Jagdpanzer* was located, we heard a couple of muffled blows.

Stolz immediately had the vehicle turn. We saw a squad of American infantry that had knocked out our sister vehicle. We opened fire with our machine gun, sending the infantry scurrying and giving the crew some breathing room to dismount before their vehicle went up in flames.

We then rolled towards our comrades, who had taken cover in a house. They came running out and climbed up onto the rear deck. We then received orders from the platoon leader to swing north. We could hear the dull sounds of fighting coming from that direction through the thick armor of the fighting compartment. Schönrath had already fired up two pockets of resistance. An American armored car, racing to the south, suddenly appeared in front of our vehicle. A quick round slammed into its rear. Before it could disappear behind the houses, an explosion caused by igniting gasoline blew the vehicle apart.

While the tank destroyers were committed, Bayerlein had *Hauptmann* Ritgen's tanks engage and destroy the tank obstacle. It was a hasty obstacle constructed out of felled trees, so a few rounds from Ritgen's tanks succeeded in blowing it apart. Ritgen then had his tanks deploy and advance on the village. He wanted to make sure the tank destroyers were not caught in a trap.

The grenadiers also dismounted and advanced. The artillery prepared to fire on the town. It had been prevented from setting up previously due to the narrow roads and the woods. Bayerlein moved forward in his *SPW*. His vehicle lurched out of the way when it started receiving fire from well-concealed positions. He ordered Ritgen to have his tanks attack the enemy pocket of resistance.

Ritgen's 2nd Battalion moved out. As it turned dark, the garish muzzle flashes from the main guns seemed even more brilliant than normal. Main-gun rounds slammed into antitank-gun positions. One of the American guns was silenced. One of the German tanks was hit, losing its track. It was immobilized, but it could still offer fire support.

Bayerlein watched the progress of the engagement, calling up support, where available, but generally leaving his commanders on the ground the flexibility to conduct the actual fight.

Ritgen's tanks rolled forward by bounds, some offering support, while others advanced. The grenadiers followed at a short distance. They knew better than to bunch up behind the tanks, which attracted all of the enemy's attention and fire. Machine-gun tracers arced through the evening air. Some Americans threw in the towel and gave up. Where the resistance was more determined, the engineers used demo charges. In the end, the combined arms of the division succeeded in wresting Wiltz from the enemy.

"Herr General, radio message from corps!"

The signals officer passed the message that had just arrived to the general. It directed the division to take Bastogne as soon as possible. It indicated that Bastogne had a fuel dump with millions of gallons of fuel.

Bayerlein directed his forces to prepare to continue the advance as soon as possible. The *Kampfgruppe* soon moved out and reached Nieder-Wampach at 2155 hours, although the main body of the division was still fArther back. From Nieder-Wampach, the distance to Bastogne was fifteen kilometers.

When his advance guard started receiving fire, Bayerlein directed his forces to halt.

"It looks like we have three options here, Kauffmann!" he said, turning to his operations officer. "We can either turn to the north and reach Longvilly along the good road from St. Vith, or continue to march on this road. The third option is to take the secondary road up ahead that leads directly to Magaret. From Magaret, it is exactly six kilometers to Bastogne."

"The last option's the best one, *Herr General,* as long as the map is correct. If only we knew whether the road to Margaret is trafficable."

Bayerlein looked at the map again. The division had tortured itself all day long advancing along muddy secondary roads. On top of everything else, the portion of the division that was in the southern column was intertwined with elements of the *26. Volks-Grenadier-Division.*

Lüttwitz wanted Bastogne taken that night, however. He was pressing for it, since signals intelligence had intercepted a message that the U.S. 82nd and 101st Airborne Divisions were approaching Bastogne from France. Lüttwitz was himself under pressure to ensure that he reached Bastogne quickly, and the *PLD* was the closest division to the prize objective. It was important for the important traffic hub to fall into German hands.

At that moment, a civilian was brought to Bayerlein's *SPW*. He had been picked up by the advance guard. Bayerlein had the man asked what he knew about road conditions to Magaret. The man replied that the road was in good shape. That settled the question for Bayerlein. The *Kampfgruppe* rolled out along the road leading directly to Margaret. It shortened the distance to Bastogne considerably. Whether it was defended?

After two kilometers, however, the improved road surface stopped. The route turned into another dirt road that would soon be a sea of mud once the tanks and other tracked vehicles moved along it. At that point, however, Bayerlein felt he had no other choice: "Keep moving!" For the division to have turned around at that point would have cost too much time.

The men harbored the illusion that the road would soon return to asphalt. On the contrary: it became even worse. More and more vehicles became stuck, further slowing the progress of the division, until it eventually reached a snail's pace. It was not until 0205 hours on 19 December that the lead tanks reached Magaret.

The civilian at the crossroads had influenced history, even if it was not a deliberate act. As a result of the slowing down of the division, Bastogne was saved and the course of the battle was changed.

It was at Magaret that the advance guard of the division encountered the enemy. A nighttime firefight broke out. The tanks that had made it that far fired at the silhouettes of the enemy. As a result of the fires that ensued, a tank commander reported that it was an American medical element. Once the report was submitted up the chain of command, Bayerlein immediately had his elements cease fire.

Another Belgian was interrogated: "Did you see American tanks?"

"A large American tank column rolled through here several hours ago," came the reply.

"Where was it headed?"

"Towards Longvilly."

"How many were there?"

"There were at least fifty tanks and just as many other armored vehicles."

Bayerlein immediately ordered reconnaissance to be conducted along the road to Longvilly. Armored cars were also sent south. The Belgian's statements were confirmed. Numerous tanks had moved through the area not too long ago. That meant that the enemy was somewhere to the rear of the *PLD*, probably at Longvilly.

As was later determined, an armored element of thirty tanks had rolled forward to the broken terrain and hills around Longvilly to bolster the defenses there. A platoon from the divisional reconnaissance squadron was dispatched to continue the reconnaissance towards Longvilly. The rest of the reconnaissance battalion sent out patrols to all sides. Bayerlein did not want to roll into the middle of what could become a pocket for his division. He needed information before he could continue his advance on Bastogne.

As late as the previous day—18 December—there had only been a U.S. corps headquarters in Bastogne. Scattered elements from the U.S. 28th Infantry Division, which had made their way across the Our back to the city, reported that the forces up front had been smashed. The closest reserves that could come to the aid of Bastogne were a combat command of the U.S. 10th Armored Division. It was immediately ordered forward and arrived in Bastogne as the sun was setting on 18 December. The American battle group immediately set about establishing obstacles on the roads leading into Bastogne from the east and northeast. They hoped to be able to hold up the Germans until the U.S. 101st Airborne Division could arrive.

The U.S. airborne division was 160 kilometers away in Reims. What happened next on the American side was reported in an article by war correspondents Robert Richards and Richard C. Hottelet. The surprise of the German offensive and the desperate situation in and around Bastogne is made clear in the article:[3]

> The small man with the broad face and the star on each shoulder prepared to go to the "Champagne Bowl," as our football games were called. It was supposed to be a real free-for-all, just like the 101st Airborne Division of the U.S. Army liked them. It was almost as if we were back home. Football with snow, wine and a clear sun. And with two regimental teams that had been great rivals for years. We were resting and had earned the privilege of having a little fun.
>
> Then a message summoned the small man—our Brigadier General McAuliffe, who referred to himself as the "Old Crock," just like everyone else—inside.[4] It was a text that had a homemade code:
>
> "Court's excited. Jim's taking off tomorrow. You have until Tuesday to move out."
>
> Now, Tuesday was the 19th of December, and this message, which was incomprehensible to the Germans, was clear enough for the

---

3. Translator's Note: Since the article—perhaps a radio broadcast—is not further referenced, the original English cannot be located. The text has been reverse-translated back into English from the German.

4. Translator's Note: Brigadier General Anthony McAuliffe was the divisional artillery commander for the 101st Airborne Division. He was given acting command of the division for the first week at Bastogne. He had jumped into Normandy and had ridden a glider into Holland during Operation "Market Garden." After the Battle of

general who commanded our division. Court meant that Lieutenant General Courtney H. Hodges, [Commander in Chief of the] U.S. First Army, was in a jam. The reference to Jim was that a comrade of McAuliffe was already on the way to help, and now someone had also offered the 101st [Airborne] Division, which was resting. Why? Old Crock didn't know himself, but he assumed that things were bad.

And boy were they bad! Up to the north, in the main headquarters, the commanding general looked at a large black and white map that covered the wall. A sinister tree entered in red pencil was spreading over the map. It was a tree that was on its side. It had large roots in the east and a trunk with a lot of branches heading west over roads, hills, rivers and villages. That's the way it was on Sunday, when McAuliffe received his message. And that tree growing rapidly was the template for the German breakthrough. The start of the worst defeat for the Army of the USA since Bataan.

The tree had been growing in length every hour for thirty-six hours. The red pencil was attempting to keep pace with the German tanks that had broken through the Allied front that were breaking through to the west. For one and a half days, the completely exhausted men in the main U.S. headquarters had received telephone calls. They then got up and added more to the tree and planted small flags on the map. The flags indicated the identified German divisions. One by one, they dotted the map, until the area looked like a hall of fame for the German Army. Names appeared like the 1st *SS Panzer-Division*, which bore the name of Adolf Hitler, and the *Panzer-Lehr-Division* of the former Chief of Staff of the "Desert Fox" in Africa, *Generalleutnant* Bayerlein.

That's how it all started for us and for McAuliffe. And while the general was busy searching for Bastogne on the map, the telephone rang again. It was a familiar voice from the corps headquarters: "This morning, we said Tuesday. Sorry, but you have to leave today at 1400 hours. Break all the records. It's really pressing."

Old Crock sent out a drumbeat for his men. It was even more difficult for him, since he was only the acting division commander. Trucks of all sizes were procured. Our division was a collection of young men who had jumped into Normandy and penetrated into Carentan. We had only been resting for the last sixteen days. And

---

the Bulge, McAuliffe was given command of the U.S. 103rd Infantry Division, which he commanded from January to July 1945.

when they pressed to the trucks in wild throngs and saw Old Crock, they called out: "Hell, Crock, why don't you give us roller skates?"

And then they took off. The 502nd and the 506th rode together. They were supposed to have played each other that day in the "Champagne Bowl," but now they were headed for the real thing to the north. The hardest action they would see during the war.

That was at 1400 hours on Monday, 18 December. At the same time, thousands of German tanks had already swallowed and digested all sorts of U.S. armored and infantry divisions. Nine German infantry divisions, six armored divisions and one airborne divisions had already been identified. And there were more in the east that were earmarked to reinforce the thrust west.

The German tree spread out more and more to the west, and our staff officers shook their heads as they marked the maps with German reconnaissance units ranging far ahead of their units. More and more blue flags were removed from the map. Those were our overrun units.

No more than fifteen minutes away from our corps headquarters, German paratroopers had jumped in and ambushed vehicles that were moving all alone. The Germans devoured one blue flag after the other. Only one remained stuck in the map. It was the one for Bastogne.

And that one was only still there because Colonel William L. Roberts from Louisiana was there with his 10th Armored Division. "The Stone," as we called Roberts, had refused to pull back. He had worked his way into Bastogne and was defending the city.

McAuliffe had moved ahead of his forces and reached Bastogne Monday evening. During the night, the advance guard rolled into the city, and the main body arrived in the early morning hours. One regiment threw itself to the northern edges of the city, towards Noville, where the *Panzer-Lehr-Division* was approaching the city.

Around 0530 hours, Bayerlein decided to renew the advance on Bastogne. If he had not been lured by the civilian into the mud bath, the division would have already been in the city, since the units of the U.S. 10th Armored Division were too weak to offer effective resistance to the *PLD*.

After one kilometer, the lead tank of the 1st Company of the *PLR* ran over a mine and was knocked out. Bayerlein ordered his engineers forward. As always, *Hauptmann* Kunze was with his men, assisting in the removal of the extensive mine obstacle. The advance guard of the division then reached the rail station at Neffe, right outside the city of Bastogne.

At the same time that Neffe was reached, Colonel Julian Ewell's 1st and 2nd Battalions of the U.S. 501st Parachute Infantry Regiment were advancing on Neffe from Bastogne. McAuliffe had instructed the regimental commander to advance, seek enemy contact and attack.

Ewell's men were able to take high ground to the east of Bastogne. He was able to set up antitank guns before the tanks of the *PLD* arrived. The rest of the regiment was brought forward. The U.S. forces had arrived at the last minute. The few hours that the *PLD* had spent in the mud hole outside of Margaret would decide the battle in the favor of the enemy.

In the morning fog, the tanks of the division rolled forward. Bitter fighting soon broke out for the northern entrance to Bastogne. The *Panzer IV's* and *Panthers* of the division attempted to take the high ground. But the dug-in enemy had the advantage in the wooded terrain. Nine German tanks were knocked out. They lit up the morning as burning torches. A few armored cars and *SPW's* that attempted to go around the high ground were engaged by infantry positions on the flanks.

The grenadiers of *PGLR 901* and *PGLR 902* then attacked. The units of the regiments tried to break the blocking position for three hours. Bathed in fog, engaged from the flanks and at a disadvantage due to the terrain, Bayerlein broke off the fighting. The division had closed to within 2,300 meters of the city, but its attacked irretrievably bogged down.

Bayerlein called the *Flak* battalion forward. It had been committed at Moiry and Remagne in a flank-guard role.

At Noville, where the *2. Panzer-Division* was also engaged with American forces at the same time as the *PLD*, the soldiers of Major Desobry held their positions. Attacked on three sides, they turned back all attacks. At Longvilly, Lieutenant Colonel Cherry fought against elements of the *PLD*. His men were cut off. They fought their way through the thinly held German blocking positions and re-established their own defensive positions further back. In the southern portion of the all-round defense, the American defenders also held out. Lieutenant Colonel James O'Hara, who defended in that sector, later stated: "It was only possible for us to divert the German armored avalanche. We couldn't stop it."

While the *PGLR 902* and a portion of the division's heavy weapons bogged down outside of Bastogne and dug in together with the *26. Volks-Grenadier-Division*, von Manteuffel appeared at Bayerlein's field command post.

"Advance past Bastogne to the south and take St. Hubert!"

Leaving behind the aforementioned formation, Bayerlein reorganized and continued the advance, as directed. During the morning hours of 20

December, the division encountered an American transport column that was attempting to reach Bastogne from the southwest. After a short skirmish, the column was wiped out and fifty-five trucks and fifteen jeeps fell into the hands of the Germans. A short while later, the division encountered a blocking position manned by U.S. engineers. The advance was stopped for a short while.

The tank destroyers were able to eliminate the engineers who were guarding their obstacles from the flanks. American tanks supporting there were also knocked out. *Unteroffizier* Job was able to add another tank to his score. The blocking position was eliminated, the enemy ejected and, a few hours later, the *PLD* was at Morhet, twenty kilometers west of Bastogne.

Here is the overall situation according to von Manteuffel's writings:

It would have meant giving up all thoughts of offensive action [on 19 December] if the *5. Panzer-Armee* had employed all the forces of the *XXXXVII. Panzer-Korps* to take Bastogne while temporarily calling off movement west, especially since the friendly forces to the right of that corps, the *116. Panzer-Division*, was in the process of attacking Houffalize. The field army command therefore ordered the *2. Panzer-Division* to take Noville, northwest of Bastogne, and continue moving west without delay. The *PLD* was to move directly on Bastogne with elements to support the *26. Volks-Grenadier-Division*, but it was to be prepared to advance west, via Sibret, southwest of Bastogne, with its remaining elements.

The situation continued to develop to the disadvantage of the *PLD*, however. The division was being slowed up by the continuing bad road network. It did not help that the attack of the *26. Volks-Grenadier-Division* outside of Bizory, northeast of Bastogne, had bogged down. The failure at Bastogne was all the more worrisome, since the forces of the *5. Panzer-Armee* had already been characterized as insufficient for carrying out both missions it was saddled with: advancing on the Meuse and covering the long and exposed southern flank of the overall offensive while, at the same time, sealing off Bastogne. What had been feared all along by the Germans was starting to develop: Bastogne became the building block for the enemy to start bringing in ever more forces for a future counteroffensive.

On 20 December, the *2. Panzer-Division* succeeded in reaching the Noville area. It took Ourtheuville at midnight, where it was able to capture an intact bridge over the Ourthe. The division left behind security elements and continued its advance westward.

That same day, there was hardly any further advance against Bastogne proper, since the resistance there was steadily increasing. Nevertheless, the field army continued to insist on its capture.

On 21 December, the weather cleared up enough with the cloud cover opening up in places that the first Allied fighter-bombers started to appear over the area of operations of the two field armies, even if only in limited numbers. As a result of a lack of fuel, the *2. Panzer-Division* was only able to make a limited advance and had to content itself that day with expanding its bridgehead over the Ourthe as far as Tenneville (north of Ourtheuville).

The *PLD* continued its advance in the direction of the Meuse by reaching Morhet. The reconnaissance battalion, reinforced by the divisional engineers, was able to make it as far as a line defined by Tillet–Gerimont–Amberloup, all of which were about halfway to St. Hubert. The *26. Volks-Grenadier-Division* was able to take Sibret after a hard fight. The attacks against Bastogne—both from the north and the south—miscarried.

The encirclement of Bastogne, at least in the east between Champs and Senonchamps, east of the city, was completed with the weak forces in position there. The tanks of the *2. Panzer-Division* got a late start on 22 December, due to continuing fuel problems. It did not have sufficient combat power available to take the heavily occupied high ground around Marche. It left behind a *Kampfgruppe* to seal off the area, with the rest of the division occupying Hargimont and On (halfway to Rochefort–Marche) on 22 December.

On 22 December, the Anglo-American air forces increased their sorties. Despite that, the *Panzer-Lehr-Division* advanced on St. Hubert, which was taken during the night.

The *7. Armee* reported at the same time that the *5. Fallschirmjäger-Division* had been attacked several times during the day.

✠

Fifteen of Bayerlein's tanks reached Forrieres at 1600 hours on 23 December. One and a half hours later, Rochefort could be seen by the lead elements of the division's two *Kampfgruppen*. *Major* von Born-Fallois moved at the head of his reconnaissance elements to the city limits and reported that it was clear of the enemy. This later turned out to be incorrect.

By then, it was dark. The entrance to the city led through a type of bottleneck. Despite that, Bayerlein told his men to continue: "Close your eyes and go!"

The fifteen tanks of the battle group started to move out. As soon as they were in the middle of the bottleneck, they were greeted by fire from guns located on both sides of the surrounding high ground, which the reconnaissance battalion had not identified.

The fight for Rochefort had started. The first two tanks encountered an obstacle and were immobilized when they tried to bypass it and ran over mines. Their tracks were blown off. The crews dismounted and attempted to repair the damage, all the while receiving direct enemy fire. Bayerlein had his engineers and some grenadiers from the 2nd Battalion of *PGLR 901* fan out through the woods and onto the high ground to try to silence the enemy.

The next tank overran the barricade and crushed it under its tracks. The advance started to pick up momentum again. Rumbling and roaring, the tanks reached the center of the town. They were greeted there by American antitank guns and field pieces. The enemy had chosen his positions carefully, and the guns mutually supported one another while taking all of the crossroads and key points under interlocking fires. The fighting for Rochefort lasted the entire night.

Obergefreiter Schüßler, who was assigned to the 7th Company of *PGLR 901* of *Oberleutnant* Mahr, has provided a firsthand account of that fighting:

"Dismount!" the platoon leader ordered when there was a crashing noise ahead of us and one of our tanks was transformed into a red-glowing torch in the space of a few seconds that filled the night with tongues of fire.

Next to me, my No. 2, Norbert Peltz, jumped out, and Höfer, my No. 3, practically landed on my back. We ran behind our platoon leader. I heard the rattling of steel, and then the darkness was torn by two or three pyrotechnics going into the air. That was immediately followed by the rattling of automatic weapons.

The tank we had been riding on rolled forward a bit, ran into a low garden wall and knocked it over. The turret traversed and the long trunk of the main gun spat out a long stream of fire. The enemy machine gun, which had fired at us from ten meters away at the edge of the city, disappeared with a crunching impact.

"Follow me . . . quick . . . quick!"

We ran on. Someone behind me fell with a jarring cry. An arrow of tracers turned on us and threw us behind the cover of a wall. I brought up the machine gun on its bipod, and when I saw the tracers burn out, I aimed for the point of origin.

When it started being lit up there again, I pulled the trigger. The machine gun shuddered in my hands. The bolt ate the belt of ammo and spit out the empty casings. The impacts could be heard crashing over in the distance. The enemy machine gun fell quiet abruptly. Off to my left, the second machine gun of our squad barked. Its rattling resounded in our ears. The dry cracks of the main guns hammered away, with the enemy's antitank guns filling the intervals. The enemy apparently wanted to hold this town with all the means at his disposal. A long shadow appeared next to me. I swung the machine gun around and was just about to shoot, when Peltz, who was next to me, grabbed my arm.

"He's one of ours!" he called out.

It was *Leutnant* Becker, a platoon leader in the 6th Company, which had also been held up, just like we had been.

"*Gruppe Schüßler*, get over here!" Becker ordered.

We crawled over to him.

"What is it, *Herr Leutnant?*"

"The 6th is being held up by a couple of machine guns over there in the houses. We're going to go around the houses and take out the machine guns." There were mortar rounds bursting over there, where the officer was pointing.

"The heavy platoon's already started. It's time for us."

The houses covered in moonlight looked like they were in a dream. But as soon as we saw the bright muzzle flashes, we knew that the peacefulness was but an illusion. We hurried along the way, reached a house and took cover behind it. Hand grenades were being tossed from one of the neighboring houses. The crack of the detonations was swallowed up in three bursts of machine-gun fire.

"Keep going . . . keep going!"

Then we reached the back courtyard of the building. As I was running, I saw the brilliant flashes of the bursting mortar rounds; I saw the "dark mice" descend on the houses and impact on the roof.

"Man, we're supposed to go in there. Our own mortars will turn us into mincemeat!" Höfer whispered behind me.

"Get up . . . go!"

With a lurch, *Leutnant* Becker rose. We pushed ourselves off the ground and ran after him to the back door of the house. A mortar round slammed into the courtyard five meters in front of the officer. But Becker had heard the incoming round and ducked for cover in time.

He surfaced again out of the smoke of the impact. He reached the door and kicked it open. As I reached the dark hallway, I heard him running ahead of me. Peltz crashed to the ground behind me. Ammo cans went everywhere. A door off to the side was thrown open.

"What's the matter?" one of the GI's asked.

Then a submachine gun barked. It was the submachine gun of Becker up ahead. Everyone was accounted for from my section on the ground floor of the house. Fire was being sprayed in our direction. I fired as I ran. Kramschneider was also firing. A hand grenade flew over our heads into the room where the Americans were. Its ear-deafening blast had us hit the deck. Then the three enemy machine guns, which had been set up between sand bags along the windows, fell silent.

Leutnant Becker fired the prearranged aerial pyrotechnic. The mortar fire and the rattling of our machine guns fell silent, and the men of the 6th Company came running forward.

"Keep going . . . don't stop now!"

Oberleutnant Winter, the commander of the 6th Company, showed up at the head of his company.

✠

The fighting for Rochefort continued throughout the night. The tanks continued firing, but only individually. Three or four had been knocked out; the remainder pulled out of the built-up area, where they were extremely vulnerable. They waited for the rest of the ground elements to take up their positions around the town, in order to then proceed in a concentric fashion.

As it started to turn first light on 23 December, the town was completely encircled. An hour later, it was completely in German hands. The enemy had put up a tough fight and inflicted heavy casualties on the *PLD*.

Bayerlein summoned his commanders. He directed the *PALA 130* to reconnoiter south in the direction of Libramont. *Major* von Born-Fallois's men determined the town was filled with enemy. Although there was an engagement with U.S. forces there, the battalion rejoined the division in accordance with its orders.

That same day, the division crossed the Lesse to the northwest of Rochefort on the intact bridge. The *PALA 130* moved rapidly through American positions and reached Ciergnon, halfway between Rochefort and Dinant. As such, von Born Fallois's men were the farthest west of all the German formations, with the exception of *Kampfgruppe Peiper* of the *1. SS-Panzer-Division "Leibstandarte SS Adolf Hitler."*

The reconnaissance battalion took Ciergnon during the afternoon of 24 December, after a bitter fight that required the reconnaissance troopers to give it their best. Whenever the enemy resistance got stiffer, von Born-Fallois was there to rally his men forward. It was thanks to his tireless efforts that some of his sections were not cut off or destroyed.

When von Born-Fallois radioed back to the division command post that Ciergnon had been taken, Bayerlein believed for a moment that perhaps his men would do it after all, that they might be the first to the Meuse and thus be the first ones to accomplish the first stage of the offensive.

But only a few minutes later, another report filtered in, which negated all thoughts of any further advance. The lead elements of the *2. Panzer-Division*, which were north of the *PLD* at Marche had been interdicted by the enemy and thrown back after hard fighting. Von Manteuffel had thereupon ordered the *9. Panzer-Division* forward, but it was unable to move far due to a lack of fuel. It did not look like the *2. Panzer-Division* would be able to be relieved.

The *PLD* then received orders to launch an immediate attack in the direction of Humain and Buissenville to relieve those elements of the *2. Panzer-Division* encircled there. Moving rapidly, Bayerlein regrouped his division and formed two *Kampfgruppen* for the relief attacks. The first battle group, which had twelve tanks, was directed towards Humain, while the second group, which had only five tanks, was instructed to take Buissenville.

While the one battle group was able to take Humain in a direct attack, the effort against Buissenville failed. During their march through Havrenne, the men of the *PLD* saw proof of what was happening to their beleaguered comrades in the *2. Panzer-Division*: The remnants of the divisional artillery had been shot up there. Around Humain, the burnt-out *SPW's* of an entire company were found. The battle group that had been directed to Buissenville encountered ten knocked-out German tanks right outside the village. Monitoring Allied radio transmissions, Bayerlein's signals intelligence personnel were able to determine that at least thirty tanks of the *2. Panzer-Division* were encircled northeast of the *PLD*. Bayerlein then redirected his efforts in that direction to relieve the encircled tankers.

How had the desperate situation arisen in the sector of the *2. Panzer-Division*? Von Manteuffel outlines the events in his book, *Die Schlacht in den Ardennen*:

During its advance on 23 December, the *2. Panzer-Division* had had to defend against continuing enemy pressure from the north and had to detach elements again and again to protect its northern flank. That was the case at Hogne and Harvesin, to the west of Marche. The division's reconnaissance battalion reached Foy–Notre Dame that day, east of Dinant . . .

The forces of the division had to be divided into two groups, each fighting to all sides, to defend around Conneux. But the lack of fuel, which soon became noticeable, and the later onset of a lack of ammunition weakened the division's combat power, with the result that it had to yield to the enemy's superior numbers. On 24 December, the *2. Panzer-Division* was turned back west of Marche. The division, which had advanced to within five kilometers east of the Meuse at Dinant, was threatened with destruction. Elements of the division moving to the lead battle groups ran out of fuel on the way. The reconnaissance battalion, which fought bravely, succumbed to the enemy's superiority. In the face of increasing enemy pressure, the bulk of the *2. Panzer-Division* was pulled back to Rochefort. As a result, the *XXXXVII. Panzer-Korps* transitioned to the defense (after the *LVIII. Panzer-Korps* had not succeeded in breaking through the American lines between Soy–Hotton–Grandmenil).

The forward command post of the *PLD* was established in Humain during the evening of 24 December. The forward elements of the divisional headquarters experienced Christmas 1944 there. From the window of a hotel on the marketplace in St. Hubert, where the main body of the divisional headquarters had established itself, Bayerlein saw the first bombers fly in at noon on Christmas Day and drop their bomb loads on the city. They were followed by fighter-bombers. One of them dove to barely twenty meters off the ground and fired into the windows of the hotel. Although it did not cause any damage, it put a damper on any holiday spirits that existed.

The Allied air forces started a concerted bombing campaign with the onset of flying weather. The front lines were bombed as if on a "conveyer belt." Most of the damage was caused in Barrière and Champlon, where the wrecks of divisional vehicles smoldered after the attacks.

The main Allied airpower effort was directed against the *2. Panzer-Division*, which was in the Hargimont area. Though his binoculars, Bayerlein could see the gliders heading in towards Bastogne. Completely surrounded by this point, the city was being supplied from the air.

Although the *Kampfgruppen* of the *PLD* were generally not being attacked in their main lines of resistance at this point, it was a different story for the division's logistical elements. The rear-area services at Morhet, Tilet, Sibret and St. Hubert suffered heavy casualties. A *Flak* battery that attempted to reply to the attack of P-38 Lightnings simply disappeared under a hail of bombs. Hardly any men of the battery survived. But the heaviest loss the division had to take was the complete destruction of both of its armored maintenance facilities, which were swept up in a maelstrom of fire. They had been ordered to remain behind in Bergisch-Gladbach and Koblenz because of the lack of fuel, but Bayerlein had ordered them forward anyway in order to get his tanks and other armored vehicles repaired as quickly as possible and back into the fight.

On that same Christmas Day, the third maintenance facility of the division—also its largest—which was stuck at the rail station at Birresborn, was heavily bombed and effectively lost.

There was little fuel to be had. Every drop of fuel had to be brought forward by truck from the large depot at Troisdorf. The division had already lost thirty fuel trucks on their long march to the front. That figure does not include those trucks that got stuck in the mud, turned over or just broke down.

In the middle of the precarious fuel situation, an order from Model arrived indicating that all vehicles that were not needed for a direct combat role were to give up their fuel to the armored vehicles. Bayerlein refused to carry out the order; he saw the day coming when even his tanks would not have any fuel.

On that Christmas Day, aerial observers also appeared in the skies, in addition to the bombers, fighter-bombers and fighters. They directed the ground artillery onto any and all targets they could identify. Some eight armored cars and an equal number of trucks fell victim to indirect artillery fires. Bayerlein gave the Allied pilots his grudging respect; they were great at what they did. Although he requested *Luftwaffe* support, no German aircraft were ever seen in the skies.

During the night of 25–26 December, the *PLD* also pulled back to Rochefort. The withdrawal was also accompanied by the loss of another eight trucks and several *Kübelwagen*, which all fell victim to U.S. Army Air Force Lightnings.

On the morning of 26 December, the division reached Custinne. It was there that tanks of the U.S. 2nd Armored Division attacked the flank guards and rearguard of the division. They had been driving individual groups of the *2. Panzer-Division* in front of them, and the German forces reported that a portion of the main body of the division had been wiped out. The U.S. attack

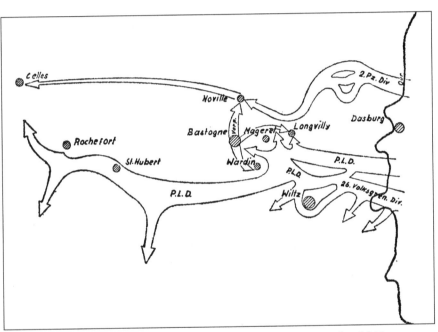

Advance of the *Panzer-Lehr-Division* from 16 to 31 December 1944.

was turned back. Elements of the 2nd Battalion of *PLR 130* succeeded in knocking out seven tanks of the U.S. advance guard.[5]

In his headquarters in La Roche, an old palace in the Ardennes, von Manteuffel briefed Hitler's special emissary, *Major* Johann-Mayer, on the situation. The picture was not a pretty one. He did not pull any punches and recommended that the planned thrust to Antwerp be called off immediately. If the Germans were to accomplish anything at all, then the *5. Panzer-Armee* needed to be pivoted north immediately. It would then be possible to score a partial success by capturing all of the American forces east of the Meuse.

Johann-Mayer was convinced by von Manteuffel's arguments. He called the *Führer* Headquarters and talked to Jodl, presenting him with von Manteuffel's arguments. Jodl then spoke to von Manteuffel directly: "The *Führer* has not made a decision yet."

"But you know the decision has to be made now, immediately!" Von Manteuffel did not hold back his anger. "Moreover . . . I need more support."

"I can only give you one more armored division," Jodl replied, continuing: "And don't forget: The *Führer* does not want you to take even a single step back. Advance! Never retreat!"

Von Manteuffel replaced the handset.

That day he had issued orders to also go over to the defense at Bastogne, since the available forces and means were insufficient to resume the attack on the city, which the supreme command continued to insist upon.

✠

In the ring outside of Bastogne, the grenadiers of *PGLR 902* had been involved in uninterrupted, bitter fighting ever since 19 December. Attacks were conducted on 22 December by all of the forces surrounding the city, but they were all turned back. The last big attack on Bastogne was conducted on Christmas Day. The German artillery conducted a one-hour preparation. At 0300 hours on 25 December, the *26. Volks-Grenadier-Division* and the *15. Panzergrenadier-Division* attacked from the northwest, while the *5. Fallschirmjäger-Division* moved out from the southeast towards the city. *PGLR 902* fought as part of the *26. Volks-Grenadier-Division.* Von Poschinger's men moved behind the advancing tanks and approached the American main line of resistance.

---

5. At this time, *I./PLR 130* was serving as an independent unit fighting in Hungary. *II./PLR 130* was a mixed battalion as follows:

    5th Company equipped with Panthers.
    6th Company equipped with Panzer IVs.
    7th Company equipped with Panthers.
    8th Company equipped with Panzer IVs.

The village of Champs was taken. Wild close-in combat ensued. Men fell and died in the snow; death yielded a rich harvest on both sides. Of the German tanks employed in the attack, some twenty-seven remained behind on the battlefield, burning torches.

In the end, the German attack bogged down. That signaled the end of any reasonable expectation of being able to take the city. Once again, we will let Richards and Hottelet pick up the narrative:

We already knew that Patton's men (U.S. Third Army) were only a few miles south of Bastogne. The "brass hat" ordered the American 4th Armored Division to step on it, after a message was received from Bastogne that clearly demonstrated the danger of the hour. He likewise fired up the U.S. 80th Infantry Division to hurry as quickly as possible, since the men of the U.S. 9th Armored Division, the 10th Armored Division, the 28th Infantry Division, as well as the paratroopers of the 101st Airborne Division were in a bad situation in Bastogne.

The city of Bastogne was completely destroyed. All that was left were ruins and rubble from houses. In peace, Bastogne had been an ugly city. In war, it was even uglier. Like a soldier whose face had been wounded by a rifle bullet.

The defense of Bastogne was removed from the spotlight at that point and switched to the relief attack that was being conducted by two of the most famous divisions in Patton's Third Army. They were the 4th Armored Division, which was referred to as "Roosevelt's butchers" by the Germans and feared by them, and the Blue-Ridge Mountain Boys of the 80th Infantry Division. They were coming from a successful fight in the south, and they were coming with the confidence of soldiers who had already encountered the Germans and had beat them back across all of France.

The 80th Infantry Division had been resting in the vicinity of St. Avold in Belgium. It had received orders on 19 December to march to Bastogne. The 4th Armored Division had arrived like a rocket. It had covered the 240 kilometers from Fenstrange to Bastogne in the space of forty-eight hours. It had fought its way through along the Arlon–Bastogne road, and both of the divisions had their first serious fighting around Chaumont. The locality changed hands three times. The tanks fought . . . the infantry fought . . . and the snow was littered with the bodies of the fallen.

There were two men who gave wings to the attack: Lieutenant Colonel George Jacques, who commanded the 53rd Armored Infantry,

and Lieutenant Colonel Creighton Abrams, who commanded the
37th Armored.

On 26 December, Abrams smoked the last of his Christmas cigars.
He was in Clochimont, standing erect in [the hatch of his] Sherman
command tank, when he stated: "We're going to Bastogne today!"

The tanks of the 37th Armored rolled as far as Assenois, just a few
hundred meters northwest of Bastogne. They came so quickly that
friendly artillery took out a number of its lead tanks and armored
cars. Lieutenant Hoggess moved forward with his four Shermans.
Firing with everything they had, they rolled through the siege ring
and opened a gap. He was followed by Captain William Dwight and
behind him were the half-tracks of the 80th [Infantry] Division. Then,
all at once, they were through. Lieutenant Hoggess called out to the
individuals he saw in front of him: "Hello! Come on out!"

He was not certain whether they were friendlies or Germans. An
American officer came out of the house. It was Lieutenant Webster
from the 101st [Airborne Division's] engineers.

"I'm damned happy to see you!" Webster said.

They had actually reached the city and broken through the
German siege ring. And General McAuliffe, our "Old Crock," jumped
into his vehicle and rolled towards the tanks. It was exactly 1710 hours
on 26 December when he reached the command tank of Captain
William Dwight. He still knew nothing of the one small blue flag that
had held out on its own. He had no clue that he had assumed a role
of historical importance. He also said nothing heroic when he shook
Dwight's hand. No, "Old Crock" simply said: "Captain, I'm happy to
see you!"

Bastogne had been saved. Bastogne would be able to hold out
against any German combat forces.

On the night of 26–27 December, the *PLD* reached the area around
Rochefort. Bayerlein established his headquarters in a chateau in Zilly. Zilly
was a dot on the map north of La Vacherie.

On the morning of 28 December, the 3rd Company of *PJLA 130*
was screening when it was caught by surprise in an American attack. The
acting company commander, *Oberleutnant* Wagner, was surprised when he
dismounted his vehicle in front of a farmer's house. The crew had to abandon
its vehicle in a panic. All of the classified documents Wagner had had with
him were left behind.

On that same day, *Leutnant* Schönrath rolled forward in the tank destroyer of *Oberfeldwebel* Stolz in an effort to recover the lost documents. The tank destroyer headed west, looking for the last known location of Wagner's vehicle. Schönrath was not having any luck and was about to turn around when three U.S. tanks came rolling out of the woods behind him.

"Hook to the left!" Schönrath ordered his driver.

Krenstedt turned the vehicle, while *Unteroffizier* Job began to peer earnestly through his sights. Everything depended on who was the fastest.

When the vehicle had pivoted left, Job had enough in his sights to go to work. The first Sherman was in his sights. The Sherman started to traverse its turret in the direction of the *Jagdpanzer*, but it was too late for it. Job's round set it ablaze. Krenstedt pivoted some more to help Job acquire the next target. The second round was already in the breechblock, when Job took up a sight picture on the second tank. The second round left the barrel soon thereafter, and the next Yank tank was set alight. By then, the third enemy tank had started firing. Its first round was over and slammed into a hedge behind the *Jagdpanzer* Job then let loose with his third round. Three rounds . . . three kills.

"Let's get the hell out of here!" Schönrath ordered. The *Jagdpanzer* moved out at speed, returning to the German lines. The documents were not recovered, but the division had three fewer enemy tanks to contend with.

✠

On 29 December, the U.S. Third Army was allocated an additional two divisions. They were the U.S. 87th Infantry Division and the U.S. 3rd Armored Division, which were advancing on Bastogne from the southwest. On the morning of 30 December, their lead elements reached an area between five and ten kilometers west of Sibret. With those fresh divisions, Patton hoped to cut off the German forces west of Bastogne—the *2. Panzer-Division*, the *PLD* and the *26. Volks-Grenadier-Division*—by attacking to the north in the direction of Houffalize.

On the same day, von Manteuffel had issued orders to the *PLD*—with *Volks-Grenadier-Regiment 77* of the *26. Volks-Grenadier-Division* in support—to attack the Bastogne corridor and interdict it. The division was to advance from the west and northwest to the southeast. At the same time, the *1. SS-Panzer-Division "Leibstandarte SS Adolf Hitler"* and the *167. Volks-Grenadier-Division* were to advance from east to west. The pincers were to close south of Bastogne and finally cut off the city, once and for all.

The *PLD* and the elements of the *26. Volks-Grenadier-Division* ran right into the attacking elements of the U.S. 11th Armored Division, which had started its attack north at 0300 hours. A short, sharp skirmish ensued. Using the few remaining 88's available along with a handful of tanks, the forces of the *PLD* were able to hold up the U.S. attack and then force it back. The attack launched by the *"Leibstandarte"* was able to reach Villers-la-bonne-Eau before it was halted there by the forces of the U.S. 35th Infantry Division.

Those were the last combat operations of the *PLD* in 1944. At 0105 hours on 1 January 1945, Adolf Hitler delivered his last New Year's address to the nation. Speaking in a voice filled with confidence, he stated:

> This people and this state and its leading men are unshakable in their will and unflinching in their fanatical determination to fight this war through under all circumstances to a successful conclusion . . . . The world needs to know that this state will never capitulate . . .
>
> So, like the phoenix from the ashes, the German will has once again risen like never before from the rubble of our cities. We will fight until the origins of our enemy will one day find an end. German spirit and German willpower will force that! That, my comrades, will enter history as the miracle of the twentieth century.
>
> In this hour, I therefore pledge to the almighty as the speaker of Germany that we will loyally and unflappably fulfill our duties in the New Year, firm in the belief that the hour will come in which victory will finally turn to those to whom it is the most deserving: the greater German *Reich*!

That same morning, Patton had an order-of-the-day sent out to the soldiers of his field army. It was just as long as Hitler's speech. It concluded by stating:

> I cannot find any better expression of my feelings than to call upon the immortal words of General Scott at Chapultepec:
> "Brave rifles, brave, battle-tested riflemen! You have been baptized in fire and blood and have emerged steel!"

So began the first day of 1945, which would see almost five more months of terrible fighting on German soil.

The Allied counteroffensive started early on 3 January 1945. Its objective was to reach the Houfalize area from the north and south with strong forces in order to cut off all of the German forces west of that line, including the *PLD*.

The Allied plan did not develop as envisioned. The heavy snowfall helped the German forces, who knew a thing or two about withdrawing along the roads from their experience in the Soviet Union. Thanks to the brave actions of the rearguards, the main bodies were able to withdraw. One of the rearguards was the *PLD*. Bayerlein, who still maintained his headquarters in Zilly, received orders on 5 January to hold a line running St. Hubert–Pironpre "until the last round."

From that day forward, the *PLD* conducted a stubborn delaying action and only moved at night. A number of hard skirmishes and engagements were fought. In the period from 11 to 15 January alone, more than fifty-three of the division's armored vehicles had to be abandoned and blown up along the side of the roads due to a lack of fuel or a mechanical breakdown, which could not be repaired in time.

With the return of better flying weather, the Allied air forces seemed to hit the *PLD* especially hard again. Vitally needed fuel was also targeted. A large rail transport with fuel was lost. The Allied targeting also made most of the road around Houffalize virtually untrafficable. The bad roads forced some of the fuel to be brought forward during the day, which made for easy targets for the fighter-bombers.

On 13 January, when the division, with the divisional engineers in the lead, pulled through Houffalize, bombers and fighter-bombers struck all of the roads leading to the east with a vengeance. The division was fortunate in that it only lost several vehicles and no personnel to the attacks. Other formations were not quite so lucky.

The Ardennes offensive was over for the Germans. *Oberst* Gerhardt, the commander of the *PLR*, summed it all up later on:

When the Ardennes offensive was ordered, our division had been barely one half reconstituted and equipped. But it was given a full combat rating. In reality, this was the situation: The armored formations had been battered in combat and were a force that had not been completely outfitted. Their soldiers deeply mistrusted the senior command and the ability to conduct a fight against fresh forces that were magnificently outfitted.

That was the mood we were in when the operations order reached us. The long-range objectives stood in stark contrast with the forces actually on hand and the stockpiles of fuel and ammunition available. On top of all that was the fact that in our case we were employed on the left wing of the *5. Panzer-Armee* and the only thing available to screen the left flank was a newly formed *"Volks-Grenadier-Division,"* which consisted of combat-inexperienced rear-area and home-front soldiers whose combat value was a big zero due to a lack of experience, primitive training, old age and poor equipment.

Correspondingly, the entire operation—from Rundstedt on down to the simplest grenadier—was considered to be an act of desperation, whose failure was pre-ordained. It seemed to us we were like the besieged in a fortress, who had to make a final desperate breakout attempt in order to save face before we finally had to capitulate.

That point was driven home to most by the fact that our division commander, *Generalleutnant* Bayerlein, was personally present in the lead attack forces, something that was, in and by itself, not his job. He justified it by saying it was all or nothing and he was not married, so it did not matter if he fell.

To that end, we employed only enough men up front that could be used as tank crews. They rest remained behind to screen the supply routes, since we could not trust that to the forces that were following us. Also telling for this offensive being an act of desperation was the fact that when we objected that the amount of fuel quantities was completely insufficient, we were informed we had to take the enemy's fuel dump as quickly as possible and fuel up there, even though they had to know that our thoroughbred tank engines could only use a special type of fuel. The only thing they did was attach a special detail, which was intended to test any possible captured fuel stocks for their ability to be used by us.

A further hindrance was the fact that no reconnaissance was to be conducted—on express orders from the Armed Forces High Command—so as not to endanger operational security. The main roads—based on the map—were to be reserved for logistics and the motorized forces, while the horse-drawn infantry divisions received the secondary roads.

When the advance started, it turned out that the secondary roads were untrafficable in the winter weather, even for the light *Panje* carts,[6] with the result that everything, in the end, pressed together on the one or two roads behind our division. That led to complete chaos,

---

6. Translator's Note: A *Panje* cart was the German Army's slang term for any small and generally primitive horse-drawn wagon or cart. It came from the fighting in the Soviet Union, where the carts were often the only way of moving logistical supplies around in the dead of winter on the Soviet Union's extremely poor road network. The *Panje* was the small Russian packhorse used to pull the carts.

especially since most of the cart drivers were Russians who hardly understood German and understandably showed little inclination to help restore order or expose themselves to danger.

As a result, the few motorized supply vehicles of the *PLD* also got caught up in the mess, especially at night, and remained stuck or only moved at a walking pace, whereby staff officers had to precede them in order to force their right-of-way.

When the original plan—prior to continuing the advance, Bastogne was to be taken by the *PLD* so as to secure the presumed stockpiles there, especially the fuel—was tossed aside and the *PLD* was to advance past Bastogne to the south and leave the taking of Bastogne to the following infantry divisions, the disaster started. When the weather cleared and allowed the enemy to employ airpower, which had not been possible on the first two days, then it was clear to any prudent man that the offensive had practically bogged down on the third day and it was then imperative to return to the lines of departure to avoid a complete disaster. What we had predicted occurred. The *PLD* had to be halted, because the rear divisions did not succeed in their mission of screening the left flank, let alone take Bastogne, and soon our right flank was also exposed, since the 2. *Panzer-Division*, which was advancing to the right of us, was unable to make progress. As a result, the enemy had the opportunity to attack our lead elements from two sides and to take the only supply route under artillery fire from both the north and south and, as a result, practically interdict it.

After the division had held out in that extraordinarily precarious situations for several days, without the situation next to us or behind us changing, we were also ordered back to our lines of departure— almost too late. As a result, the operation had failed. The last faith in the leadership on the part of the forces in the field was lost and irreplaceable materiel sacrificed.

With regard to the promised big employment of the *Luftwaffe*, there was a single action—almost having the effect of a demonstration— on the part of a few hundred fighter-bombers and bombers, which perhaps slowed down the course of events but could not change them. If there had been flying weather on the first day, then the offensive would most certainly have bogged down that day, since we did not have anything to employ against the enemy air forces.

The purpose of this offensive was all the more incomprehensible to the forces in the field, since we knew how difficult the fighting on the Eastern Front was and how few forces were available there. And we also knew how much more dangerous the Russian enemy was for our homeland. Since it had been clear to us by 1943 at the latest that the war could not be won, it would have been more understandable to us if all of the forces still available had been committed to the Eastern Front, where the fighting still had a purpose. But we had a hard time buying into the Ardennes operation. And we were capable of making a judgment call after all of the campaigns we had participated in. In my case: Poland, France, Russia, Africa, Italy and, once again, France.

✠

PGLR 901 was pulled out of the line on 15 January and was sent to Fischbach to stage. The regiment remained there until 20 January. On the way there, the 9th Company, the self-propelled infantry gun company, was hit from the air, with many soldiers being killed or wounded. After the attack was over, the company was effectively reduced to its headquarters section and one platoon. The remaining platoon was then committed near Weiler and Wallhausen under the leadership of *Leutnant* Gierke. The rest of the regiment was pulled back across the *Westwall*, whereupon it assembled at Reif.

On 26 January, Gierke's platoon got into a tight spot. The platoon had to pull back in the direction of Gemünd, pressed hard by the pursuing enemy. Gemünd was the first zone of defense along the *Westwall*. Once there, the platoon was pulled out of the line and sent to rejoin its company and regiment in Baden. Using its last remaining fuel, the platoon reached the new assembly area on 28 January. The platoon's immobilized vehicles remained behind in Reif under the care of *Stabsfeldwebel* Wollesen. On 29 January, one gun had to be blown up. One of the platoon's *Maultier*[7] prime movers, which was in the middle of the main line of resistance without any fuel, also suffered the same fate. It was not until 5 February that enough fuel arrived that Wollesen was able to rejoin the rest of his company.

✠

Approximately 200 men of the *PLD*—representing all of the division's regiments and troop elements—reached Hoscheid, where they were impressed into the defense of the town against the Americans advancing from the north. It was an eerie situation, and the signs of dissolution among the various

---

7. The *Maultier* (Mule) was a semi-tracked supply vehicle based on the Opel two-ton truck.

formations were increasing. By 21 January, most of the division had gathered in and around the town. The men of the division saw mighty aerial formations gather above the town to assemble for a bombing run. Fortunately, it was not intended for them; instead, the target was the bridges at Dasburg.

When Bayerlein moved to his new command post in Übereisenbach in his staff car, he had to cross the only bridge that was still intact at Gemünd. After a few days of bad weather and the resultant lack of aerial attacks, the traffic had moved along the road leading to the bridge and over it without any concerns. On 21 January, the sun came out, however, and the roads on both sides of the bridge were jammed with vehicles of all types. As soon as the weather cleared, the fighter-bombers pounced from the heavens and hit everything that had not quickly disappeared under cover. The area around Hosingen was especially hard hit.

When Bayerlein reached Hosingen that evening, he was barely able to make his way through the burning wrecks of vehicles. Dead horses and burnt-out trucks were lying on their sides. The general counted more than 300 shot-up and burning vehicles. The entire, gigantic column must have panicked. Vehicles had collided with others. In their efforts to get off the road as quickly as possible, they were hurried along by death. For many a kilometer, it was only the bridge at Gemünd and another one at Dasburg that lead across the Our to the east.

On 23 January, Hoscheid was lost, and the *PLD* had to pull back behind the *Westwall*, where the division regrouped. Once the final status reports were received from all of the subordinate elements, it was determined that the division had been practically destroyed again in the five and a half weeks since the offensive in the Ardennes had started. Only ten tanks and six tank destroyers were operational. There were only 400 grenadiers in the lines. The various ground combat elements had suffered casualties of up to 80 percent of their authorized end strengths. Only the rear-area services had been spared somewhat. They were able to report an end strength of nearly 5,000 men. Some 30 halftracks and 200 trucks had been destroyed, primarily from the air.

Once again, the *PLD* had ceased to exist for all practical purposes. It was moved to the area south of Neuerburg to undergo a battlefield reconstitution. Once there, it received additional orders moving it towards Cologne, with the intent of holding up the Allied advance through the *Reichswald* in the direction of Kalkar and Goch–Üdem.

Montgomery was preparing his new offensive under the code name of Operation "Veritable." His forces were to move out along a line running Nijmegen–Kleve–Gennep–Kevelaer–Geldern. It was intended to overrun and eliminate the German forces arrayed along the near banks of the Lower

Rhine. Montgomery wanted to prevent the German forces from being able to pull back along the right bank of the Rhine between Rees and Wesel. The days preceding the offensive were filled with a suspicious silence.

The *PLD* reached its new area of operations on 6 February. Its *Panther* battalion was issued a full complement of tanks—sixty vehicles in all[8]—and the two mechanized infantry regiments were given considerable replacements. The next day, Bayerlein was surprised when he learned he would be transferred into the unassigned officer manpower pool in anticipation of assignment to a higher-level command. His successor was *Oberst* Horst Niemack (promoted to *Generalmajor* on 1 April 1945), a highly decorated armor officer in his own right.[9] On 24 March, Bayerlein became the commanding general of the *LIII. Armee-Korps*, which was also employed in the West and had three *Volks-Grenadier* divisions allocated to it. Bayerlein's corps was given the mission of defending the sector from Jülich to Düren against the anticipated Allied attack.

Early in the morning of 8 February, the German main line of resistance started to receive incoming artillery fire. The barrage had commenced at 0440 hours, signaling the start of the Allied offensive. The Allied gunners fired for twelve straight hours, employing more than 2,000 guns, which rained steel through the air. When the guns ceased their artillery preparation, they were followed by huge numbers of bombers, fighter-bombers and fighters over the German main line of resistance, raining bombs and rockets and strafing everything that moved. Once the initial preparation was completed, the Canadian First Army moved out between the Meuse and the Rhine. The British XXX Corps advanced through the Reichswald in the direction of Goch and, farther to the south, the U.S. Ninth Army advanced from Düren across the Rur. The U.S. field army was aiming its efforts in taking a section of the Rhine south of Wesel, between the mouth of the Lippe there and the ferry crossing at Voerde–Mehrum.

In order to hold out against the superior Allied numbers, the levees along the Rhine between Emmerich and Pannerden were opened up early on 8

---

8. More recent research indicates that the number of *Panthers* was in fact thirty. See Nevenkin, Kamen, *Fire Brigades: The Panzer Divisions, 1943–1945* (Manitoba: J.J. Fedorowicz Publishing, 2008).

9. Author's Note: Niemack was the 69th recipient of the Swords to the Oak Leaves to the Knight's Cross of the Iron Cross on 6 June 1944 for his actions in the fighting east of the Sareth on the Eastern Front while commanding *Panzer-Füsilier-Regiment "Großdeutschland"* of the *Panzergrenadier-Division* of the same name. He had received the first two levels of the Knight's Cross as the commander of *Aufklärungs-Abteilung 5*. It had been intended for Niemack to command *Panzer-Grenadier-Division "Großdeutschland,"* replacing von Manteuffel, but he was badly wounded in the Doblen area of operations and incapacitated for several months. He was a rising star in the German military, and he became a general officer at the age of thirty-five. After the war, he served in the *Bundeswehr*, where he also attained general officer rank.

February, when it was realized the offensive was taking place. As a result, the high waters of the Rhine flowed into the area of combat operations north of the Nijmegen Highway–Kleve–Kalkar on the west side of the river. For the next nine days, the Reichswald was transformed into the incarnation of hell on earth.

On 22 February, after the Allies had cleared the Reichswald, Operation "Blockbuster" was launched, with the intent of seeing British Commonwealth and U.S. forces link up as part of the master plan. It was here that elements of the *PLD* were employed against Horrocks's XXX Corps, which was rolling forward like a riptide, sweeping everything out of its way. Despite their best efforts, the soldiers of the *PLD* were unable to do more than slow down the materiel might of the Allies.

After the division was pulled back, it was given the mission of advancing to the south to link up with the divisions of Bayerlein's corps thrusting northward. The Germans wanted to pinch off the lead enemy armored elements, which had already reached Glehn.

The pincer movement was launched on 27 February, but the *PLD* bogged down on the first day of the attack. Bayerlein's corps met with better success advancing from the south, and it took Kapellen that morning. Towards noon, however, the advancing elements were engaged by Lightnings and Typhoons, with six tanks receiving direct hits. Others were immobilized by the bombs and rockets. Bayerlein's forces also came to a standstill. During the evening of 27 February, U.S. tanks slammed into the left flank of the corps and forced it back out of Kapellen.

The *PLD* was involved in defensive fighting outside of Schiefbahn. The Americans were able to reach the village and take it. If the Americans continued their rapid advance, most of the combat elements of the division—especially *PGLR 901* and *PGLR 902*—were in danger of being cut off. The only way out was to attack through Schiefbahn, which Niemack ordered. If the village were retaken, then enough time would be won to allow the mechanized infantry to disengage and move back.

The tanks of *PLR 130* and the tank destroyers of *PJLA 130* assembled and launched an attack. Mechanized infantry followed. Once again, *Unteroffizier* Job has provided a firsthand account of operations:

In Normandy, our crew had to bail out three times while under the command of the experienced *Oberfeldwebel* Erich Stolz. One tank [destroyer] was shot out from under us. The two others had to be abandoned in the Falaise Pocket, since they were extensively damaged. But we had always made it through and had also survived the Ardennes offensive and the Allied artillery barrage at Üdem.

We were alerted one evening towards the end of February 1945. We were directed to conduct an immediate counterattack to eject the American tanks from Schiefbahn, which were advancing in the direction of the Rhine. In addition to the 3rd Company of *PJLA 130*, there were also a few tanks from the tank regiment that attacked. Elements of the 1st, 2nd and 3rd Companies of the *PGLR 901* were likewise attached, as was a heavy platoon with heavy machine guns and mortars.

Oberfeldwebel Stolz, who had climbed aboard our *Jagdpanzer* again as its commander, followed closely behind the *Jagdpanzer* of the platoon leader.

When *Leutnant* Schönrath saw and heard the firing of the enemy tanks at the crossroads right outside of Schiefbahn, he had the platoon disperse to both sides of the road. We then identified the positions from which the enemy was firing. Machine-gun fired rattled among the roar of the main guns, and the mechanized infantry, which had mounted our *Jagdpanzer*, had to press themselves flat in order not to be swept off [the rear deck] by the incoming lead.

The four tanks of *PLR 130*, which were moving off to our right, started to fire. I could see the impacting rounds through my gun optics. Then I saw an enemy and lined him up in the sights. When another blinding flash shot out of the concealed position, I aimed a half a meter low and fired.

Bushes fluttered up in the air, and a Yank tank appeared under the disappearing camouflage. The second round ripped its turret off before it could even fire.

All of the tanks [and tank destroyers] were engaged at this point. The reports of guns firing and the sounds of rounds impacting could only be heard in a muffled manner within the steel walls of the fighting compartment. *Oberfeldwebel* Stolz continuously called out his observations and orders to us, so that Ömmes Krenstedt, our driver, who had already carted us around some 3,000 kilometers through Normandy and in the Ardennes, could traverse the vehicle, enabling me to acquire targets.

Thirty meters off to the right of us, an American main-gun round hammered into one of our tank destroyers. Although I could not identify anything through my sights, I indirectly saw the glimmer of the flames and knew that my comrade's tank destroyer had been set alight. For half a second, I contemplated the comrades who were there in the burning coffin. Had they been able to get out?

Then a heavy blow shook our vehicle. There was a crash. It seemed as though a round had penetrated.

"Jupp" Heller, our loader, almost dropped his round when our *Jagdpanzer* jerked backwards and then raced forward with a jolt.

Ömmes had immediately thrown the vehicle into gear and was trying to get the vehicle out of harm's way by flooring it out of there. As a result, the second round intended for us missed. It passed through the spot where we had been and struck a tree to the rear.

I fired at an identified enemy tank. All of the other tanks [and tank destroyers] were also firing. The night was cut by lances of flame. Sheets of flame blazed skyward. Tanks burned with thick columns of smoke. But our attack stalled in the face of the enemy's defensive fires. The enemy was firing with tanks and antitank guns in a broad semicircle around Schiefbahn. Our grenadiers were knocked off the tanks by machine-gun salvoes.

"How are we supposed to get through there?" Heller yelled, enraged.

"Don't get your tail feathers in a spin," Krenstedt replied.

Before Heller could respond, the acting company commander's voice came over the radio: "Assemble at Dora 12!"

We rolled back, and *Oberleutnant* Wagner told us that we were then going to attack from the southwest, along with a couple of *Panthers*. Mortars would be in support. At the same time, it was intended to penetrate into Schiefbahn from the east with another group.

We headed out. Everyone was informed they had ten rounds available for firing, which was a lot at that stage.

"If we attack first, then load like there's no tomorrow, Heller!" I told the loader when we had reached the attack position. Heller, who hailed from Augsburg, nodded. He understood his craft and knew that the speed of firing was dependent upon him. The guy who survived was the guy who fired quickly and was the quickest. We had learned that from nearly five years of fighting in almost all the countries of Europe.

We started hearing the firing from the eastern attack force echo through the night. Then there was machine-gun fire from the main body of grenadiers, who had taken up covered positions behind the tanks.

Leutnant Schönrath radioed everyone to get ready.

"Button up!"

Heller reported that the main gun and coaxial machine gun were ready for firing.

At that point, the only thing that could be heard was the muffled roar of main guns firing.

All of a sudden, Stolz called out: "Tanks!"

I quickly had the first one in my optics. It was black, outlined against the light background of the nighttime sky. It was rolling out of some vegetation barely fifty meters away. I fired, and a brilliant red flame filled the sights. I couldn't tell: Was the enemy tank burning or had we been the ones hit? But it was the enemy who had been lit up with the first round.

"Keep going . . . keep going!" Those were the orders we received. We advanced. The handful of mechanized infantry that had hitched a ride tried to make themselves small behind the fighting compartment, when we were sprayed with machine-gun fire and the bullets ricocheted off the armor. Muzzle flashes could be seen firing simultaneously on three sides through the night. The two *Panthers* from the regiment fired, soon joined by us. We fired with everything we had.

Leutnant Schönrath directed us. He then issued orders to move out. *Feldwebel* Dückert's *Jagdpanzer* eliminated one of the Yank tanks that had had lurched out towards us by surprise. We then saw another one. The first round I fired stopped it; the second round turned it into a burning torch at the side entryway into the village.

We reached Schiefbahn. The night turned raving mad. A tank pushed its way up next to us. We did not realize it, until it fired and its round grazed the side of our vehicle, hammering our ears.

Ömmes pivoted quickly in the direction of the threat. I traversed the gun as far as it would go in its relatively fixed position. The enemy got off an additional round and it missed as a result of our pivoting action. I acquired a sight picture and fired. The enemy tank was powerless against our round. The round bored into the enemy tank and exploded.

"Keep moving!"

All of the tank destroyers were firing. Schönrath ordered us to head for the middle of the village, where we set up a defensive perimeter around the marketplace.

An enemy tank destroyer pushed its way into the marketplace from a side street. It was soon joined by another four. Dückert's and Schönrath's vehicles fired at about the same time we did. Three flames lanced out into the darkness. Three hammer blows indicated that all of us had hit steel. Two sheets of flame rose skyward from two of the tank destroyers. The third one—it was the one we had engaged—rolled a bit forward, and I took up another sight picture. My round hit it between the turret and the hull, and ripped off the turret like a matchstick. The crew tried to dismount, but as it was doing so, the ready racks on the vehicles started exploding, soon taking the entire vehicle with it. The remaining enemy vehicles hurriedly withdrew.

A few German grenadiers arrived. Everything seemed somewhat surreal in the darkness and the flickering light from the flames of the burning tank destroyers. The mechanized infantry assaulted a house on the far side of the market place. Two enemy machine guns were firing from there.

Schönrath ordered us to take the basement under fire. We took up a sight picture and fired a high-explosive round. We advanced a bit and reached the far end of the marketplace, where we saw a bunch of enemy tanks approaching from the west. The armored fighting started anew. We knocked out two of the advancing tanks. Dückert accounted for another two, while Schönrath's crew got another one as it was turning to vacate the killing zone.

We then assembled at the western outskirts of Schiefbahn. We had driven the Yanks out and owned the village. That meant that our encircled comrades would then be able to pull back without interruption.

The grenadiers mopped up the rest of the village. One assault detachment took forty Americans in a basement prisoner. They had fought with bitter desperation, since they thought they would be relieved by an immediate counterattack on the part of their tanks. It took several hand grenades to convince them their hopes were not going to be realized.

While we were successful, we had also suffered heavy casualties. Two of Schönrath's *Jagdpanzer* had been knocked out in that nighttime duel.

In a division order-of-the-day on 2 March, the following account of the fighting to take Schiefbahn was given:

The companies are to be informed of the following acts of bravery from within the division:

While retaking Schiefbahn on 1 March 1945, *Unteroffizier* Eduard Job of the *3./PJLA 130* knocked out five enemy tanks in intense night fighting. It should be noted that Job has knocked out thirty-eight enemy tanks as a gunner on a tank destroyer.

Job, who was already a recipient of the German Cross in Gold, was entered into the Honor Roll of the German Army and received the Honor Roll Clasp, a rarely awarded decoration.

CHAPTER 13

To the Bitter End

The men of the *PLD* offered bitter resistance to Lieutenant General Horrocks's XXX Corps as they pulled back to the north from Schiefbahn in the direction of Xanten and in the Wesel bridgehead. Veen was the site of one of the last major tank engagements of the Second World War, and it was a fight that cost both sides heavily. In the end, however, the few German tanks had to yield to the overwhelming numerical superiority of the Allies.

Once again, *Unteroffizier* Job was in the thick of the fighting. The men of the antitank battalion had been committed outside of Rheinberg, the southern bulwark of the defenses around the Wesel bridgehead. Job provides the narrative:

> When we attempted to open fire on the attacking tanks, I was unable to traverse or elevate and depress my main gun any more. Something was jamming the traversing gears.
>
> "Get going . . . fire!" *Oberfeldwebel* Stolz cried out.
>
> If only I could! Instead, the enemy fired. Fortunately, the tank did not hit. The round screamed overhead and slammed into the ruins behind us.
>
> "Get going . . . fire . . . fire!" the gun commander called out again. "It's firing at us again!"
>
> I feverishly looked for what was wrong. Suddenly, I discovered an antitank round that had gotten stuck in the traversing mechanism. It was removed in a hurry. I was once again able to move the gun.
>
> After the second round, the enemy tank was in flames. The enemy's half-tracks, which were also rolling forward, raked our vehicle with their small-caliber weapons, causing it to clang and clatter all over our armor. They were knocked out with a few quick rounds.
>
> Once again, our company was involved in tough defensive fighting. We knew there wasn't much more that could be done, but our comrades were heading to the ferry at Rheinberg, which was still intact. We were screening their crossing over the Rhine.
>
> We were also wanting to head in the direction of Rheinberg and the ferry, when three American tanks that had broken through appeared in front of us. They apparently also wanted to get to the

ferry. We were the last tank destroyer [to move out]. We had to turn to stop the pursuing enemy. I saw one of the Yank tanks head directly towards us. At a distance of no more than forty meters, I slammed a round into the front hull. At that point, everything went quickly.

The tank continued moving ahead—not under control but, nonetheless, directly towards us. Before we could turn, before Ömmes Krenstedt could get the tank destroyer out of the collision course, the enemy tank smacked into our front slope. Our tank destroyer lurched backwards, throwing us against weapons and equipment. [Due to the force of the impact, the] Yank tank turned, moved at a right angle away from us and then collided with the wall of a house, which rained down upon it.

Oberfeldwebel Stolz immediately left his hatch and held the dismounting Americans in check, while the two other tanks were knocked out by our other comrades, who had immediately turned around after hearing the main-gun fire.

The delaying action to Rheinberg marked the end of combat actions for the *PLD* on the west bank of the Rhine. The individual battle groups crossed the river and regrouped on the far side. The main body of *PGLR 902*, for instance, was located in the Neviges–Heiligenhaus area on 7 March. It proved difficult to regroup as a division, and most of the elements fought on their own. *Hauptfeldwebel* Wollensen, who had previously been assigned with the infantry gun platoon of the heavy company of *PGLR 901*, recounts his experiences after being reassigned to the 1st Battalion of the regiment:

On 26 March, we were alerted and immediately headed in the direction of Striefen (Sieg province). We were directed to establish a blocking position there to stop the enemy attacking from the Remagen area.

Intense fighting followed, and one of my best men, who had survived the entire war without incident up to that point, was killed. The fighting for Striefen lasted until the morning of 27 March. Striefen was set ablaze, and the pressure of the enemy grew stronger by the hour. The 1st Battalion of *PGLR 901* slowly pulled back through Adscheid and Katzwinkel in the direction of Niedersorge. We were able to catch our breath there for a short while.

But the Americans soon attacked with fresh units. The enemy advanced so rapidly with his tanks and mechanized forces into our provisional positions that the self-propelled infantry-gun platoon, which was with the 4th Company, could not change position in time and all of the men were taken prisoner.

My company was positioned on the high ground at Wormbach and was able to hold that position through all of 3 April. The attacking enemy forces were tossed back again and again and sustained heavy casualties. But the pressure grew too intense there, as well, and we slowly pulled back to Altenhundem (Sauerland). We were relieved there and immediately headed for Neuenrade, where we were to be committed again. We were not afforded any days of rest.

It was quite a sight along the road to Neuenrade. Units were marching in every direction. Among them were a few "lone wolves," who were rounded up by the military police and were integrated into larger groups. We were also "fortunate" in receiving one such platoon. That evening, I directed the [straggler] platoon into position. When it dawned the next day, it had completely disappeared without a trace. But we didn't shed any tears at its departure. You couldn't depend on a bunch like that. It was different with the men of our division. They held their positions until they were told to pull back.

At 1800 hours on 4 April, we discussed operations at the battalion's headquarters in Neuenrade. In the middle of the briefing, there was heavy artillery firing, followed a short while later by a large armored attack. We ran to our companies and tried to get out of Neuenrade. There were explosions everywhere. The enemy had occupied the high ground around the city. We were sitting in a trap.

Despite that, some were able to sneak out individually. Most remained. My company, all of forty-six rifles strong, gradually assembled in a house at the outskirts of the city. Our *Hiwi*, our brave and terrific Odilawadse, was given civilian clothes and sent into the city to see what was happening.[1] Two hours later, he came back and reported that Neuenrade was full of enemy tanks and that most of the 1st Battalion of *PGLR 901* had already been taken prisoner.

The night passed quietly. Nothing stirred in our area. We then disengaged from the enemy.

During the night of 12–13 April 1945, we were moving in three small groups in order to find a weak point to infiltrate through the enemy. In the process, we lost *Obergefreiter* Weninger. That did it for

---

1. Translator's Note: *Hilfsfreiwilliger*. These "volunteer auxiliaries" were Soviets who had been captured by the Germans and chose to remain in service with the German Army. They generally performed duties in the rear area or the trains so that more soldiers could be released for combat duties. At the end of the war, most German formations took extraordinary measures to ensure their *Hiwis* did not fall into Soviet hands, which generally meant immediate execution.

me; I knew everything was lost at that point. I had the machine-gun posts pulled in and all of the weapons destroyed. No more spilling of blood—that was the only thing I could do for the men assigned to me, who had held out to the very end. Then the end came.

At 0715 hours on 13 April 1945, we were surrounded by heavily armed Americans and had to and drop our equipment. The march into captivity started which, fortunately, only lasted a few months for everyone. We were taken to Sinzig.

The treatment at the camp was bad. The rations were even worse. We vegetated out in the open until wc wcrc finally released.

One more word about the men. They also showed their best side in captivity. Comradeship was not just a word on a piece of paper for us. They all maintained astounding discipline up to the last day. I was proud of these eighteen-year-olds, for whom I had the privilege of helping and leading in difficult times.

Just like *PGLR 901*, the other regiments and divisional troops of the *PLD* were alerted on 22 March and committed in the Ruhr Pocket in an effort to ward off the expected Allied attack north of the Ruhr. Desperate attacks were launched in an effort to break out, but the sheer numbers of the Allied forces made such efforts fruitless. Niemack was badly wounded in the fighting and flown out of the pocket on orders of *Generalfeldmarschall* Model, the Commander in Chief of the trapped forces of *Heeresgruppe B*. Niemack was replaced in command by *Oberst* Paul von Hauser, who had commanded *PGLR 901*.

The division was forced back through Medebach, Rhadern and Hillershausen. Soon most of the remaining *Flak* defenses of the division were gone. To the west of Alt-Stenberg, many of the tanks of *PLR 130* were destroyed or immobilized from the air. During the night of 1–2 April, the division was pulled back to Winterberg.

On 4 April and again on 5 April, the division was attacked by U.S. forces north of Winterberg. There was heavy fighting in the area around the *Kahle Aste*—the highest hilltop in the Sauerland, with a peak measuring 841 meters—and Silbach. The main burden of the fighting was borne by the grenadiers of *PGLR 902*, with *Oberstleutnant Ritter* von Poschinger falling at the head of his regiment. He was joined in death by *Oberleutnant* Rasmus, the commander of the 4th Company of the regiment, with his company being savagely battered in the fighting.

Succeeding von Poschinger in command on the battlefield was *Hauptmann* Klein. He led the regiment back through Altena and Hemer to Iserlohn, where he and his men were taken prisoner on 15 April. Klein had been the sixth commander of the regiment in the course of the fighting since June 1944.

The last few armored vehicles hid in the woods of the Sauerland region after 5 April. They watched as columns of American tanks and vehicles streamed past on the roads. The men were no longer capable of offering any effective resistance against the vast numerical superiority. What had once been the best-equipped armored division of the German Army had been reduced to a total of twenty tanks and tank destroyers and ten tracked vehicles. On 9 April, Werl was lost. Two days later, the Allies reached Dortmund.

The pocket grew ever smaller around the division. On 15 April, the main body of the division surrendered. By then, it had only 2,460 men, eight tanks and self-propelled guns, fifty other types of armored vehicles and one operational battery. Not far away from the area where the main body surrendered was *Oberfeldwebel* Stolz and his *Jagdpanzer*. Once the news of the surrender reached the crew, they dismounted their vehicle, which had been a faithful servant to them for more than 3,000 kilometers, and blew it up. They then marched into captivity.

Several small groups of the division managed to avoid captivity in the Ruhr Pocket. Two have been identified and a fair amount is known about them, with both coming from the 2nd Battalion of *PLR 130*.

The first group comprised 131 tankers of the battalion. Their account has been provided by *Dr.-Ing.* Wilhelm Cursiefen, who was the battalion engineer at the end of the war:

> We reached Bayrischzell with 131 men after a real odyssey that led through Wittenberge, Dresden, Regensburg, Munich and Miesbach. We went into a side valley towards Kufstein, which ended at Zipfelwirt.
>
> After Regensburg, I was the senior officer and was responsible for those 131 men. We still had forty vehicles, including the heavy machine vehicle, a three-axled monster, which had helped us a great deal in the past. The vehicle had to be left behind in Miesbach with a broken differential.
>
> That bunch of 131 men maintained the best of discipline until the very end. On 5 May, we held a council of war: *Leutnant* Mann,

our staff administrative official, all of the senior noncommissioned officers and me.

Any further combat operations would have been crazy. I had all of the remaining money distributed as pay and after we had talked to all of the men, we decided that *Leutnant* Mann and I would attempt contact with the Americans the next day. We put on our black *Panzer* uniforms and discarded our camouflage outfits.

We took off during the afternoon of 7 May. A *Feldwebel* drove us in the *Volkswagen* as far as the last curve before reaching Bayrischzell. At the entrance to the road was an American tank. We—*Leutnant* Mann and I—dismounted and marched towards the tank. When we reached it, we had to remove our pistols and, after a while, a jeep appeared, which took us to Schliersee. It was there that an American major accepted the surrender of our 131 men.

The next morning, we went back to our guys in a three-quarter-ton truck. Just before getting there, the Americans had us dismount. They didn't quite trust us. So we had to move ahead of them. We reached our men. We had our last breakfast as free men. Then we told them to form up. We reminded them to keep calm and stay together.

All of the men put on their awards, even those they normally kept in their pockets. It was something that went without saying. Then we marched off—for the first time since 6 June 1944, without worrying about the air.

In Bayrischzell, we had an "overwhelming" reception. We were guided by heavily armed jeeps. Pulled up in front of the railway station. *Hauptfeldwebel* Trenczek had the men dismount and form up. Our *Hauptfeldwebel* was a man the likes of which you seldom encountered. The American major received our report.

We surrendered our weapons. We went on to Kufstein, where we wound up in a large yard. The "God-damned *Panzer-Lehr*" was shown to one spot on the lawn.

The next day, we continued on to Rosenheim. One hundred men to a lowboy. At the camp in Rosenheim, we were subjected to nightly shakedowns with an eye towards any items of value.

We then continued on in the direction of Heilbronn. There was gunfire in the camp. Blood was spilled for a little bit of drinking water, which was rarer than something to eat.

We then went on to Mannheim from Heilbronn, which we were only to happy to leave, even if the new objective was uncertain. I was separated from my men there. I only saw a few of them again after that. The fate of many of them is forever cloaked in secrecy. They had survived the war perhaps only to perhaps perish somewhere else.

In conclusion, I only wish to state one other thing: The men, no matter what rank they wore, remained loyal to one another in the best of comradeship and maintained exemplary discipline and a sense of duty to the very end. Things that you just couldn't quite take for granted anymore, as you can well imagine. We were the last men of the *PLD*, a division that had been in combat in all of the major fighting from the start of the invasion until the end of the war and had been bled white more than once.

The second group of men was outfitted with the *Jagdpanther* at the factory and actually saw one more combat engagement before the end of the war, separate from the division. That group's exploits have been compiled by Martin Block, a modern researcher:[2]

Late in March 1945, the remaining tanks of *PLR 130* were concentrated into the 1st Battalion. The tankless crews and supply elements of the 2nd Battalion under *Hauptmann* von Schlippenbach just managed escape the closing "Ruhr-Pocket" and moved to the Armor School at Bergen, where they arrived on 4 April 1945.

The acting school commander, *Oberst* Grosan, wanted to incorporate the men into his local *Kampfgruppe*, comprised of various elements based at the school. But then a telephone call from a high-ranking *Panzer* officer in Berlin stated that *Hauptmann* von Schlippenbach and his unit were to be issued some thirty brand-new *Jagdpanther* at MIAG in Braunschweig. Following that, the 2nd Battalion of *PLR 130* was not to return to *Kampfgruppe Grosan*. Instead, it was to report to Military District XI in Hanover.

5 and 6 April 1945
Hauptmann von Schlippenbach reported to the military district commander, *General* Lichen, in Hanover to receive his orders. Meanwhile, the men of the battalion went directly to Braunschweig, where they picked up thirty-five *Jagdpanther*.

---

2. Translator's Note: Extracted and edited from a posting by Martin Block on Missing-Lynx.com (www.network54.com/Forum/47207/thread/1241644888/Jagdpanther+823), accessed on 4 April 2011.

7 April 1945

During the day, the men of the battalion familiarized themselves with the new vehicles and prepared them for combat. Fuel and ammunition were acquired and the 8.8-centimeter main guns calibrated. The 5th through 8th Companies received eight *Jagdpanther* apiece, while the headquarters company received three.

Von Schlippenbach had some conversations with the local area commander for Braunschweig, *General* Veit, and other officers. These conversations left von Schlippenbach with the impression that the continuation of war, at least against the Western Allies, was senseless.

At dusk, the battalion left Braunschweig and moved westward about thirty-five kilometers on the *Autobahn*. In the area of Edemissen–Haemelerwald–Burgdorf, the battalion formed a screening line facing west to southwest, with the 5th Company on the right and the 8th Company on the left. It remained idle in those positions for several days.

11 April 1945

The battalion engaged in its first and only combat action against U.S. forces on this date. The U.S. 11th Cavalry Regiment pushed eastward from Burgdorf, and thus made contact with the *Jagdpanther* on the left flank of the battalion. Details about this action are scarce, but what is known is that von Schlippenbach's *Jagdpanther* was knocked out. Von Schlippenbach was either wounded or suffered from shock, and *Oberleutnant* von Falkenhayn had to take over command.

In the afternoon, two *Jagdpanther* under *Feldwebel* Dette knocked out two U.S. tanks and secured the bridge over the Oker River in Meinersen. While changing positions, the steering system on Dette's *Jagdpanther* failed. It remained stationary in the middle of the road and was shot-up and set on fire by a U.S. fighter-bomber shortly afterward. In addition, several trucks also went up in flames as a result of more violent U.S. fighter-bomber attacks.

Additional combat took place on the extreme left flank of the battalion near Edemissen. There, two *Jagdpanther* stopped an assault by Combat Command R of the U.S. 5th Armored Division for about two hours. They claimed the destruction of at least three U.S. tanks. Numerical superiority finally forced the *Jagdpanther* to pull back.

Near the village of Abbensen, a *Jagdpanther* platoon under *Feldwebel* Feuerpfeil had a brief meeting with members of *SS-Kampfgruppe Wiking* before noon. *Feldwebel* Feuerpfeil adamantly refused to accompany the battle group as its commander had demanded, and after a heated exchange of words, the *SS* force moved on into in the direction of Uetze.

In the evening, *Oberleutnant* von Falkenhayn held a briefing with all the remaining *Jagdpanther* commanders. It appeared to many of the men that the war was lost and to continue fighting was senseless. Von Falkenhayn allowed his men to destroy their *Jagdpanther* and to split up in order to make for home. Some of the crews were still willing to continue the fight, while others were happy at the prospect that they would come out of the war in one piece.

One of those willing to continue fighting, a *Leutnant*, assembled nine *Jagdpanther*. His plan was to move east until he reestablished contact with friendly forces. All of the others made their *Jagdpanther* unusable and tried to avoid capture.

12 April 1945

In the morning, the *Leutnant* and his remaining nine *Jagdpanther* arrived at Wendesberg, about seven kilometers northwest of Braunschweig, where they quickly realized that they were in a dead-end. All of the bridges to the south over the Weser–Elbe Canal had already been destroyed. In the north, on the *Autobahn*, endless columns of U.S. forces could be seen moving. To the east, there was only a small bridge over the Oker River left, too weak to carry the heavy weight of a *Jagdpanther*. The *Leutnant* finally ordered his crews to destroy their *Jagdpanther* and split up.

The 2nd Battalion of *PLR 130* had ceased to exist as a combat formation.

Let us conclude our narrative with some final comments by the man who is most closely associated with the division, *Generalleutnant* Bayerlein:

Without the oppressive superiority of the Allied air forces, the invasion would have never met with success. Although a landing in Normandy under the collective protection of the assembled naval artillery would have succeeded against the local defense, it would have taken no more than four days before the German armored divisions advancing from their assembly areas had pushed the Allies back into the sea.

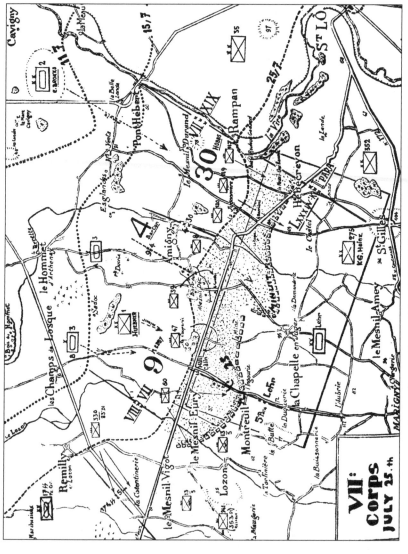

Area of operations of the U.S. VII Corps on 15 July 1944.

Rank Comparisons

U.S. ARMY	BRITISH ARMY	GERMAN ARMY
Enlisted Men		
Private	Private	*Schütze*
Private First Class	Private 1st Class	*Oberschütze*
Corporal	Lance Corporal	*Gefreiter*
Senior Corporal	Corporal	*Obergefreiter*
Staff Corporal		*Stabsgefreiter*
Noncommissioned Officers		
Sergeant	Sergeant	*Unteroffizier*
	Staff Sergeant	*Unterfeldwebel*
Staff Sergeant	Technical Sergeant	*Feldwebel*
Sergeant First Class	Master Sergeant	*Oberfeldwebel*
Master Sergeant	Sergeant Major	*Hauptfeldwebel*
Sergeant Major		*Stabsfeldwebel*
Officers		
Second Lieutenant	Second Lieutenant	*Leutnant*
First Lieutenant	First Lieutenant	*Oberleutnant*
Captain	Captain	*Hauptman*
Major	Major	*Major*
Lieutenant Colonel	Lieutenant Colonel	*Oberst Leutnant*
Colonel	Colonel	*Oberst*
Brigadier General	Brigadier General	*Generalmajor*
Major General	Major General	*Generalleutnant*
Lieutenant General	Lieutenant General	*General der Fallschirmjäger, etc.*
General	General	*Generaloberst*
General of the Army	Field Marshal	*Feldmarschall*

APPENDIX B

Selected Knight's Cross Recipients of the Division

Generalleutnant Fritz Bayerlein

Fritz Bayerlein was born on 14 January 1899 in Würzburg. After completing secondary school, he entered military service in the *2. Jäger-Bataillon Aschaffenburg* on 5 June 1917. After the end of the Great War, he was accepted into the *Reichswehr*, where he was promoted to *Leutnant* on 1 January 1922.

He was accepted as a general-staff officer and soon started a series of assignments typical for that career field. As a *Hauptmann*, he served on the staff of the *15. Infanterie-Division*. He was promoted to *Major* on 31 May 1938, where he served with the *XV. Armee-Korps*. On 1 April 1939, Bayerlein became *Generalleutnant* Schaal's operations officer in the *10. Panzer-Division*, which was in the process of being formed. He served in that capacity in both Poland and France. In recognition of his superior work, he was promoted to *Oberstleutnant* on 1 September 1940. *Generaloberst* Guderian requested the services of the gifted officer on his headquarters staff. Together with Guderian, Bayerlein participated in the armored thrusts and raids far into the Soviet Union. Bayerlein was then picked to become *Generaloberst* Rommel's Chief of Staff for the *Deutsches Afrika-Korps* in North Africa.

Bayerlein formed a close bond with Rommel. Following the fighting at Sidi Rezegh, he was awarded the Knight's Cross to the Iron Cross on 26 December 1941.

On 1 April 1942, Bayerlein was promoted to *Oberst*. He later became the Chief of Staff for *Panzergruppe Afrika*, when the original *DAK* was expanded beyond a corps. In that capacity, he frequently assumed acting command of the fighting forces in North Africa. When *General Ritter* von Thoma was captured by the British at El Alamein, Bayerlein assumed command of the *DAK* and led it on its long retreat to Tunisia.

When General Messe assumed command of *Panzerarmee Afrika* at the Mareth Position in February 1943, Rommel insisted that Bayerlein become the Italian general's chief of staff. Thanks to Bayerlein, the German-Italian force was eventually able to extract itself from the dangerous position at Mareth. As a result, Bayerlein later received the Oak Leaves to the Knight's Cross to the Iron Cross on 6 July 1943.

In March 1943, he was promoted to *Generalmajor*. He was flown out of Africa before the capitulation of the Axis forces there in May. He commanded the *3. Panzer-Division* from 3 October 1943. Shortly after his forty-fifth birthday, Bayerlein was entrusted with command of the newly forming *PLD* on 10 January 1944. Guderian had recommended his appointment to that position. His exploits and accomplishments as division commander are detailed in the main body of the text.

Fritz Bayerlein passed away on 30 January 1970 in his native city of Würzburg.

Generalmajor Horst Niemack

Horst Niemack was born the son of a businessman in Hanover on 10 March 1909. As a child, he was already riding horses, a passion that was nurtured by his maternal grandfather, who was a well-known veterinarian and horse fancier.

After receiving his college-preparatory diploma in April 1927, Niemack entered the *Reichswehr* as an officer candidate. Four years later, he was commissioned a *Leutnant* in *Reiter-Regiment 18* in Bad Cannstadt (Stuttgart). The regiment had been formed in 1919 from a long lineage of famous cavalry regiments dating back through imperial times.

Between 1930 and 1939, Niemack participated in most of the large horse tournaments in Germany. By 1934, he had been awarded the German Horseman Award in Gold. In 1936, he was an instructor at the cavalry school, where he worked with cavalry and artillery officers attending courses there. Two years later, he was promoted to *Rittmeister* (*Hauptmann*) and placed in charge of the hunting stables at the school.

In October 1939, Niemack was assigned to *Aufklärungs-Abteilung 5* of the *5. Infanterie-Division* as a troop commander. In April 1940, he was given command of the battalion. He distinguished himself in the campaign in the West in 1940, where his battalion formed the nucleus of the division's advance guard. He was among the first across the Meuse, and his forces raced ahead through enemy resistance across the Aisne and as far as the Marne. He led from the front and was personally credited with knocking out enemy vehicles.

Along the Marne, Niemack's battalion was credited with cutting off the retreat for large enemy elements. Acting on his own initiative, Niemack advanced on the Marne at Damery, a decision that ultimately saw him awarded the Knight's Cross to the Iron Cross on 13 July, the only *Rittmeister* in the German Army to be so honored during the 1940 fighting in France.

At the start of the campaign in the East, the *5. Infanterie-Division* was in the vicinity of the Lithuanian border. On 22 June 1941, Niemack's battalion forced a crossing over the Memel. Niemack's forces then blocked the retreat route for a Soviet corps and held a sector ten kilometers in width for three days, thus sealing the pocket at Bialystok. On 10 August 1941, Niemack became the thirtieth individual of the German Armed Forces to be honored with the Oak Leaves to the Knight's Cross to the Iron Cross.

Badly wounded in the fighting, Niemack was sent to Germany for convalescence. He was promoted to *Major* and assigned to the Cavalry Instructor Group at the School for Mobile Forces in Potsdam (Krampnitz). In February 1943, after being promoted to *Oberstleutnant*, he was assigned command of *Panzergrenadier-Regiment 26* of the *24. Panzer-Division*, which was being reconstituted after most of it had been wiped out at Stalingrad. Niemack was reassigned from that command before the division was recommitted to combat operations. On 15 October of the same year, Niemack received command of *Panzer-Füsilier-Regiment "Großdeutschland"* of *Panzer-Grenadier-Division "Großdeutschland."* He successfully commanded that regiment until he was badly wounded on 24 August 1944. Up to that point, his name was associated with the intense fighting around Kriwoj Rog, Ljubimowka, Targul Frumos, Wilkowischken, Schaulen and Doblen. It was for the fighting in Rumania at Targul Frumos—a largely unknown but hugely successful tactical operation on the part of von Manteuffel's *"Großdeutschland"*—that Niemack later received his Swords to the Oak Leaves to the Knight's Cross to the Iron Cross (sixty-ninth recipient on 4 June 1944).

On 7 February 1945, Niemack assumed command of the *PLD*, and his leadership of the division is examined in the main body of the book. Although he was flown out of the Ruhr Pocket on the express orders of *Generalfeldmarschall* Model after being wounded, he was eventually taken prisoner by the British at the military hospital in Eutin.

After the war, Niemack resumed his interest in equestrian activities. He also entered the *Bundeswehr*, where he rose to the rank of reserve *Brigade-General.* He passed away at Groß Hehlen (Celle) on 7 April 1992.

Oberst **Rudolf Gerhardt**

Rudolf Gerhardt was born in Greiz (Thuringia) on 26 March 1896. After receiving his college preparatory diploma, he entered military service with the *Thüringisches Infanterie-Regiment Nr. 96* on 7 August 1914. By 24 September of the same year, he was on active duty with his regiment in southern Poland. In November, he became an *Unteroffizier*, and he received the Iron Cross,

Second Class, the following month, as well as being wounded for the first time on 26 November 1914.

On 22 March 1915, Gerhardt was commissioned a *Leutnant*. He was wounded for the second time on 11 August 1915 and was sent back to a military hospital in Germany. After convalescing, he attended a three-month course in Erfurt. In March 1916, he was reassigned to another infantry regiment and sent to the Western Front.

As an acting company commander, he fought at Fort Douaumont and, in the fall of 1916, at the Battle of the Somme. On 13 October, he was wounded for the third time. He was again returned to Germany to convalesce, and he received the Iron Cross, First Class, on 15 October.

On 2 January 1917, Gerhardt returned to his old regiment, which had also been sent to the Western Front. After recovering, he returned to the regiment, becoming the battalion adjutant on 20 August 1918. Wounded a fourth time in 2 September 1918, he again had to be evacuated. That was followed by a short tour as a liaison officer, followed then by duties as regimental adjutant. He remained in the *Reichswehr* for a short time after the war ended, leaving active service on 31 July 1919.

In October 1934, Gerhardt returned to active service as a *Hauptmann*. He was assigned to the *Kraftfahr-Lehr-Kommando* in Zossen, which served as a cover for the development of the fledgling *Panzertruppe*. In October 1935, he was assigned to *Panzer-Regiment 1* of the *1. Panzer-Division* in Erfurt, where he became a company commander in October 1935. A year later, his company formed the cadre to assist in the formation of *Panzer-Regiment 7* in Ohrdruf (Thuringia). In April 1938, that regiment moved to Vaihingen (Stuttgart).

On 1 January 1939, Gerhardt was promoted to *Major*. He was given command of *Panzer-Abteilung 66* in Eisenach and took it into combat in Poland in September. He was wounded there, on 8 September 1939, for the fifth time, qualifying him for the Wound Badge in Gold. He also received the 1939 Clasp to both of his Iron Crosses. On 28 October, he returned to *Panzer-Regiment 7*, where he assumed command of one of the battalions, which he commanded during the campaign in the West and then during *Operation "Barbarossa."* By 22 September of that year, he had been awarded the Knight's Cross to the Iron Cross for his leadership in combat. Two months later, on 12 November, he assumed acting command of the regiment.

On 1 January 1942, he was promoted to *Oberstleutnant* and on 18 December 1942 to *Oberst*. The division returned to France a short while later for reconstitution. It was intended to send it to the Caucasus. Instead, it was sent to Italy and then on to Tunisia. During the crossing, the regiment suffered large losses in materiel. It was an uphill battle in Tunisia, fighting against an enemy who commanded the skies and who possessed overwhelming numbers. On 23 April, Gerhardt was wounded for the sixth time and had to be evacuated to Germany.

After convalescing, Gerhardt was assigned to *Generalfeldmarschall* Kesselring's headquarters in Rome, where he served as the senior weapons officer. In November 1943, he was sent back to Fallingbostel in Germany to assume command of the *Panzer-Lehr-Regiment*. He led the regiment until January 1945, when he was reassigned to attend a course for future general officers. On 20 March 1945, he was acting commander of *26. Panzer-Division*. He was captured by the Americans on 6 May 1945. He passed away in Münster (Westphalia) on 10 November 1964.

Generalmajor Georg Scholze

Georg Scholze, the son of a large landholder, was born on 21 August 1897 in Löbau in Saxony. He served in the Great War as a *Leutnant*, where he earned both classes of the Iron Cross serving as a platoon leader and battalion adjutant. At the end of the war, he left active military service with the rank of *Oberleutnant*. He then resumed his schooling, which had been interrupted, and received his college-preparatory degree. He worked in agriculture until 1923, when he transferred to the *Reichswehr* as a civilian responsible for border affairs. He married in 1926 and fathered five children.

He was recalled to active duty in 1935, where he served as a *Hauptmann* and company commander in *Infanterie-Regiment Potsdam*, which later became *Infanterie-Regiment 9*. Promoted to *Major* on 1 January 1937, he was assigned to the headquarters of the *III. Armee-Korps*, serving as an adjutant for personnel affairs.

In 1938, he assumed acting command of the 2nd Battalion of the *Infanterie-Lehr-Regiment* at the infantry school at Döberitz-Elzgrund in facilities originally built for the 1936 Olympics.

The school battalion, which consisted of highly qualified instructor personnel drawn from infantry regiments all over Germany, participated in the campaign in the West. The entire regiment, re-designated as *Infanterie-Regiment 900*, under the command of *Oberstleutnant* Müller-Bülow, then fought in the Soviet Union at Olita and Kalinin. It was in the East that Scholze, who had been promoted to *Oberstleutnant* on 1 June 1940, received the 1939 Clasps to his Great War Iron Crosses.

The regiment returned to its home garrison after the winter fighting of 1941–42. Once there, the regiment was reorganized and redesignated as *Lehr-Regiment (mot) 901* and Scholze, by then an *Oberst*, assumed command. In December 1942, the regiment was again dispatched to the Eastern Front, where it was committed near Starobjelsk under the operational control of the *19. Panzer-Division*. The regiment acquitted itself well, and Scholze was awarded the Knight's Cross on 26 February 1943. The regiment received two separate mentions in armed forces daily reports.

The regiment was sent back to Germany for reconstitution and then sent to Dalmatia to conduct antipartisan operations. In December 1943, the regiment returned to Germany, where it was integrated into the newly forming *PLD*. Scholze participated in the initial round of fighting of the regiment in Normandy, but he was reassigned in July, relinquishing command to *Oberst* Paul von Hauser.

Initially, he served on the military mission to Rumania. In January 1945, he assumed command of the *20. Panzergrenadier-Division*. On 14 April, his wife and four of his children were killed in a bombing raid on Potsdam; only a son survived the war. On 20 April 1945, he was promoted to *Generalmajor*, with an official date-of-rank listed as 1 February 1945. On 23 April 1945, Scholze committed suicide, after elements of his division were encircled around Berlin.

Hauptmann Karl Philipps

Karl Philipps was born the second of five sons to a Protestant minister on 8 May 1920 at Höxter (Weser). He attended school in the Spandau section of Berlin, where he completed his college preparatory studies in 1938. Following that, he performed his six months of compulsory labor service and then entered the military on 1 October 1938, being assigned to *Schützen-Regiment 3* of the *3. Panzer-Division* in Eberswalde.

In 1939, he was nominated to become an officer candidate and saw service in Poland in that capacity. As a squad leader, he was awarded the Iron Cross Second Class.

Following the campaign in Poland, Philipps attended officer-candidate school in Wünsdorf. Upon completion, he was commissioned a *Leutnant*. He participated in the campaign in the West as a platoon leader in the 2nd Battalion of the *Panzer-Lehr-Regiment*, but he was badly wounded and had to be medically evacuated to Germany. He returned to his battalion after convalescence. By then, the battalion had been integrated into *Lehr-Brigade 900*, and Philipps was designated a rifle platoon leader, participating in the drive on Kalinin and the subsequent hard winter fighting. It was during that period that Philipps was presented with the Iron Cross, First Class. He was later assigned liaison officer duties and then became the brigade adjutant.

Philipps was promoted to *Oberleutnant* and went with his commander, *Oberst* Scholze, back into the Soviet Union. He assumed acting command of the 5th Company of the *Panzergrenadier-Lehr-Regiment* and saw lots of tough fighting around Starobjelsk. Philipps received a glowing evaluation report and was also awarded the German Cross in Gold.

In the fall of 1943, Philipps went with his regiment to the Balkans, where it was primarily engaged in antipartisan warfare against Tito's forces. In tough fighting around Banja Luka, *Kampfgruppe Philipps* particularly distinguished itself, and the young officer was awarded the Knight's Cross on 7 April 1944.

Phillips is mentioned frequently in the text with regard to his actions while assigned to the *PLD*. It should be mentioned again, however, that Philipps received the Army Honor Roll Clasp for his actions around Tilly.

In the course of a counterattack on 11 July 1944, Philipps was captured by the enemy. He was sent to an officers camp in the United States and later became the camp adjutant. Returning home after the war, Philipps completed his studies and became a minister. He served a mining community in the Ruhr area and later became the superintendent of the church district of Gladbeck-Bottrop. He passed away in Gladbeck on 5 May 1982.

APPENDIX C

Other Knight's Cross Recipients Assigned to the *Panzer-Lehr-Division*

Major Joachim Barth
Knight's Cross as a *Hauptmann*, on 17 December 1942 while assigned as the commander of *Panzerjäger-Abteilung 13* (*13. Panzer-Division*).[1]

Major Gert von Born-Fallois
Knight's Cross on 2 January 1945 while assigned as the commander of *PALA 130*.

Major Walter Brandt
Knight's Cross on 18 July 1944 as commander of *PPLB 130*.

Feldwebel Rudolf Brasche
Knight's Cross on 9 November 1942 as an *Obergefreiter*, while assigned as a squad leader in the 4th Company of *Panzergrenadier-Regiment 93* (*13. Panzer-Division*).

Oberst Joachim Gutmann
Knight's Cross on 18 September 1942 as an *Oberstleutnant*. while assigned as the commander of *Panzergrenadier-Regiment 11* (*9. Panzer-Division*).

Oberst Paul *Freiherr* von Hauser
Knight's Cross on 25 January 1943 as a *Hauptmann*, while assigned as the commander of *Kradschützen-Bataillon 61* (*11. Panzer-Division*). Oak Leaves as an *Oberstleutnant* and commander of *Panzergrenadier Lehr Regiment 901* on 28 October 1944.

---

1. Translator's Note: All of the dates given for the receipt of the Knight's Cross stem from Veit Scherzer's book on Knight's Cross recipients, which represents the latest and most thorough exploration of the topic in print. Veit Scherzer, *Die Ritterkreuzträger, Die Inhaber des Ritterkreuzes des Eisernen Kreuzes 1939–1945* (Ranis/Jena: Scherzers Militaire-Verlag, 2005). Kurowski's dates are based on information contained in the von Seemen book, which was the only one available at the time and filled with numerous mistakes.

Major Joachim *Ritter* von Poschinger

Knight's Cross on 25 January 1945 while assigned as acting commander of *PGLR 902*. Final rank, *Oberstleutnant*.

Oberstleutnant (posthumous) *Prinz* Wilhelm von Schönburg-Waldenburg

Knight's Cross on 18 May 1941 as a *Hauptmann*, while assigned as the commander of the 1st Company of *Panzer-Regiment 31* (*5. Panzer-Division*).

Stabsarzt Dr. Hans-Joachim Schulz-Merkel

Knight's Cross on 23 December 1943 while assigned as the battalion surgeon of the 1st Battalion of *Panzer-Regiment 35* (*4. Panzer-Division*). Final rank, *Oberstabartz*.

Major Konrad Uthe

Knight's Cross on 12 August 1944 (posthumous) as the commander of *PGLR 901*. Final rank, *Oberstleutnant* (posthumous).

Oberstleutnant (posthumous) Willi Welsch

Knight's Cross as a *Hauptmann*, on 29 September 1941 while assigned as the commander of the 2nd Company of *Schützen-Regiment 110* (*11. Panzer-Division*).

APPENDIX D

Division Manning Charts and Rosters

Headquarters

Division Commanders: *Generalleutnant* Fritz Bayerlein, *Generalmajor* Horst Niemack, *Oberst* Paul von Hauser (acting commander)

Operations Officer: *Oberstleutnant i.G.* Kurt Kauffmann

Logistics Officer: *Major i.G.* Berend Werncke

Division Adjutant: *Hauptmann* Otto Kuhnow

Liaison Officer: *Hauptmann* Alexander Hartdegen

Assistant Operations Officers: *Hauptmann Freiherr* von Funck, *Hauptmann* Anselm Hübner

Assistant Logistics Officer: *Oberleutnant d.R.* Christian von Hesse

Rations Trains: *Hauptmann* Rudolf Matthey

Baggage Trains: *Oberleutnant* August Plür

Quartermaster: *Oberleutnant d.R.* Walter Dahm

Division Ammunition Officer: *Oberleutnant* Armin Bez

Technical Specialist: Kurt Balko

Weaponry Specialist: Otto Preuß

Paymasters: *Stabszahlmeister* Erich Kalass, *Oberzahlmeister* Hermann Brauer, *Oberzahlmeister* Erich Geppert and *Oberzahlmeister* Wilhelm Zöllmer

Division Surgeon: *Dr.* Wolfgang Schmidt

Assistant Division Surgeon: *Dr.* Wilhelm Heinemann

Division Judge: *Kriegsgerichtsrat Dr.* Ludwig Schwarzmann

Foreign Intelligence Technician: *Leutnant d.R.* Friedrich Fischer

French Translator: *Sonderführer* Edgar Beutel

English Translator: *Sonderführer* Herbert Koziol

Protestant Chaplain: Reverend Hans-Thilo Liebe

Catholic Chaplain: Father Wilhelm Hausmann

Division Major Commands and Troops

PGLR 901: *Oberst* Georg Scholze, *Oberst* Paul von Hauser

PGLR 902: *Oberst* Karl Marzahn (until January 1944), *Oberst* Joachim Gutmann (until 10 June 1944), *Oberstleutnant* Willi Welsch (killed on 27 July 1944), *Major* Otto Kuhnow (missing-in-action on 22 November 1944), *Oberstleutnant Ritter* von Poschinger (killed on 4 April 1945), and *Hauptmann* Klein.

PLR 130: *Oberst* Rudolf Gerhardt
   I./PLR 130: *Major* Markowski
   II./PLR 130: *Oberstleutnant* von Schönburg-Waldenburg
PALR 130: *Oberst* Luxenberger
PJLA 130: *Major* Joachim Barth
PALA 130: *Major* Gert von Born-Fallois
PPLB 130: *Major* Walter Brandt; *Hauptmann* Kunze (effective August 1944)
PNLA 130: *Major d.R.* Hermann Derfflinger
HFA 311: *Hauptmann* Gustav Weinkopf

APPENDIX E

Manning Roster of
Panzergrenadier-Lehr-Regiment 901
(June 1944)

Regimental Commander: *Oberst* Scholze

Regimental Adjutant: *Hauptmann* Ehricht

Liaison Officers: *Leutnant* Schulte and *Oberleutnant* Hinz

Signals Officer: *Oberleutnant* Möller

Maintenance Officer: *Oberleutnant* Schneider

I./PGLR 901

Battalion Commander: *Major* Uthe

Battalion Adjutant: *Oberleutnant* Gehrke

Paymaster: *Oberzahlmeister* Schmalisch

Company Commanders:

    1./PGLR 901: *Oberleutnant* Monz

    2./PGLR 901: *Oberleutnant* Mersiowski

    3./PGLR 901: *Hauptmann* Salzmann

    4./PGLR 901: ?

II./PGLR 901

Battalion Commander: *Major* Schöne

Battalion Adjutant: *Oberleutnant* Lankhorst; *Leutnant* Genin

Paymaster: *Oberzahlmeister* Block

Battalion Surgeon: *Stabsarzt Dr.* Selzer

Liaison Officer: *Leutnant* Rheinländer

Company Commanders:

    5./PGLR 901: *Hauptmann Philipps* with *Leutnant* Hillermann as a platoon
    leader

    6./PGLR 901: *Oberleutnant* Winter with *Leutnant* Genin as a platoon
    leader

    7./PGLR 901: *Oberleutnant* Mahr

    8./PGLR 901: *Hauptmann* Pfitzner

Regimental Troops:

    9. (s.I.G.)/PGLR 901: *Hauptmann* Hennecke (*Oberleutnant*
    Lankhorst starting in September 1944)

    10. (Flak)/PGLR 901: *Oberleutnant* Klein

Manning Roster of the Headquarters Company of *Panzergrenadier-Lehr-Regiment 902*

Activation Oversight: *Oberleutnant* Rahneberg (later transferred to *PGLR 901*)

Antitank Platoon Leader: *Oberleutnant* Rasmus (later commander of the *4./ PGLR 902*)

Motorcycle Platoon Leader: *Leutnant* Kieborz (missing in action)

Signals Platoon Leader: *Leutnant* Kleine-Hering (signals officer until the end of the war)

Flamethrower Platoon Leader: *Leutnant* Röder

Heavy Infantry Gun Platoon Leader: *Leutnant* Vogt

Losses within the Headquarters and Headquarters Company of *PGLR 902*

Type of Loss	Officers	Noncommissioned Officers	Enlisted Personnel
Killed	4	3	10
Missing	1	5	29
Wounded	2	9	25

Engagements and Battles of the *Panzer-Lehr-Division*

Lehr-Brigade 900 (mot)

Winter 1941–42	Between Leningrad and Moscow (Kalinin)

Panzergrenadier-Lehr-Regiment 901

December 1941– March 1943	Starobjelsk (attached to the *19. Panzer-Division*)
Fall 1943	Dalmatia (antipartisan operations)

Panzer-Lehr-Division

8–9 June 1944	Attack on Ellon
9–17 June 1944	Defensive fighting in the areas of La Bell Épine–St. Pièves and Braurey
10–11 June 1944	Fighting in the vicinity of Tilly, Villers-Bocage and Evrécy
11–13 June 1944	Defensive fighting in the vicinity of Marcel
13–14 June 1944	Offensive operations at Tilly-Lingèvres, La Belle Épine and Villers-Bocage
	(ten days of fighting along the line Tilly–La Belle Épine)
16–17 June 1944	Mopping up in the Cachty–Mauperthine area
18 June 1944	Fighting at Fontenay–Hottot–Percy
9–16 July 1944	Defensive fighting in the area Pt. Hebert–Le-Camps
10 July 1944	Le Losque
11 July 1944	Attack on the Vire Canal
15 July 1944	Defensive fighting around Le Mesnil

16–17 July 1944	Fighting at Durandt–Sadot
24 July 1944	Hebricrevon
25–27 July 1944	Battle at St. Lô–Perriers
26 July 1944	Defensive fighting and counterattack around St. Gilles
1–10 August 1944	Fighting at Argentan, Alencon and Soissons
13 August 1944	Defensive fighting around Bouci
21 November– 4 December 1944	Offensive and defensive operations in the area around Saarluckenheim
22 November 1944	Counterattack against the Zabern Depression
2 December 1944	Defensive fighting on the Isenbuhl (mountain)
16 December– 5 February 1945	Ardennes offensive: offensive and defensive operations against and around Bastogne, St. Hubert, Celles and Rochefort
6 February– 6 March 1945	Defensive fighting on the lower Rhine and at the Wesel bridgehead
1 March 1945	Night attack at Schiefbahn
21 March– 15 April 1945	Defensive fighting in the Ruhr–Sauerland area, Winterberg and Altena; Ruhr Pocket

APPENDIX H

Panzer-Lehr-Division Order of Battle[1]

Stab/Panzer-Lehr-Division
Headquarters group, including anti-aircraft, map, engineer and signals units.

Panzer-Lehr-Regiment 130
Consisted of *Stab* (headquarters), *I. (Panther)* and *II Abteilung*.

I. Abteilung
The *Abteilung* was organized as a *Panther-Abteilung* consisting of a headquarters group, a headquarters company and four *Panther* companies (1, 2, 3, 4).

II. Abteilung
Consisted of a headquarters group, a headquarters company and four *Panzer* companies (5, 6, 7, 8) with *Panzer IV*.

Panzergrenadier-Lehr-Regiment 902
Comprised a headquarters group and the *I.* and *II. Bataillon*.

I. Bataillon
Headquarters group and three (1, 2, 3) armored *Panzergrenadier* companies and one (4) heavy armored *Panzergrenadier* company plus a supply company.

II. Bataillon
Headquarters group and three (5, 6, 7) armored *Panzergrenadier* companies and one (8) heavy armored *Panzergrenadier* company plus a supply company.

Panzergrenadier-Lehr-Regiment 901
Comprised a headquarters group and the *I.* and *II. Bataillon*.

I. Bataillon
Headquarters group and three (1, 2, 3) armored *Panzergrenadier* companies and one (4) heavy armored *Panzergrenadier* company plus a supply company.

II. Bataillon
Headquarters group and three (5, 6, 7) armored *Panzergrenadier* companies and one (8) heavy armored *Panzergrenadier* company plus a supply company.

Panzer-Artillerie-Regiment 130
Initially comprised a headquarters group and *I. Abteilung* (self-propelled), *II.* and *III. Abteilung* (heavy). However, changes to the organization of the regiment were made in April and November 1944.

1. Compiled with material from the author and reference to Kamen Nevenkin, *Fire Brigades: The Panzer Divisions* (Winnipeg: J.J. Fedorowicz Publishing, 2008).

I. Abteilung

Headquarters, headquarters battery (motorized), three batteries (1, 2, 3) of light field guns, motorized.

II. Abteilung

Headquarters, headquarters battery (heavy), two batteries (4, 5) of light field guns, self-propelled and one battery (6) of heavy field guns, self-propelled).

III. Abteilung

Headquarters, headquarters battery (motorized), three batteries (7, 8, 9) of heavy field guns (motorized). These batteries were equipped with captured Soviet 15.2-cm howitzers and supplies of shells were limited.

Heeres-Flak-Artillerie-Abteilung 311

Headquarters group and three heavy *Flak* batteries.

Panzerjager-Lehr-Abteilung 130

Headquarters group, headquarters company, two *Jagdpanzer* companies with *Jagdpanzer IV* and one company with towed *PaK 40* antitank guns.

Panzer-Aufklärungs-Lehr-Abteilung 130

Reconnaissance *Abteilung* consisting of a headquarters group, two armored car companies and three armored reconnaissance companies (half-track).

Panzer-Pionier-Lehr Bataillon 130

Headquarters group, headquarters company (motorized), three armored engineer companies.

Panzer-Nachrichten-Abteilung 130

Signals *Abteilung* with two companies.

Feldersatz-Bataillon 130

Field replacement battalion with a headquarters company and four other companies.

Select Bibliography

Primary Sources

Bayerlein, Fritz. *Die PLD vom D-Tag bis zum V-Tag*, manuscript.

Brasche, Rudolf. *Kampfberichte der 1./901*, manuscript.

Bradtke. *Heeres-Flak-Abteilung 311*, manuscript.

Cursiefsen. *Dr.-Ing.* Wilhelm, *Die letzten Tage*, manuscript.

Daily logs of the *Panzer-Lehr-Division* (provided by *Freiherr* von Funck and Anselm Hübner).

Ehricht, Gerhard. *Bericht des Panzergrenadier-Lehr-Regiments 901* and "*Stellenbesetzungsliste*," manuscript and list.

Ernst, R. *Panzerschlacht von Tilly*, manuscript.

Gerhardt, Rudolf. *Von Wunstorf bis zu den Ardennen*, manuscript.

Hilter, Friedrich. *Panzerhusaren mit Anhänger*, first-hand account.

Job, Eduard. *Kampfberichte der 3./Pz.Jäg.Lehr-Abt. 130*, manuscript

Kiefer, Martin. *Erlebnisse aus dem Sanitätsdient beim II./Pz.Gren.Lehr-Rgt. 901*, manuscript.

Lankhorst. *Stellenbesetzung Pz.Gren.Lehr-Rgt. 901*, list.

Neumann, *Dr.* Johannes. "*Die Kämpfe eines Pz.Gren.Lehr-Regimentes am Donez*," firsthand account.

—. *Ein Minute vor zwölf*, firsthand account.

—. *Augen zu und durch*, firsthand account.

—. *Stolze Stunden für ein Lehr-Regiment*, firsthand account.

Oventrop. *Südlich Rshew am 5.8.1941*, manuscript.

—. *Der Gegenangriff vom 8.8.1941*, manuscript.

Stolpe, Erich. *Die Stabskompanie des Regiments 902*, manuscript.

Thies, Ernst. *Sie kommen*, manuscript.

Tönnes, Walter. *Das Panzer-Pi.-Lehr-Bataillon 130*, manuscript.

Wollensen, Richard. *Die 9. (s.I.G.-Sfl.) Pz.Gren.Lehr-Rgt. 901*, manuscript and division association periodical.

Secondary Sources

Alman, Karl. *Großlandung Seinebucht*. Rastatt, 1960.

Bernhard, Herbert. *Dann brach die Hölle los*. Wesel, 1954.

Bernig, Heinrich H. *Duell der Giganten*. Balve, 1961.

Carell, Paul. *Die Wüstenfüchse*. Hamburg, 1958.

—. *Sie kommen*. Oldenburg, 1960.

Churchill, Winston. *Memoiren, Volume 5, 2nd Book*. Hamburg, 1949.

Cramer, Hans. *Die Panzer-Aufklärungs-Lehr-Abteilung*. Minden, no year.

Eisenhower, Dwight D. *Invasion*. Hamburg, 1949.

Hayn, Friedrich. *Die Invasion*. Heidelberg, 1954.

Hoffmann, Karl. *"Panzer-Lehr-Regiment 130 im Einsatz."* Division association periodical.

—. *Invasion 1944*. Division association periodical.

—. *Zur Geschichte der Panzer-Lehr-Truppe*. Division association periodical.

—. *Gefechtseinsätze der PLD*. Division association periodical.

Hottelet, Richard C., and Robert Richards. *Bastogne—Wie wir Rundstedt aufhhielten*.

Keilig, Wolf (editor). *Rangliste des deutschen Heeres, 1944*.

—. *Das Deutsche Heer 1939–1945*. Bad Nauheim, 1955.

Kesselring, Albert. *Soldat bis zum letzten Tag*. Bonn, 1953.

Kollatz, Karl. *Tiger vor!* Rastatt, 1961.

—. *Generalleutnant Fritz Bayerlein*. Rastatt, 1961.

—. *Generalmajor Horst Niemack*. Rastatt, 1961.

—. *Feldwebel Rudolf Brasche*. Rastatt, 1961.

Korten, Hans-Joachim. *Oberst Georg Scholze*. Rastatt, 1959.

—. *Die Lehrbrigade 900 bei Kalinin*. Division association periodical.

Maertz, Joseph. *Luxemburg in der Rundstedt-Offensive*.

Manteuffel, Hasso von. *Die Schlacht in den Ardennen 1944/45*. Frankfurt am Main, 1960.

Meyer, Kurt. *Grenadiere*, Munich.

Podzun, Hans-Henning. *Das Deutsche Heer 1939*. Bad Nauheim, 1953.

Rommel, Erwin. *Krieg ohne Haß*. Heidenheim, 1950.

Ruge, Friedrich. *Rommel und die Invasion*. Stuttgart, 1959.

Seemen, Gerhard von. *Die Ritterkreuzträger 1939–1945*. Bad Nauheim, 1955.

Schulz, Johannes. *Unternehmen Overlord*, Balve. 1961.

Speidel, Hans. *Die Invasion*.

Toland, John. *Ardennenschlacht 1944*. Bern, 1960.

Wilmot, Chester. *Der Kampf um Europa*. Braunschweig, 1949.